TRANSLATION FROM THE SAME AUTHOR

From Gandhi to Vinoba

LANZA DEL VASTO

Return to the Source

A TRANSLATION OF
Le Pèlerinage aux Sources
BY JEAN SIDGWICK

RIDER · LONDON

RIDER & COMPANY
178–202 Great Portland Street, London W1

AN IMPRINT OF THE HUTCHINSON GROUP

London Melbourne Sydney
Auckland Johannesburg Cape Town
and agencies throughout the world

First published in English 1971

303·61

First published in France under the title
Le Pèlerinage aux Sources

© Denoël 1943

English translation © Rider & Company 1971

*This book has been set in Imprint type, printed in Great Britain
on antique wove paper by Anchor Press, and
bound by Wm. Brendon, both of Tiptree, Essex*

ISBN 0 09 107060 0 (cased)
      0 09 107061 9 (paper)

CONTENTS

PUBLISHER'S INTRODUCTION

Return to the Source was first published in France where about a million copies have been sold and it has already been translated into several other languages. Well known in Europe, India and South America, the name of Lanza del Vasto has remained somewhat of a stranger to the majority of Englishmen, the work of Shantidas—the man Gandhi himself named Servant of Peace— being up till now largely ignored in this country. However, in these days of an ever more positive conversation between East and West, both on the political and religious level, and in this decade where increasingly more people are looking towards the East for a return to first principles and a greater simplicity, the very man who is said 'to keep Gandhi alive in the West' can no longer remain unknown to England. One of his books, *From Gandhi to Vinoba*, was published by Rider and Company in 1956 but with this first translation into the English language of *Return to the Source*, we are pleased to offer a book which is perhaps of greater relevance today than when it was first written some thirty years ago. A personal account of the author's awakening to what has subsequently become his life task, *Return to the Source* provides the bridge and explanation for the work of the thirty foregoing years and Vasto's work today.

Born in 1901, in San Vito dei Normanni, Lanza del Vasto is descended from an illustrious family already celebrated in the tenth century; a family which can count emperors of the Occident and Norman kings of Sicily amongst its members.

As a child he learnt several languages and pursued his formal education to a Doctorate of Philosophy, an attainment which, however, could never satisfy him. Possessed from an early age by an incurable thirst for a better comprehension of the essence of things, Vasto found that for him 'philosophy and all the sciences put together cannot account for the existence of a fly'. It was at this point, as he tells us in his recollections, *Les Enfances d'une Pensée,** that he stopped in order to take to the road and to the sea, to question the world straight in the eyes. For, born with an artist's vision and compelled by a deeply spiritual approach to his surrounding world, it is life itself which has always been Vasto's true subject, the art of living, his most fervent pursuit.

His ceaseless questioning and urge for true knowledge has never allowed him any rest on all levels, and since finishing his studies at university, the author's world has known no frontiers. Material gain and professional status could never content him and not having chosen any particular career, he left home when the family fortunes collapsed, not wishing to be a burden to his parents. He never returned except for the occasional visit. For several years he travelled widely in Europe, staying a while in every capital, earning a living by whatever means possible. A scholar, he was able to teach Latin, and a talented artist and craftsman, his gifts in drawing, painting and engraving helped along the way and added to a basic appreciation of every type of manual labour. Always rejecting profit and the comforts of convenience, and guided by an implicit trust in God, he refused to stay put in any one place, experiencing poverty, hunger and, at times, ridicule. But ever observant, ever curious, he sought in every situation and every trade a fresh meaning of truth and a more genuine contact with human beings.

In 1936 Vasto embarked upon what was to be his most significant journey to date, the one which was to provide the definition of his life task. It is this journey, the impressions gained, the people encountered and the lessons learned which the author offers us in *Return to the Source.*

Aged thirty-five, Vasto finally left Europe to travel across India, mostly on foot, motivated by his search for 'that distance that sharpens sight and makes one see clearly . . . this clarity whose name is Detachment'. The journey took over a year and, impelled by his initial search for wisdom, the author travelled far both overland and in spirit, clearing his view, defining his aim. In this vividly written account, Vasto the poet, the artist, and the man invites the reader

* Published 1970, 'Edition Denoël', Paris.

to travel with him, sharing his emotions, his enthusiasms, his hunger and fatigue and above all his ceaseless compulsion to keep going, to travel farther, to experience all things in order to learn. For *Return to the Source* provides a truly lyrical exposition of a pilgrimage—a journey which is distinguished through its lack of laid-out plan; one which creates its own direction in accordance with the inner urge which surely guides both on the physical and spiritual plane. At his most poetic or his most serious, the author never loses his sense of humour and objectivity and as an initiation into the age-old wisdom and culture of India the book's renown and influence has already been considerable. From Ceylon to Wardha, from the banks of the Ganges to Port Said, Vasto continued his quest with open eyes, struggling, noting, evaluating, and at every step strengthening his purpose.

And his quest was certainly to find an answer, the answer which has become his life's mission. As we learn from the account, an early meeting with the Ramana Maharshi, who for the Hindus is God personified, convinced Vasto that not all the serenity of the East could ever satisfy his roving Western mind, and it was at this point that his route took its most positive turning—'I hold that charity is worth even more than wisdom. That is why I shall go to Wardha, to Gandhi. Yes, to learn how to become a better Christian'.

It is this stay at Wardha which provides the central core of the account and the basis for his work today. With Gandhi, whose convinced disciple he became, he learnt the true meaning of the philosophy of non-violence. He fully accepted the aims and methods of Gandhi's thought, the community at Wardha serving as the model for Vasto's own.

For since his return to Europe, Vasto, now known as Shantidas, has worked ceaselessly to uphold Gandhi's aims in the Western hemisphere. Through his work he has attempted to find one solution to the many problems of our confused and war-torn time. Following the precepts given by his master, Vasto asks for politics without violence, production without machines, society without exploitation, religion without intolerance. His fundamental principle is to implant love and truth, his method a return to the earth and to craftsmanship, manual work and a simple life; the whole held together by an accent on the common basis of all religions.

Once back in France, he made his message very clear and in 1944 as war was drawing to a close, several people sought him out to form a small group in Paris, working at weaving and carving. In 1948, the first rural community was founded in Tournier. Named the 'Ark', it was open to all, but by 1953 it had become clear that a fresh start would have to be made on a stricter basis. So Tournier too was abandoned and in its turn a much larger successor near Bollène. By now to be a member—or companion—one had to be a novice for three years and then be admitted by unanimous vote.

The problem of ever expanding members has now been solved, at least for the moment, by the acquisition of la Borie Noble, the Noble Borough, a domain of 2,000 acres, of which about 100 are now cultivated, situated some sixty miles north west of Montpellier overlooking the Herault plain to the south. When the companions first moved there in 1963, there was nothing but a ruined house, but since then an impressive group of buildings has been built from stones found in a drowned valley where a reservoir was then being established.

The Ark as it now stands comprises several communities, each of them grouping ideally from thirty to fifty men, women and children. Each community is under the authority of a patriarch designated by Shantidas, the head of the whole Order. Run on a thoroughgoing application of Gandhian ideas, the community is self-supporting; however, relations with the surrounding villages and people are good and the older children board at the local lycée.

In the Ark an effort is made to apply non-violence at all levels; to find a unity in life, to give an inner preparation to external action. And to this end every companion devotes each day of his life. He vows before God to progress along the way of non-violence and of truth, and also takes the vow of purification, of poverty, of service and of work, of responsibility and co-responsibility, and finally of obedience. If he falls short of what is expected of him, he must do penance. If he observes a shortcoming in someone else who is not prepared to atone for it, he must take it upon himself to do penance in his stead. This self-imposed sanction is the only one admitted, a sanction which is eminently non-violent. It is, as Shantidas says, the 'gem' of a rule which lays down a rhythm of life, the manner of dress, the hours of work, the times of prayer.

The achievement of a rhythm and a harmony is indeed the central precept of the Ark's Constitution: 'the aim of manual labour is not only to obtain one's daily bread by pure means, but to bring about an inner harmonisation between body and soul'. And to this end there is no stop. Entirely unmechanised, all the labour is done by hand or horse-drawn plough, and the only electricity on the estate is that used to grind flour for home-baked bread. Prayer, ritual festivities, music, study and spiritual exercises all play a large part in the daily life of the community where all activities are carefully balanced and alternated. Meals are simple and, naturally, vegetarian, rice providing the staple basis. Singing is an important factor at the community, and indeed Shantidas and his wife, Chanterelle, are internationally recognised for their musical talents quite independently of their other work. Clothes are home-spun and handicrafts of every type are practised and encouraged, beauty being the end for each thing produced.

All the members of the Ark, bear, like those of a Noah's ark, a name from the animal kingdom or a name of a flower. Like that of Noah, the Ark is afloat on the waters of a world that is submerging, its people struggling for help. It is an islet of calm and peace: a way of life, thoroughly Christian, a nucleus of believers, mostly Catholics—but which in no way excludes those of other faiths, who find that the path of non-violence helps them to live as Christians. It is a society of free men, ruled with dignity, complete with its own school, musicians and doctor. All decisions affecting the life of the community are taken at a Council of the companions every week and unanimity is obtained, if necessary, by resorting to a period of reflection in silence and then fasting. Vows are re-peated each year and a companion may be allowed by the council to make a lifelong vow after seven years which entitles him to be known as a Son of the Ark.

People sympathetic to the cause of the community may train there for short periods, while some of the companions are allowed to work outside the community itself. There are also 'allies', that is, people who have promised to observe the teachings of the Ark, without, however, living in the community.

And over all, founder and inspiration, presides Shantidas him-self, an imposing figure, now in his seventies. As patriarch of the Order he urges each in turn to act upon himself, to bring about inner conversion. He asks every man to change his inclinations, reduce his needs, mend his ways: conquer himself. He recommends fasting and silence once a week, penance according to one's religion, and daily bodily exercises so as to gain mastery and knowledge of oneself. Prayer, meditation and moments of recollection also all go towards preparation for a life of devotion and dedication. No stranger to work himself, Shantidas stresses its necessity; both inner work demanded for self mastery and outer physical labour with one's hands; the quest for the Kingdom of God as constant inspiration.

Shantidas' conviction has never faltered and his influence amongst his followers is strong; however, the success of his mission, though certain, is naturally not startling in such an age as we live in. Nevertheless in France itself about a 1000 have been inspired by the Ark and been drawn into its organisation. Gatherings are held at La Borie and there people of every race, language and religion gather on the hillside to listen to the word of the master. Shantidas does not only wait for some to come to him, but often travels abroad preaching his message. 'The Pilgrim', as he is called, has visited South America several times, and wherever he goes in the world, be it Spain, Belgium, Switzerland, Italy or the Lebanon, there are always organised groups of the friends of the Ark ready to welcome him and acknowledge his word.

Like his own master, Gandhi, Shantidas has always remained a realist. As he has kept his objectivity in even the most inspired of his literary work, so he has achieved this in his daily life. Though for the greater extent withdrawn himself in person from the turmoil of the twentieth century, he remains intensely aware of its problems and recognises the difficulties of converting the general mass of humanity to his particular way of life. However, all his efforts have always been directed towards finding a practical solution at every level, and in order to be able to be of use outside the community itself, a separate organisation was established in February 1958 under the name of 'Action Civique Non-violente'. The organisation, while linked to the Ark, remains independent of it, its aim being to unite people of differing views in the movement dedicated to non-violent political action. The movement, though still not holding a vast membership, is capable of attracting a fair amount of mass support, and can count upon volunteers from among the companions and a small devoted and trained 'army' from companions is always ready, under Shantidas' orders, to participate in any action.

The Non-violent Civic Action provides a headquarters for campaigns, supplies information, enrols members and maintains contacts with other pacifist movements in France and abroad. It publishes its own news sheet and trains volunteers.

The campaigns held have been modest affairs, but nevertheless significant. At the time of the war in Algeria, from June 1959 to the summer of 1960, action was started against the internment camps where Algerians were detained on the ground of being 'suspected persons'. Volunteers turned up at these camps and demanded to be arrested on the very same grounds. The desired result was not fully achieved but, in a new effort, help was given to those refusing to undertake military service in Algeria. This was much more successful for although the idea of substituting civil for military service in Algeria was never realised, the French Government did eventually recognise the right of conscientious objection to military service.

Beginning in the autumn of 1960, sites were opened where anyone refusing to serve in Algeria could come with pick and shovel, on some job of work of service to the community; and would be supported at the moment of arrest by volunteers all claiming to be the wanted person, so that the police had to arrest not one person, but half a dozen. Five leaders of the Non-violent Civic Action, charged with inciting the military to disobedience were tried and given short suspended sentences in November 1961. The government finally promised to introduce the necessary legislation when Louis Lecoin, a conscientious objector of the first World War, who had spent over ten years in prison, began a fast to death. The Bill, which put an end to an obligation dating from the Revolution, was finally passed in December 1963. Other demonstrations have been held against the manufacture of nuclear weapons.

The strength of the Non-violent Civic Action movement in France lies, like all to do with the community, not so much in the number of its supporters, but in the purity and vigour of its actions and its connection with a spiritual force, the Ark. Indeed, the Ark today stands as the true training ground for non-violence at every level.

Since that first pilgrimage in 1936 made by an enthusiastic, inquisitive and sensitive young man, Shantidas' efforts have been tireless. He has himself undertaken fasts: with Danilo Dolci in December 1956: one of twenty days in France in protest against cases of torture in Algeria in 1957 and one of forty days in Rome which coincided with the Papal encyclical 'Pacem in Terris' in 1963. An idealist in the best sense of the word, it has always been his solid grasp of reality and positiveness of approach, reflected in all his work, whether humanitarian, artistic or literary, which has distinguished Shantidas from the well-meaning but often misdirected and impractical dreamer.

Pilgrimages to India and across the world are no new phenomenon; there have always been men willing to leave all in search of themselves, and no more so than nowadays in this particular decade where, daily, thousands of young people trek to Katmandu and the frontiers of Tibet. What sets the few, men such as Lanza del Vasto, apart from the general mass is indeed their real sense of purpose and conviction: for thirty years ago Vasto set out to seek for truth not content to look only for his soul. His account in *Return to the Source* provides an inspiration for the general reader and must surely add a fresh dimension to the one who already knows the route.

And thirty years later, Vasto's achievement cannot be denied. Since those youthful wanderings, so passionately described, this man has created an Order, open to all believers, whatever their religion. An Order with its own Rule; its vows; its dress, handspun and handwoven, white on holidays and coloured on week-days; and its symbol, a wooden cross worn night and day round the neck.

A patriarchal Order, uniting both families and single persons in one large family exchanging each evening a kiss of peace; an extended family with Chanterelle, Shantidas' wife and his closest collaborator, as its mother.

A working Order, which as a rule empties its coffers each summer lest it should become rich—as once happened to the monks of Western Europe; and which has, as another of its rules, a respect for beauty and refusal to tolerate things ugly even if convenient, practical and expedient.

A non-violent Order, where even in matters of food there must be no taking of life. An Order which is not a sect, where East and

West can meet, where all of whatever class, race, nation or religion can become reconciled.

A revolutionary Order, since it has undertaken to work as stated in the Ark's Constitution, for 'the only revolution from which good can result, the Gandhi revolution'.

I

CEYLON

OR THE STUPEFACTION OF
THE NEWCOMER

CEYLON, *December 1936*

Here I am then, just off the ship, all alone, white of skin, self-conscious and bewildered, pestered by people trying to sell me things, by others promising me all kinds of pleasure or imploring me for alms, by volunteers eager to take me to the temple of Buddha or to the house where the nice ladies are.

As in a dream, I move through the colourful, dark-faced crowd and wander past the city's mean arcades, turn away from them and go step by step down to the shore.

On the horizon I watch the trail of smoke from the disappearing ship, the last fragment of a world I have left. And now, only a perfectly empty future. My feet, accustomed to the planks of the ship, feel the firm earth plunging and heaving. The perpetual croaking of the crows hollows out the distance. From a clump of glossy-leaved trees, plumes of rose-tipped stamens rise; the overblown flowers are falling one by one.

I think to myself, 'Detachment was what I wanted and now I have got it.' The thought strikes me dumb. Like someone about to die, I think of my early years, for the beginning and the end of a life meet to form a circle.

From the shore in front of me comes the low-pitched roar and rush of the surf: it brings back the sound of the beaches of my childhood. Sea, oh sea, everywhere the same, sea that I hear but which does not speak, sea that I love but which loves me not, inhuman link between all manner of men.

And here on this tropical beach I have found the fresh, paddling feet of my childhood again.

2

—Tell me, what is there to be gained from going far away?

—The distance that sharpens sight and makes one see clearly, the distance that stretches links and makes one love strongly; this clarity whose name is Detachment.

3

No doubt it is true that Europe exploits this poor country—as nation to nation, and on an abstract plane. But it is just as true to say that the hapless European who lands here is immediately and mercilessly fleeced, man to man, and in the most blatant, excessive and humiliating manner.

The grandest hotel in New York would scarcely charge me more than does this sordid one in Colombo, where the linoleum and the washbasins stink, where by day ferocious sunlight flashes through the loosened slats of the blinds and at night one wakes up itching alarmingly.

The insistence of the shopkeepers and the demands of the beggars border on persecution.

If I had an honest servant (I mean one who would be content with his wages, supplemented by various tips, plus a reasonable percentage of petty thefts) I could send him out shopping and, by letting like deal with like, offer myself the luxury of saving some money. But delivered up defenceless to the merchants, the most I can do is to attend my own defeat with dignity and calculate from time to time how much longer I can live on my resources. I can see these coming to an end more and more quickly. But I have no intention of asking for help from home. So I shall just have to make do with what I have, that being the rule of the game.

Nevertheless, I must admit that there is no joy in my heart as I see the day of reckoning draw near. I expect no more humanity from the people around than if I were among fish at the bottom of the sea. In fact, I find them so quick at laying their hands on me, so sharp-eyed and so sharp-toothed that I feel they are bound to devour me alive when they have finished skinning me.

4

COLOMBO, *December 1936*

On each side of the passage, tiled roofs slope down to shoulder level. Under this canopy the vendors squat among their wares. Fruit is piled in great heaps of colour. There are a few butchers' stalls with red chopping blocks. Cobblers are stitching away at square-shaped sandals.

The houses with their rooms bare of all furniture open on to the street where cooking and other tasks are done.

On one threshold a woman is shaving her husband. A youth is lying asleep in the middle of the street, his head pillowed on a soft heap of dust. His teeth glisten, for he is smiling in his dream. Two young men with supple haunches come along hand in hand. At the corner, near a milestone, a man squats with his elbows on his knees and his hands at the ends of his long forearms hang like cloths at the ends of two sticks.

Women pass. They have high, square shoulders and, swathed in colour from head to heel, they look like flames. Their hips are narrow and set high, they have palm-tree waists and legs like bamboo plants and carry themselves like queens, but the look in their eyes is that of shy little girls. They carry their children naked, astride a hip-bone. One of them accosts me. She wants to sell me a green leaf, a nut and a white paste that one rolls up in a leaf and chews, which makes one spit red.

When we arrived in port there were birds like frail sea-gulls flying around with wings as tapering as those of swallows. Their movement in flight was touchingly graceful and delicate. They live on the garbage in the port. The women here are like the sea-gulls and their flight.

When you are close to a tree you can admire the leaves one by one. All gleam and none of them is void of grace. Similarly the women passing in the street here look like each other, as do the leaves on the same tree.

The men, slim, nimble and straight, carry their heads high. From the back, tightly wrapped in their robes, which are white with coloured hems, they look like graceful long-limbed girls. Sometimes the beauty of a gold jewel sets off their dark skins.

Their smile is sweet and reveals dazzling teeth between full
lips. Their eyes, black and of a lovely oval shape, present their
sadness to the blazing sun.

5

I am beginning to distinguish the differences in this many-coloured
crowd. The Cingalese swathed in purple cloth that falls smooth
and flat from the waist to the feet with a blue or violet hem
running from the loins to the heel. Indians from the north wearing
European shirts with the tails loose over their white cotton gowns.
Pariahs short-clad or sometimes wearing only a rope of twisted
rag that cuts in between their buttocks and is attached back and
front to a string tied below the waist. Brahmins wearing ear-rings
and marked between the eyes with a red spot. Shivites with their
foreheads smeared with ashes. Vishnuites marked with three
vertical stripes above the nose. Old men from Kandy with tortoise-
shell combs crowning their hair-buns. Shaved Moslems wearing
red fezes or green turbans. Afghans with embroidered waistcoats,
slippers and baggy trousers gathered in at the ankles. Bonzes
clad in saffron- or sulphur-coloured robes, their shaved heads
protected by black or yellow parasols.

No greetings pass between them, but there is no quarrelling
either. They tramp the same pavement in silence. They do not
speak the same language, have nothing to do with each other,
do not eat between the same walls, do not drink at the same wells.
They do not like each other enough to exchange glances nor hate
each other valiantly enough to fight.

Side by side, like horse and ox in the same farmyard.

6

A black giant with a scarlet loin-cloth comes running against the
current of the crowd. His head is crowned and plumed with a
big basket of pineapples. As soon as a man here has a weight to
carry or a cart to pull, he starts running. He rushes towards the spot
where he can relieve himself of his burden and stretch out in
the shade. It may be that he will not find this spot till his day is
over. Perhaps he will not find it till all his days are over. And even

in the sleep of death he will be troubled by the harassing thought that tomorrow he will have to begin all over again, be born and reborn to the point of exhaustion, die and die again, times without number, and run and search again in order to expiate the immemorial mass of sins, the one massive, immemorial sin from which all others spring; the attachment of ignorance.

7

THE ROAD FROM COLOMBO TO KANDY, *January 1937*

It's a good three days' walk from Colombo to Kandy, the capital of the hills. Under the hot sun the countryside spreads green, for the sea-breezes carry wind and rain wide over the land.

A well-kept road cuts through the drenched plain. A cow is browsing with her hooves deep in water.

Green everywhere on the ground. Green in its original state, becoming banana yellow in the full glare of the sun. The green of the trees remains darker and gleams.

A black peasant with a rose-coloured loin-cloth is running behind the wooden plough with which he is scratching the earth. His little humpbacked ox is no bigger than a donkey and trots like one. On every road one meets these oxen, yoked alone or in pairs to carts covered with matted palm-leaves. They are the only beasts of burden on the island, apart from elephants and men.

A girl is bathing in the pond. She dives in fully clothed. Her loosened hair becomes an eel in the water. She comes out with her wet clothes clinging to her skin in the glory of nakedness.

The ditches are inhabited by tortoises whose shells cluck as they enter the stream where they plunge out of sight in clouds of mud. The soil has become so soft and wet that the mass of the trees has sunk and the branches rest on the ooze, their reversed image falls in twice deeper.

From the patchwork of the rice-fields a blue bird rises like an arrow and lodges in a clump of radiant palms.

Here the ground begins to rise towards the mountains. The rice-fields lie one above the other in terraces each rigorously level, their edges following the natural outline of the slope so that all the land visible is encased in perfectly fitting irregular scales ascending the hill.

Beyond, the wood begins. The hill suddenly humps its back like a buffalo, followed in the distance by other hills, but blue. Falling waters and spirals of smoke accompany its rising.

From this height the palm-trees appear head first; their rope-like trunks fathom the slope. Below, the forest stretches its scaly backbone, flickers its fins and plumes, its wings and lizard feet, its tongues of blood or fire.

One tree is hung with leaves like crimson butterflies, another holds up brilliantly coloured goblets, yet another has a purple top. Down there, a tree is shining like a solitary autumn, brilliant as a topaz, for rain has hung a luminous veil on that side of the valley. The air smells of cut grass and the nectar of flowers.

The plain, flattened in the middle by the brilliance of the sunlight, hollowed out by shadows on the left, and lit here and there by the long, roving shanks of the rain, is wide enough to house several seasons side by side.

The forest around Kandy is free from wild beasts. Nevertheless, at night it becomes fearful to the lonely traveller. When the toads and night-birds tune up and sound like the drums and flutes of the temple, when the greenery that turns even day into night has closed up behind him, when the fireflies light up on the chandeliers of the high branches, then something more terrible than wild beasts takes his breath away: the presence of God in this leafy dwelling-place so closely reminiscent of the first Paradise.

8

KANDY, *January 1937*

The temple of Buddha is a little fortress surrounded by a double rampart and a moat and flanked by big round towers with flattish, pointed roofs.

At nightfall the drum sounds incessantly: two short beats and two long, accompanied by a shrill pandemonium of flutes which catches you by the throat and makes you feel dizzy.

Carrying my sandals, I cross the bridge. My feet savour the wet paving in the courtyard. Not without a feeling of awe, I advance between the granite columns and through the sculptured porches. With care and politeness I ease aside the rumps of the faithful kneeling round the wall, their faces hidden between their knees, and make my way into the steep staircase that leads to the sanctuary.

This is a narrow closet at the end of an arcade decorated with ivory, gold and silver, which opens directly on to the sacrificial table. The statue of Buddha behind it sparkles with carbuncles and uncut stones. The lamps, the votive flowers and the pious warmth of the worshippers have made the air unbreathable.

Everyone has brought an offering of flowers; some carrying them on trays, others in the palms of their hands. The priest in his fiery robe takes them and scatters them on the stone altar.

The fiendish paintings on the outer wall, the infernal music in the courtyard, had not prepared me for sacrifice so touching, so fitting for the Blessed One, the 'Thus did he depart', the Gentle One. For he taught that thou shalt not kill and that each of us must learn how to die, die completely and for ever, die well, die without any risk of return to this world of suffering, of illness and repeated deaths, this world of attachment and ignorance.

9

Having chanced to surprise an angler on the bank of a lake which was so thickly populated with tortoises and fish that the water was brown, I asked him, 'Aren't you a worshipper of Buddha? How is it that you have taken the liberty of murdering this fish?'

'The Commandment,' explained the pious man, 'does not forbid us to eat, but only to kill. It doesn't forbid us to let a hook hang in the water. I only took my hook back and then the fish went and died on the bank.'

*　　*

The mountains and trees and the scattered town of Kandy lie round a lake ringed with heavy stone embroidery.

It was one of the many great reservoirs dug out for the kings long ago, when canals radiated throughout the island then alive and joyful with fresh water, and rich in its harvests, its temples and towns. Today the jungle and the swamp, with their wild beasts and their fevers, have invaded three-quarters of the arable land,

and great numbers of its over-numerous population wander starving through the finest garden in the world.

10

It is called the Bodh-tree, the Fig-tree of Illumination. At the foot of such a tree young Gautama entered Deliverance, but moved by compassion, he came back to show the way to men, as well as to gods and animals.

There is nothing of a fig-tree about this one—unless you give this name to all tropical plants. As a matter of fact, the fig-tree, with its grey trunk twisted like an elephant's and its broad leaves with their capriciously curling outline, glossy on the top side and dull and ridged with veins underneath, is the only Mediterranean tree that bears any resemblance to the vegetation here.

But the Bodh-tree belongs to the poplar family, even though it lacks their tall, quivering, gothic slenderness. On the contrary, it spreads itself bulkily. Four men with outstretched arms could not encircle its trunk.

Unlike that of ordinary trees, its girth is increased not just by the widening rings of its sapwood but also by the massive piling up of outer growth, for the roots under the ground are continually being joined by those that keep crawling down through the forked branches and coil round the trunk like ever-tightening rope, while the tufts at the ends of the newest roots, still groping their way down, hang in mid-air.

And over this mountain of petrified entrails rises the ethereal head of the tree. Its light-coloured leaves, scarcely as big as a hand, are heart-shaped and taper finely. They keep turning this way and that on the axis of their central fibre so that the tree trembles and rustles incessantly with the multiple movement of all its leaves. Even on the breathless air where the great leafy head floats they still quiver like the gills of a resting fish.

There are Bodh-trees in the forest living in freedom, but there are others, striking in their majesty, that descend directly from an off-shoot of the Tree at Gayā under which the Blessed One meditated. They are surrounded by a platform built of stone, and in their shade, as in other temples, there is a carved niche with an altar on which the country people lay their offerings of fresh flowers at the hour of prayer.

11

ON THE TRAIN

The third-class compartments, like sheep-pens, have slatted partitions. Wooden benches would be superfluous here, since everybody sits cross-legged on the floor just as at home.

A woman is eating as she squats, her long hair brushing the feet of the passengers. She scrabbles with her fingers in a big bowlful of rice and peppers, inserts four fingers neatly between her teeth and with her thumb shoves the food into her mouth. From time to time she dips a copper cup into a big basin full of water and drinks. The laughing-eyed child in front of her, naked, fat, black, sleek and beautiful as a Buddha, stretches out its hands: it wants some too!

A Moslem with a fez stands out from the others because of his impressive corpulence. Raising his eyebrows, he looks at his rings and then, very majestically, belches.

The countryside and the heat of the day come in through all the open windows and so do the cinders and smoke from the train, not to mention dust and insects.

A thin old man beside me begins to shiver and his teeth chatter. He pulls a rough, striped woollen blanket over himself and rolls himself up in it to his neck; his head falls back and his long teeth show, like those of a thirsty horse.

Facing us, a woman who is probably his daughter has begun to weep without moving. Three tears glisten beside the garnet stud in her nostril. The old man gets up suddenly, jostling the woman who is eating, and vomits out of the window to an accompaniment of loud sobbing. Then he stretches out on the floor. I push a basket under his head and help him to pull the blanket up over his knees. Whereupon he rests his long, black hand lightly on mine to thank me. His daughter goes on weeping, motionless.

The train burrows its way through forests so densely bound by liana that they look more like hills than trees, and allow no insight into their secret.

12

ANURADHAPURA, *January 1937*

It is not immediately obvious that this is a town. It is true that
there is a station, a post office, a hospital and even a few houses,
but these humble buildings lie at different ends of four or five
wide, tree-lined avenues which cross on hillocky meadows lush
with green and pitted with pools of water.

Here once upon a time stood Anuradhapura, the city with the
artificial lakes that reflected the sky; the city with the palaces,
the convents and the sunny temples with roofs of gold; the city
that used to be compared to Dvarak built in the middle of the
sea by Vishvakarna, the architect of the gods.

And now it has fallen apart and lies in the grass and the puddles,
just as one longs to fall apart oneself in the clammy, sweltering air.

*

The Dagoba, which is still standing and has been cleaned up,
testifies to the city's former grandeur. It arches its back, vast
and round like the sky. It has neither beginning, nor end, nor
entrance. It is not a temple but a reliquary. Somewhere in the
grandiose, solid mass of the tower, some single hair or fragment
of bone is preserved of the One who said, 'Just as a man shudders
with horror when he thinks he has trodden on a serpent, but
laughs when he stoops and sees that it is only a rope, so I discovered one day that what I was calling "I" does not exist, and all
fear and anxiety vanished with my mistake.'

Earth and scrub have reclaimed another of the Dagobas and
turned it into a mound.

The surrounding trees, whose mass is reflected in the lake,
have rounded heads just like it.

*   *   *

Here and there in the grass lies the broken paving of a temple.
It is bordered by the loosened steps of a staircase. The road
that once led to these steps now goes through the bottom of a
pond. Each step has a small, round-bellied Buddha in the middle
and one on each side. With his globular eyes and his short legs

pulled up against his thighs, encrusted with lichen and green with moss, he looks like a jubilant little toad.

I was admiring the lion carved on the ramp, the coil of his tail, when a tail shining with life whipped the air, then vanished in a flash like a sob of light. The serpent! I shuddered, not yet knowing that I do not exist.

*

The more I meditate on this Dagoba—impenetrable, faceless and shut to the world, massively seated on its tiny, mystical treasure which the devout will not set eyes on till the end of time, and an object of derision for the profane—the more I meditate on it, the more orthodox and meaningful it appears to me.

For the temple exists only for the mindless crowd of believers, but, for the man who knows, it is in the Dagoba that the truth of this Godless religion lies.

A squatting religion in which there is no impulse towards any Object, Person or Image whatsoever; an incubation or the dense inner silence.

14[1]

The same thought translated into human form confronts me in this statue of Buddha abandoned in the midst of the fields in the shade of mighty trees.

It must be very old, judging by the erosion of the stone, and, above all, by the nobility of its conception and the perfection of its shape.

Nothing that the human will and love have ever chiselled out of stone could be purer, more gently strong or more beautiful.

The long flanks of the Sage are as smooth as a tree-trunk; his chest broadens out like the cup of a lotus. His shoulders are rounded and so are his arms and legs; his hands are folded one in the other in the dedicated attitude of contemplation. His long tapering feet are drawn up against his thighs so that his legs are wedged into each other. And on the firm base of these two flattened triangles, the majestic figure rises like a pyramid.

The crack in the stone that splits his brow like a flash of lightning has not disturbed the calm of the One who knows how to keep wayward thought on a tight rein.

His head is round like a Dagoba, round as the roundness of the absolute.

Under the taut arch of his eyebrows, his eyes look down absently. Light flows over the broad globe of his cheeks and round his placid mouth that looks as if it were about to smile.

A faint smile that we catch or lose according to the movement of the shadows and the time of day, and the gift of our watchfulness.

I am reminded of the Sphinx of Egypt—the same knowledge has given form to that Sphinx and to this Buddha, so far apart in space and time.

Yes, this Buddha is a Sphinx at the cross-roads where the ways of truth come together.

And his beauty springs from the point where nature and geometry meet, where humanity and metaphysics fuse, without the abstract losing its purity or the living creature its plenitude.

But I am talking a lot, now that I am no longer in his presence. Face to face with him, I stood dumb, silent to my very soul, such was the power of his noble affirmation of effacement.

'It is more difficult', says a text, 'to discover what is holy than to admire beauty as ordinary people do.'

But we who are of the ordinary people need beauty to admire so that it may lead us to discover what is holy.

15

I thought it was a shower—one more—on the leaves. But when I raised my head, I saw a leap, a tail, and there was the monkey looking at me and nodding his head. He had come forward on his own, leaving his army in tumult behind him.

'Greetings and glory to you, Hanumana, captain of the monkeys. Thou art come forth from beyond the strait to the country of the demons to deliver Sita the Beautiful and render her to Rama.'[2]

The divine one leaned forward and frowned in order to fathom my words, then turned aside without haste, strode along the pathway of branches, leapt, dived into the splash of greenery and swam through it with wide strokes.

And like a shoal of fish flying from wave to wave, so he and his kin flew from tree to tree on the rolling crests.

My pursuit of the monkeys brought me to the edge of the jungle, where trunks and liana were darkly intertwined. Beneath them, sluggish yellow streams lay between steep banks overhung with leaves furry like bearskin.

1. We have retained the original numbering (omitting 13).
2. It is generally accepted that the island of Lanka in the Ramayana is none other than Ceylon (*Singh-Lanka* : Lion Island).

II

MADURAI

OR THE LAZY BRAHMIN

MADURAI, *January 1937*

Madurai, the first town one reaches in the south of the peninsula after leaving Ceylon, is a huge village scorched into dust by the sun. The houses are rarely more than one storey high. There are also patches of wasteland where hovels made of mud and covered with thatch or matted palm-leaves huddle together and form villages within the town.

A dense crowd of dark-skinned people in colourful rags swarms or squats outside these huts, doing cooking and chores, or satisfying nature in the open air.

Nearly all the men have three horizontal marks of ash on their foreheads, the sign of the followers of Shiv.

Their ribs and arms, when they are bare, show the same triple stripes.

The temple of Shiv, surrounded by walls, is as big as a city. To the visitor imbued with a Latin sense of proportion and Christian sobriety it is at first sight so hideous that his head swims.

Its hugeness, or, rather, that portion of its hugeness that the eye can take in, produces a feeling not of grandeur but of oppression.

A swarm of statues seethes above the flattened architraves of the porches and over these bunches and clusters of agitated bodies, another crowded row of bodies proliferates and buds, and above this yet another row is thrown in tumult, row upon row, up to the sky in a headless pyramid.

The whole is carved out of porous, crumbly tuff that gives free rein to baroque facility and is of a brownish or greyish colour, except where patches of the original daubing remain.

But when one goes beyond the red and white striped walls of the first enclosure and the maze of passages, antechambers and paved courtyards, and the arcades with a thousand columns, and the staircases and the elephant cages and the grills of the covered market and the green artificial lakes bordered with flights of steps, and follows the many-coloured crowd whose hustling and scurrying spills over from the dance of the gods on the high towers blazing in the light, the dividing line between ugliness and beauty, between the natural and the monstrous, between what is right and what is queer, between the diabolical and the divine, wavers, and the triumphal flood of life sweeps it quite away.

A vision flashed through my mind of the Temple at Jerusalem when the whole of Israel had gathered there for the passover and Jesus was teaching in the courtyard of the Gentiles. And as I passed by the stalls on which fruit, food, pots and pans and holy beads were set out pell-mell and the cool shops, heady with the perfumes of flowers, where the garland-makers carried on their prosperous trade, I saw him in person, arming himself with a knotted rope and preparing to overturn the tables of the merchants.

2

Shiv the smiling, whose smile is as taut as a bow, the Great Destroyer who dances on the earth with fire, fever and plague, does not dwell alone in this palace. His whole family lives with him and has a part in his magnificence.

The Goddess resides in a pavilion opposite his apartments. They can often be seen together in the rooms and walks of the temple. He holds her hand, or else gallantly helps her to mount the bull which usually serves to transport him, or he seats her on one of his knees.

On these occasions he is serene and she smiling. She is then Sati, the wife, Ooma the Gracious, Gauri the Golden.

Her name is Purvati, the Earth, and like the earth she is quiet and motherly, whereas the Sun which has gone howling up into the sky 'takes all creatures up in his rage'.

But as soon as she is out of his presence the Kindly Mother

begins to resemble her husband. Her face darkens; her eyes dilate
and whiten; she sticks out her tongue, and two fangs jut out
of her chaps; eight or ten arms sprout from her simultaneously,
brandishing harpoons, tridents, arrows and other weapons;
the beads she tells are skulls and she is mounted on a lion. She
has become Kali the Black, Durga the Inaccessible, Karala the
Horrible. Not, however, for her worshippers, who cling all the
more closely to her cloak, crying 'Mother! my mother!', vowing
her 'ineffable love' and singing moving hymns to her as we do
to the Virgin Mary.

Their two sons hold state in various quarters of the same
Royal Seat. One is called Skanda and rides a peacock. He is
a handsome young man, yet nobody here seems to take him very
seriously: he is the God of Armies.

His glory is dimmed by that of Ganesh, his brother, who is not
only as valorous as he but is possessed of different and rarer
qualities.

One meets this young prince riding a rat. His belly is swollen
and his head is that of an elephant. It would be very foolish,
however, to let oneself be put off by his coarse appearance.
Divine Ganesh is the patron of people of fine judgement who are
not misled by outward appearances. His small, jewel-like eyes are
shrewdly critical and twinkle mockingly. Through his powerful
trunk comes the inspiration of poets and thinkers.

His fidelity, like that of the elephant, is unshakable. The guard-
ian of his mother's door, he defended her threshold against Shiv
himself when he tried to force it, and it was only by ruse that all the
demons and all the gods together, in league with his father,
overcame his resistance.

Like the elephant's, his is the gravity of the substance of the
earth and the darkness of the powers under it. His swollen belly,
a royal globe, is the fruit in which all the hidden treasures of the
kingdoms ripen.

Like the elephant, he holds high the sceptre and the honours of
virile power. But in him, male sap, the elixir of life capable of
engendering nations, the ambrosia of immortality, is dammed
up and controlled by a mighty effort of continence. And seated
in the posture of an ascetic, he draws it up step by step through
his body by the joints of his backbone, then, having purified it

by unremitting meditation, brings it to the crown of his head.

Whereupon, like a torrent gushing from a rock, or lightning flashing from black clouds, straight from his forehead springs the sign of the male.

And it is the single member, that of the head, the member that dominates and outreaches thought.

And this member is a magician's wand and infallibly strikes the spark of conception.

And this member is the column by which the sky rests on the abyss.

And this member is an organ, the organ of the sixth sense.

Therefore, the elephant plunges his trunk into the rivers of life, into the fountains of clarity, so as to slake with their waters the thirst of his heart and of his entrails.

As for the rat, it is a mean footling sort of demon that Ganesh has subjugated in order to punish it.

For what offence, the story does not say, but I suppose it to be the offence of all rats towards all elephants, that is to say, the impertinence of trying to resemble them, in which they succeed only in the measure of rats, and by their tails.

Vanity of which the various species of the Envious will have to bear the consequences: namely, being crushed by the weight of their model.

3

At nightfall, when the sky is veiled with tender violet, and a rosy glow still lingers, a noisy, tumultuous crowd rushes along the esplanades, and people throng into the shadow-filled dens where feeble lamps begin to flicker.

Flutes and drums force out their holy din, the sacred parrots scream in their cages, the solemn elephant trumpets, the faithful jostle each other, bawling piously.

A woman sits on a step suckling her baby, two gangs of boys start fighting, old women sitting in a ring on the ground exchange the latest gossip.

Monks with their bony, black bodies draped in pink and their beards and hair unkempt, wait silently in single file along the wall. The stretcher-bearers who will be carrying the god in a minute or two, taking advantage of the preparatory bustle,

B

stretch out on the paving-stones in the midst of the comings and goings and turmoil of the crowd, and take a nap. The priests are busy. Naked to the waist, with shaven skulls and a cordon passing over one shoulder and under the other, they are heavily adorned with gold chains and other admirable pieces of jewellery. The turbanned guardians push back the worshippers who try to lift up the curtain behind which the statue is being encased in armour of silver encrusted with jewels and decorated with sprays of flowers.

*   *   *

Treading on each other's heels, the bigots go muttering round each pillar, stroking the feet of the statues and sometimes smearing them with saffron.

Girls from good families, clad in silks of insipid colours and wearing flowers in their hair, go up to the great bull of Shiv and, lost in inward contemplation, touch its stone genitals.

In front of a pot-bellied Ganesh an old man with an inspired face stretches out full-length, reaches out his arms palm to palm, touches the ground with his forehead, then with his nose, then with one cheek, then with the other and, bringing his hands back under his shoulders, he raises his rigid body—twice—stretches out once more and does it all over again; finally he gets up, seizes his right ear with his left hand and his left ear with the right, bends his knees as if he were going to sit—twice—straightens up again and goes off. Some put their palms together in front of their mouths, others above their heads. The kneeling women bury their foreheads between their knees.

*

When night has fallen, the bronze gates that flower with small cylinders of oil light up and blaze from top to bottom, the clamour redoubles, and the procession gets under way led by the torches blazing from trident-shaped holders.

The soft columns of the elephant sway forward past the pillars of granite, the bell round his neck clinking and a gold and purple rug flapping loosely round his flanks.

The god, invisible behind drawn curtains, rides in a sedan-chair. The priests who have shut him in after smothering him in ornaments are waving huge fans round him, and the crowd throws itself deliriously in his wake.

This people worships, not in silent contemplation, but in a frenzy of noise. And the divine image explodes into ten tempestuous arms.

They enjoy beauty, not in the crystal of a simple form, but in the molten, seething substance of Fusion, in which every being and every order are bubbles.

The joyful ceremony takes place three times a day, every day in the year.

At all hours of day and night, people bring flowers and saffron and pour milk, butter and boiled rice on to the statues. It blackens them but makes them live, shine and laugh. Dripping with grease, they leap up like wild beasts or reptiles, claws unsheathed, thighs apart and loins jubilating.

All around, the people of the town are famished and lousy. The misery of human beings here is great.

4

At Madurai I had my first deliverance. I was delivered of my trousers, my jacket and my shirt. The happy man, as everyone knows, has no shirt. Consequently, I sailed into happiness.

My new outfit is a long, wide strip of cotton, plain, white and hand-spun. You just wrap it round your loins, fold one end over the other on the left side and twist them up tightly so that they cling together, which fastens the strip without any need for a belt. With the cloth that hangs from the twist, you make a pleated flap which covers the bare side and enables you to take long strides without showing too much leg. A scarf thrown over the shoulders completes the costume.

An Englishman who had been living for many years in India once told me that if you go out in the sun bare-headed, you fall down dead. But my skull cannot have the delicate sensitivity of colonial heads, for although I have shaved it to make my deliverance complete, the sun has given it a golden glare and does not look as if he wanted to strike me unconscious.

Nevertheless, I still feel modest about my too-white body. I admire and envy the people I see, for their limbs are dark and burnished like rich metal and precious wood.

These floating veils give you the pleasure of a swimmer in clear water.

Blancheur oblige. This simple dress, full of ancient dignity, inclines the wearer to pure thoughts.

5

Let no one accuse me of vanity for talking so complacently about my style of dress. It has served me as an instrument of knowledge.

The very day I put it on, the glass cage in which I was imprisoned vanished, and I stepped into the field of human relations unimpeded.

All those for whom the foreigner was only an easy prey or a subject of curiosity turned their eyes elsewhere and vanished into space. All those who feared that contact with a foreigner or a man without caste would contaminate them—and this includes every Hindu who respects his tradition—became accessible to me. They admitted me to their confidence and to their homes. I even won the friendship of a few. Now this country is one of those where the best people hide away and everyone hides what is best in him.

As for the foreigner under the cheese-cover of the sun-helmet, I maintain that he can never get to know the Hindu. Even if he stays here thirty years to govern or to traffic, to amuse himself or to learn, and however shrewd an observer he may be, he will still not know them, for the simple reason that he will never have had a chance to meet them.

More often than not, he will remain closeted with other foreigners or be reduced to the company of his servants only. His opinion of this vast, mysterious country, thousands of years old but with no history, will have been formed from the behaviour of his 'boy'.

The latter, the supple and silent Gopal, will inevitably win his complete confidence, for he will be so respectful, so inventively and touchingly attentive that not even a woman in love could surpass him in delicacy. And Gopal will rob him.

Just as a bitch in heat trails all the dogs in the neighbourhood behind her, so does the man in the sun-helmet, wherever he goes, the yelping mob of beggars, wretches who will spoil and trample underfoot every generous feeling he has and by a trick of the trade at which they excel, drive their prey into such a fit of exasperation that he will end up by throwing them everything he has in his pockets, much as he might slap the face of an insolent boor.

It may very well happen that people with brownish skins, but irreproachably polite, will ingratiate themselves into his private life. They will never treat him otherwise than as a little king and this will make him purr with satisfaction. If need be, they will assure him, when it comes to the pinch, of the depth of their attachment, and this with tears in their eyes and quavering voices. Thanks to which he will be caught in their snares time after time.

On the umpteenth occasion, however, he will go red with rage and swear never to be caught again. The fact will have dawned on him, once and for all, that his hangers-on are not men, but snakes and octopuses. Whereupon he will arm himself so effectively with mistrust that none of them will ever be able to dupe him again. And he will be convinced that his knowledge of India is infallible.

6

It is difficult for a young man to acquire good manners when he has neither master nor parents to teach him.

The costume I have been wearing for the last half-hour only makes my ignorance of what is not done all the more unpardonable.

It is lunch-time, and I enter an eating-house. I have no sooner crossed the threshold than the host looks at my feet with astonished severity. It occurs to me just in time that I must leave my sandals at the doorway. Visibly relieved, he deigns to turn his back on me and lead me down a dark corridor.

He brings me to a halt at a trough of water, I get ready to plunge my hands and perhaps my face into it, with the dirty haste that characterises people of our kind. The good man utters a cry and rolls his eyes up till the whites show. Picking up a small copper ewer, he scoops up a little water and pours some first on my fingers, then on my feet. Just at this moment, a newcomer approaches the trough as if on purpose to prevent my committing another blunder. I note that after sprinkling his hands and feet he raises the ewer above his head and pours water into his mouth, then spits all round him. So when the host presents me with the ewer for the third time I now know what to do with it, and I gargle, snort and spurt out my jet of water with all the fuss and noise proper to distinguished people.

This done, I am brought into the dining-rooms. We pass a row of screens behind which voices can be heard, but I see no one at table. My guide leads me to an empty recess and leaves me there.

I study the wall and the vent in it through which the light descends. It is a prison wall, prison light. Having deliberated some time, I conclude that the best thing is to sit down at the foot of the wall and wait. The man comes back, spreads out in front of my crossed legs a banana-leaf, splashes it with water and sprinkles water round me in a circle, puts a pinch of salt on the tip of the leaf and begins to scoop things out of his pots with his hand. On the rim of the leaf he deposits little mounds of something that looks like peas, then some sort of mashed vegetable, then a mixture of red and green, then boiled seeds, then small round fritters, then a limp pancake, then a hard, light one like a dead leaf, after which he leaves me sitting in front of this doll's dinnerkin.

While I am still examining it, I see him coming from afar, staggering under the weight of a smoke-blackened cauldron which he finally deposits with a crash. And like a mason throwing mortar from his trowel on to a brick, he wallops handfuls of rice out of it on to my leaf until it spills over.

I am left sitting in front of the heap, alone and disarmed. Eventually, I set about it with my fingers, as I have noticed people do when I have looked through the open doorways of houses, but with less speed and skill than they, for when *they* do it, the mouthful rises of its own accord at the finger-tips, whereas my rice crumbles in my palm and the sauce runs down my wrist and smears my cheeks and chin.

Now these dishes feign to consist merely of boiled rice and harmless vegetables, but they take the skin off your mouth and burn your inside like alcohol.

I resort to the liquid of which he has poured me a bowlful. It is a brew of pepper that scalds my throat.

When I go out of the room there is smoke coming out of my ears and nostrils. The host is standing in front of the trough, ready to officiate with the copper ewer; a bath in the trough would suit me better.

I ask him how much this feast has cost. Three annas—fourpence. Fair enough.

*

Since I have been wearing my robe, my expenses have diminished, I will not say by half, but by nineteen twentieths.

With the small sum left I am now unexpectedly wealthy and able to live comfortably for months to come.

I can even occasionally give myself a treat beyond the reach of any European sahib with a tie and yellow shoes: that of giving a few pennies to those who need them but are not expecting them; or of doubling the price of an object when the price I am asked for it seems too honest.

7

At the hour of the siesta I was roused from my torpor by a deafening uproar in which the noise of thunder and the clanking of chains competed with a shrill but liturgical clamour.

It was coming from the street where bands of guttersnipes and little ragged girls had formed a procession and were yelling muddled hymns. They were clapping their hands to beat time, and swinging fans of palm-leaves round the object of the ceremony, whose ithyphallic belly they had hung with garlands of greenery.

It was a steam-roller used for road-mending, one of those machines the like of which has not been seen in Europe for very many years, long of chimney and short of breath, vomiting black smoke, dragging its aged, gouty roller and staining the roadway behind with a piddle of dirty oil.

A new incarnation of the Supreme Brahma, neither less funny nor less acceptable than many another.

8

As in other towns, Gandhi's disciples have a shop here in which they sell cloth spun and woven locally. The shop is at the same time a monastery, for every meeting of members of the party, or, rather, the order, provides an opportunity to live communally in the Gandhian way.

I was made welcome by some very young men with healthy-looking faces and good manners. I at once told them the reason for my journey to India: that it was only the great desire to meet their master that had made me come so far, and that I wanted to be taught by him and to put myself at his service.

For I had long been aware that this saint had discovered, or, rather, rediscovered, a truth that was capable of putting the soul back into life and renewing the world. But busy with my pleasures and studies I had not understood that this truth concerned me personally. It seemed to me that I had paid my debt to a truth when I had expressed and understood it. I did not at first see that truth makes demands on us, that it exacts from us something else than mere lip-service, that we owe it fidelity in all we do. Yet when the day came that, tired of my habits and disgusted by my pleasures, I decided to leave everything and go on this pilgrimage, it no longer seemed to me that I was responding to an obligation, or a demand, or a debt, but that I was answering the call of a great love, such as one flies to.

9

I used to go to the shop every day and spend an hour or two there with my new friends.

Among them there happened to be a half-wit who spent his time gaping at the ceiling. He was neither on the staff, nor a customer: he spoke to nobody and did not even introduce himself. But when I left the shop he came out on my heels and stuck to me during the whole of my stay in Madurai.

Since he looked like a countryman and was dressed like a beggar, I thought at first that some hope of gain had made him attach himself to me. But I was wrong, for not only did he turn out to be a servant to me, as well as a porter, an interpreter, a guide, a secretary and, when necessary, a confidant, without it costing me anything, but his first care was to reduce my expenses by half.

Where he had learnt English I cannot tell. He felt obliged to answer all my questions with the utmost volubility and from a distance he seemed to be carrying it off brilliantly. But if one listened to it in detail, there was neither meaning nor words in his outpour. Speaking English, for him, was above all twisting

one's mouth in a certain pretentious manner and making a
noise flow through it like the gurgling of a tap. To tell the truth,
he imitated the sound of English so well that at first I was completely taken in and spent my time saying 'I beg your pardon?',
'What?', 'What did you say?' until at last his language held no
more secrets for me.

But I had not reached the end of my troubles for all that.
He would take advantage of my willingness to understand not a
word by suddenly bringing out a comprehensible sentence and
even, by chance, an intelligent one. I would notice this only
when the remark had almost vanished into thin air and I never
succeeded in getting him to repeat it.

The result was that I gained great benefit from these conver-
sations, for they forced me to be perpetually vigilant and perpetually caught me out in flagrant inattention.

The man had a habit of winking with his left eye and half
of his face, and from time to time he would let out a startling
roar of laughter.

10

I immediately asked him who he was, what he did and where he
lived. He replied, 'I am a Brahmin,' as if that explained everything.
I put these questions to him again on several other occasions,
but never got any other answer than a burble of English.

11

The Brahmin decided that my hotel room was no longer suitable
for me. He therefore loaded himself with my luggage and carried
it laboriously all the way to the other end of the town, where
he deposited it in a yard, beside a plank lying on trestles.

'Here we are!' he said. 'Make yourself comfortable. Here is
your bed' (and he showed me the plank). 'These arches will
protect you if rain falls. There is a well and all the conveniences.'

'Is this your place?' I asked.

'My place?' said he, and he burst out with such a laugh that I
thought he was having a fit.

'But,' I insisted, 'do tell me whose place this is.'

'What are you worrying about?' he asked. 'Does one have a

place when one's home is everywhere? You are from nowhere,
so you are at home everywhere. Didn't you know that?'

I did know it. A beautiful arcade adorns our courtyard. Near
the well stands a grove of fig-trees and on these fig-trees, instead of
figs, there grow flowers like small crocuses but whose flesh and
scent are like those of tuberoses, and these are the flowers that
are woven into garlands for the temple.

12

I was to learn that my Brahmin owned nothing, did nothing,
had no home, lived on what chance offered and professed the
greatest disdain for all work.

13

When dark has fallen, lying flat on my plank whose cool hardness
does indeed suit me better than the soft hotel bed, I glide from
the sweetness of the fragrant air to the sweetness of sleep lightened
by dreams, and, when my eyes open again, my sight climbs the
starry branches of night.

But a soft footfall near the well announces that it is already
time to rise. Although the moon is still high, in two hours' time,
at the most, day will break.

The idle Brahmin, who went off last night to sleep in the streets,
has come back and is busying himself with the rope and pails of
slopping water.

I throw off my blanket and jump to his side. He is frisking
and snorting under the shower. His grey bun hangs down the
nape of his neck like a wet rag. His neck is thick-set, his shoulders
powerful, his legs slightly bandy. In the innocence of the water,
his genitals are laid bare like a shell, or a child's.

It is an offence against orthodoxy and a pollution of one's three
bodies to wash oneself with soap. One must rub oneself with oil
from head to foot, then rinse oneself lavishly. But water that has
already touched the body must not touch it again; that is why
basins and baths horrify men who are pure.

Similarly, a washed body cannot bear the touch of unwashed
clothing. Consequently, one pours water on a paving-stone

in the courtyard and rubs it clean with the palm of the hand,
then spreads out yesterday's robe on it, smears it with soap,
folds it in two, seizes it at one end and thumps and smacks the
stones with it till lather flies up all around.

When the washing has been hung on the rope, one dresses in
clean clothes. After which one proceeds to wash one's mouth
and teeth. To begin with, one rubs them with a finger. I see
my companion nibbling at a stick that looks like the liquorice
roots we used to chew on the way to school. He gives me one.
I bite it and it fills my mouth with bitter juice that makes me
grimace. What I thought was a sweetmeat is a toothbrush. The
chewed fibres at the end form a tuft to rub with; the bitterness
of the sap makes one's mouth water and refreshes the gums.

This operation lasts an hour or more, but seated on our legs
with our heels on the ground and our knees higher than our
shoulders, we can talk and spit at ease.

When dawn at last arrives, it finds us ready and renewed,
almost worthy to greet it.

Beyond the fig-tree grove, sunrays spread like a palm. The
Brahmin has turned towards them, and standing with his hands
joined above his head and his eyes lowered, he begins to proclaim
the invocation.

Kneeling in my corner, I recite the Lord's Prayer and, above
all, the Gloria, which is suitable and appropriate at all times, but
doubly so at the spring of a happy day.

14

The main business of my attendant was to satisfy public curiosity
concerning me and at the same time keep people at a distance, a
feat which he performed with remarkable skill. He had a gift for
grouping a whole crowd and keeping it at a street corner for as
much as half an hour, during which time I was able to come and
go freely.

What he said to them I never knew and do not care to know, but
it was extraordinarily well said, for the result was to petrify them.

When one is talented it is natural that one should enjoy practising one's art. So he needlessly multiplied occasions on which
to make himself useful.

He would sometimes stop at a door and take me inside. We would find about ten persons sitting there cross-legged on the floor, arms folded. The master of the house would come forward and greet me ceremoniously, then place me on a high seat. Whereupon my zealous adept would launch into a speech and they would all stare at me, round-eyed and open-mouthed, while I thought about my own affairs.

Before long, I would be given a bowl of fresh milk, fruit, and some sweet and spicy fritters. And at the end the master of the house would hang a garland of flowers round my neck like those that are hung round the phallus of the great Shiv.

My Brahmin would still be talking and waving his arms about, but it was obvious that he was busying himself solely for the sake of his art, for *he* had received neither milk, nor cakes, nor garland.

15

At first I had great difficulty in fastening my robe with nothing and twisting the cloth so as to make it hold. At any moment it was in danger of becoming undone, leaving me naked in the middle of the street. It is true that such an incident would have been of no consequence, since not even out of idle curiosity would a single head have turned to look at such an uninteresting sight. But what seemed to me even more difficult was to shove my purse into a non-existent belt.

I had tied my money into a handkerchief and carried it now in one hand, now in the other. At last, not knowing which hand to carry it in, I put it into those of my faithful follower. Thenceforward, it was he who tied or untied the knot in the handkerchief and supplied all our wants.

I felt relieved of a great weight.

16

One of my friends at the shop, taking advantage of the Brahmin's momentarily being out of earshot, said to me, 'Be careful of him! He's not dangerous, but he's little bit wrong in the head.' And he went on to tell me how this had come about. 'When he was very young he went in for yoga exercises. But his father didn't

want him to become a monk and thought it prudent to marry him
to a very beautiful woman. So our friend mixed yoga and the
woman and it muddled his wits. But now that his father is dead
and his wife is dead and he hasn't got a home any more, everything
is going much better for him.'

17

I frequent the Catholic community in Madurai and go to their
church. It was founded in the seventeenth century by an Italian
priest named Nobile, who, understanding that in order to evan-
gelise this country one must first and foremost live an evangelical
life, adopted the ways of the local priests, wearing a loin-cloth
and carrying a begging bowl, fasting and exercising himself and
singing as he walked the roads, just as they did. And that was how
he founded the Christian community which is still flourishing
here. Too flourishing. For I can find no one following in the steps
of its founder. What I have found are petty lower middle-class
functionaries wearing surplices and extremely anxious to hold
on to the protection of the government and get their grants from
Europe, for without these how could Truth subsist?

18

The Brahmin, after fumbling in the purse, fished out of it a
little bit of copper, black, defaced, worn thin and twisted. He took
it between his finger and thumb, brought it up to his nose and
squinted at it.

Then in order to contemplate it more comfortably, he seated
himself on his hams in the middle of the street. A horse galloping
at full speed towards us with its cart behind swerved and enveloped
us in a cloud of dust.

But the squatting Brahmin continued to peer at his coin and
presently I heard him saying, 'You nasty, mean, ugh! mean,
miserly, idiotic, sordid bit of trash! Ugh! you bit of dried snot!
You squashed fly! You pitiful louse! Pah! I've seen enough of
you! Out you go!' and he flicked it away so that it rolled into the
horse-dung.

Then he stood up again satisfied.

19

'How old are you?' I asked him one day.

'Seventy-three,' he answered.

Now he had a skimpy bun of grey hair such as elderly house-
wives sometimes have, and, like some old women, he had a few
short hairs sprouting from his chin, but otherwise his body
seemed sturdy and his bow legs very nimble indeed. So I com-
plimented him on his youthfulness, which really did surprise me.
But he seemed to find my surprise rather silly.

Next day, he was beginning a sentence with 'At our age—'

'I beg your pardon', I said. '*I* am not seventy-three.'

'I suppose you're not. You're probably about thirty-five?'

'And how old are you?'

'So am I.'

'Well!' I exclaimed. 'You *have* grown a lot younger in one day!'

But this remark did not trouble him in the slightest and he
continued the conversation as if nothing of the kind had been
said.

Whenever I asked him how old a building was, he would say,
'Two thousand years', or 'Ten thousand years', although the stone
and the style showed that it could not be more than two hundred
years old.

I attributed this uncertainty and confusion where dates and
periods were concerned to his mental trouble. But I had later
to admit that this lack of common sense is one of the most widespread characteristics of the Indian and portrays, so to speak, one
of the features of Hindu wisdom: indifference to time.

Having observed this, some people declare, 'The Indians are
mystics: it is not surprising that their ideas are vague and confused.' To which it must be answered that the Indians, no doubt
because they are mystics, have the most precise knowledge that
exists of the most precise thing that exists: the Number.

One must not forget that whereas geometry is an Egyptian
science that has come to us through the Greeks, arithmetic and
algebra are Indian sciences and ten centuries had already elapsed
before they reached us through the Arabs.

To begin with, the Indians invented the nought. Let no one say that that is nothing: the Orient has never produced a finer pearl.

It is by means of this hole in the hub that the admirable wheel of numbers turns. The nought has been the leaven that has raised all the human sciences.

It is by means of the nought that 10 transposes 1 on to another plane, that with ten signs only, one can fix, compose and decompose all the numbers, those of the stars or the drops in the sea. It is thanks to the nought that tens fit exactly into tens, in a chain so marvellously simple that it seems to be implicit in the very nature of things and to spring from them, although this was once very far from being obvious.

Only at the dawn of modern times did the system impose itself in Europe. It has been one of the main factors in the development of the Western sciences. Archimedes or Apollonius of Perga had to bend their great heads all night over a sum that a schoolboy can now work out in a quarter of an hour thanks to the signs he has learnt. And yet, in the fifteenth century, even in the most advanced colleges in France, no other arithmetic was taught than addition and subtraction. To learn multiplication, one had to have recourse to the famous universities of Italy.

Nought, zero, is the key to the system of numbers. *Zephirum* is the Latin transcription of the Arab word meaning zero. Italian transformed *zephirum* into *zero*. The plural, *zephira*, becomes *cifra*, from which comes *cypher*. The Genoese sailors, who were the first Europeans to adopt numerals, were accused of using a secret language, hence the other meaning of the word *cypher*. For a long time, people looked on these numerals, known as 'arabic', with aversion: as 'arabic' they were suspect. They called them magic and diabolical. (They little knew how right they were!)

But the conception of nought and of numbers contributed not merely to making calculation easier, it also led naturally to the discovery of negative numbers, and above all to that of the mathematical infinite, a disquieting thing that the Greeks had always rejected because it went against their attachment to closed perfection and to greatness of human dimensions. Whereas, in the definition of quantity called the *quotient by zero* the Indians define the infinite precisely, for the first time—yes! *define* the *infinite* in its relation with *zero*.

The metaphysical essence of numbers appears more transparent-
ly through the lighter and clearer symbol of the numeral.

That is why, long after the speculations of the Pythagoreans on
the subject of Sacred Numbers and the Golden Number have
been relegated to the museum of fine historical curiosities, the
problems raised by Indian thought have in their turn given
rise to others of which we are still far from having exhausted the
series. Infinitesimal Analysis, the Theory of Numbers and even
the recent Theory of Groups spring from that original impetus.

Greek arithmetic (which was not a science of calculation) was
concerned with the body of the number and its figure; Indian
arithmetic was concerned with its very life, that is to say, its
multiplications and its operative combinations.

That is why, before the sixth century, the Indians had already
discovered algebra.

Indians have a logic in no way inferior to that of Aristotle.
They possess knowledge of the living body, by which I mean
that they have inner knowledge of life in the body and a philosophy
of nature that Western science can neither refute nor replace.

In psychology, in aesthetics, in linguistics, in the art of poetry,
in the science of eroticism as in that of asceticism, they are
scrupulous analysts and untiring classifiers.

In the theory of music they have proved themselves to possess
accuracy, subtlety of taste, and knowledge unequalled anywhere
else in the world. In the intervals of a chromatic scale, for example,
in which our ears can only hear twelve degrees, they hear twenty-
two, to which their stringed instruments are tuned by means of
mobile frets. Their rhythm presents an even more astonishing
variety. Now music, as everyone knows, is a sensuous transcription of the knowledge of numbers. But the aptitude of the Indians
for exactitude disappears when it comes to formulating a date.
It is almost as if the elusive nature of time affected their numerals,
melting them so that they flow into each other and finally evaporate.
But their lack of precision concerning dates is due neither to
muddle-headedness nor to dreaminess, but to the deliberate
desire to turn away from what they consider vain. Is anybody
mad enough to want to count the shadows of clouds passing over
the waves of the sea? Are we going to waste our time, or rather,
our eternity, storing up in our memories what takes place in

time? Better to remember to be. Being does not pass away. What passes *is not*, but only appears, as the dream appears to the sleeper. And it is the peculiarity of the sleeper not to know that he is dreaming and to believe in his dreams. Everything that takes place in this vast world (and our life that passes) is an immense, inexplicable illusion. There is no other reason for this illusion than our ignorance. Those who awake see it for what it is. Making a study of what arises from ignorance and belongs to illusion is building on error and aggravating illusion. But constituting a science of memories of what once took place in time is falling into absurdity. This absurdity is History: a knowledge that knows nothing true. That is why the Indians will have nothing to do with it. And of their history we know nothing at all, at least, not through them.

*   *   *

All the operations and combinations possible with concrete, negative, fractional, figurative or transfinite numbers, and even the solution of the equation to the nth degree, could not help us to discover the age of the lazy Brahmin, knowledge which he does not possess himself. Since he gets along without it, let's do likewise.

20

The idle Brahmin and I often went for walks in the country by the road that runs along the banks bordering the rice-fields. We stopped one day as usual at one of the many rectangular tanks, framed in flights of stone steps, that have been dug out in this district. They are used for watering the fields during the dry season, and for bathing and drinking. We bathed and drank.

When we had dressed again, we lingered a while by the edge of the water. The Brahmin began tossing our knotted handkerchief as if it were a ball.

'Take care not to let it fall into the tank,' I said. 'We should have nothing left to live on.'

'Is *that* what you live on?'

'No,' I said, rather peeved. 'But I need it to preserve my body from hunger and my soul from care.'

'Ha! ha! I see the joke!' he guffawed. And he continued to

roar and writhe with laughter, wheeling round and slapping his thighs, while I considered him with some embarrassment.

21

I have come into the sanctuary at the hour of solitude when noon overwhelms the beggars with sleep in the shade of the arcades.

Even my faithful friend has left me and gone off the waste ground in search of some pillow of dust to his liking.

I have reached the room from which the processions start in the evening. The only light that enters it comes from the openings close to the ceiling, which is paved with granite like the floor. The sceptre of Shiv, a column of gilded bronze planted in the earth, passes through the hole in the ceiling and carries up into the sky the bull of solid gold which cannot be seen from here and which faces the gold-plated roofs of the supreme *cella* of the temple, the holy of holies.

It takes some time for the eyes to revive in the dark and discern the statues that adorn the pillars, and longer still for their meaning to light up.

Framing the entrance, a statue of Shiv three times bigger than a man takes a great dancing stride. A whirlwind of arms surrounds him with a flashing of blades, his moustache blazes, his eyebrows are jets of light, the crown of his head bursts into flame.

Opposite him a figure appears, probably feminine, for the waist is supple, the limbs round and loaded with ornaments. The left breast emerges, a woman's breast. But the right breast is flat, a warrior's cuirass of muscle. The two sides of the face, divided by the long bevel of the nose, are unequal and contradictory. It is Shiv again, the double, the ambiguous, that beauty alone recomposes, beauty and the victorious serenity of his smile.

Here he is again, dancing and threatening. One of his arms is thrusting a long spear into the throat of a little creature with intertwined limbs: Yama, the Lord of Death. From Yama's hand a net is still hanging. It goes round the pedestal and caught in it is a small, imploring child. Shiv the Destroyer is destroying destruction; for Shiv is the protector of the afflicted: the Saviour.

Here, Shiv is advancing on a chariot like those the crowd drags through the streets on solemn feast-days. The moon and the sun are

his chariot-wheels. The chariot represents the earth decorated
with all the animals that are the riches of the earth. The bow that
the god brandishes is Vishnu himself and the arrow Brahma.
The moon, the sun and the earth are saying to each other, 'Without
us, how can Shiv win victory?' So Shiv smiles. And his smile is
so powerful that the chariot goes forward of its own accord on
its wheels of stars; the bow curves itself like the ox between the
goad and the yoke, and the arrow springs forward.

With his arrow, Shiv is aiming at the pillar opposite, where the
three cities are carved in bas-relief: the city of iron, the city of
silver and the city of gold, inhabited by the demons of the belly, the
demons of the heart and the demons of the head. And he will
destroy the three cities and the demons who live in them, for
he is the destroyer of darkness, of desire and illusion: he is the
Prince of the Yogis.

Further off, he is teaching, seated on the mountain, his left
hand holding his rosary, his right raised 'in the pose of argumen-
tation', his disciples gathered in front of his crossed legs. Further off,
he rests and plays. His wife, now small, is sitting on his knee.

For he, the Prince of Ascetics, is married, whereas his worshippers, the yogis, give themselves up to chastity and vagabondage.
He has taken a wife just as the Vedic Rishis took wives. And
no doubt they practised the rites of carnal love as a form of ascetic
exercise. And Shiv, being a god, reaches the end of this perilous
road without falling.

The wedding of Shiv occupies the centre of the room. His
young wife, sister to Vishnu, stands between the two great gods,
slight and beautifully shaped. Her waist seems to bend under the
weight of her breasts, beautiful fruit offered up to love.

Happiness laughs in her face, shivers in her shoulders, plays in
her fingers, the happiness of surrender and triumph. The happiness of giving has made Vishnu's face radiant. In token, he is
pouring water from a small pitcher. The water flows like a ring
round the fingers of the three divinities and binds them with its
trembling stream. Shiv is smiling too, but only slightly and almost
with disdain. It is through condescension to the wishes and prayers
of the world that he is giving in to the marriage; his happiness and
fulfilment lie elsewhere.

The three figures are carved out of the same stone and so are the pedestal and the frieze showing the musicians and the revelling crowd who are taking part in the divine union. From this union spring the sanctuary and the town, the princes and the people of Madurai.

Where the darkness is at its deepest, I discover the last image of Shiv. He stands flat upon the pilaster, his head half thrust into the stone capital and his feet half buried in the base. A sublime spirit in the shape of a bird is flying up in search of the god's head, and a searching spirit in the shape of a frog is diving to discover what the god's feet are planted on. But neither bird nor frog can find an end to God and they come back at the foot of the pilaster in human form, side by side, imploring him with praying hands.

Although there is something of the god in each of these images made in man's image, the god himself appears in his entirety in a body which has no face.

In the darkest cell of the temple, the narrowest and barest, in the windowless room which only the Brahmins may enter, there he stands, solemn and powerfully present in the upright thrust of a colossal virile member.

This phallus is made of stone and is constantly anointed with ghee. Around it, garlands are wreathed and rich flowers heaped up; smooth-petalled, sweet and suffocating like amorous flesh.

22

Tell me now—this great devil of a god, this protector, more fear-inspiring than Satan himself, with cobras coiled round him and skulls for ornament, and horrifying weapons radiating from him, who leaps into rings of fire and stamps on the creature that he has struck down,

and dances and makes merry in the midst of panic and disaster,

and remains master of himself at the very height of orgy and of ecstasy, his smile and his pity ready as a taut bow,

whose throat is blue from drinking the venom of the Great Serpent that was about to poison the world,

the Good Shepherd, Master of the Herd,

Master of the herd of giants, vampires, ghouls, prowling spirits that haunt funeral pyres and the night wind,

Master of the flock of thieves, beggars and wandering fakirs
who clown and rave,
Himself incomprehensible and contradictory as man is,
inexplicable, irrefutable, too, like the living animal,
outrageous, but serene as the wise are,
inexorable, but wild and shy as life is and full of grace like death,
black and blazing like the phallus—
tell me now, what do they call this great devil of a god?
His name is Shiv, 'The pleasant one'.

23

It is a far cry to Buddha meditating in the tranquil shade at
Anuradhapura. Between the Wise One, steadfast in the immobility
of Truth conquered and the immaculate void of Nirvana, and
this king of dancing, of rut and fury, a great gulf opens. It is in
their very smiles that their unlikeness reaches its crowning
point: Buddha's almost imperceptible, like the white edge of a
lotus petal overlapping the whiteness of another; Shiv's like the
sharp edge of a strong sword.

Shiv and Buddha fought for the same territory—the sacred
earth of India. Shiv has conquered Buddha and driven him out of
his native land, driven him towards frozen Tibet, the flatness of
China, and the sultry islands. But here, Shiv reigns alone.

Alone, that is to say, in the company of the other supreme gods,
the other unique gods, Vishnu and Brahma, supreme as he is,
unique as he is and no more different from him than are the multiple shapes he likes to frolic in.

Buddha has climbed to the summit of the spirit and dwells
there.

But can one be wholly perfect when one is nothing else but
perfect?

Whoever has reached the highest summit is outreached by
Shiv, for Shiv outreaches him in depth.

Shiv is sublime, but just as profound as he is sublime.

What Buddha forgets and leaves behind, Shiv picks up and
keeps.

What Buddha repulses and denies, Shiv affirms and exalts—
in order to destroy it.

Whereas Buddha achieves deliverance in the light of the summit, Shiv, capering and laughing, goes down and sweeps the chimneys of hell, rakes the earth, sticks his spurs into the living, tickles the armpits of the lazy, prods the rumps of the hypocrites, whips off the turbans of the arrogant, snatches his cloak from the prude and his purse from the miser, buries the quarrellers together in the ruins of their house, sets fire to war in rotting empires, deals out pain according to the justice of chance, filters trouble and forges virtue in fire, and showers death upon all of us, death which is the signal for return, the inverted shadow of universal Deliverance.

*

'Shiv' is only a nickname, but his real name has been forgotten. His real name is Rudra. Rudra the Red Head appears in the Vedic Hymns in the midst of thunder and lightning, shaking and devastating the earth at the head of the Maruts on their galloping horses.

At that time he counted only as a valiant chieftain among the gods, but he made his fortune in the ruins, and now he has become king of kings and god of gods.

In the days when Shiv was only Rudra, there was somebody who attracted more hymns than all the gods put together, and this was Agni, the Fire of Sacrifice.

The fact is that Agni united all the gods in his person since he was their common mouth and the tongue of fire by which they devoured the victim and tasted the sacrifice.

But Rudra is more properly the untamed fire that bursts from the clouds as he pleases, sets a tree by the roadside ablaze, kills a man, and goes his way. He lies hidden everywhere, since you can strike him out of a stone or draw him from sticks by rubbing them together. He wakes and watches on the hearth, and cooks man's food. He defends the lost traveller from wild beasts in the forest at night. He lights up the bedchamber and urges the young husband and wife to the play of love. Terrible or familiar, he holds all the threads of life.

He climbs over the heads of Varuna and of Indra, his former master, and reaches the sun and the stars, which are the dwelling-places of fire. Their brilliant fire, however, is the same as that

which burns in the heart of man and that is why the secrets of
destiny are written in the celestial signs.

Then one day Shiv invented a new fire to put in the heart of
man: ascetic fire. And that day he conquered Agni and became
the lord of the gods. It is neither a goat nor a horse that the ascetic
immolates and burns in the fire of Shiv, it is not just a handful
of rice or sesame or clarified butter that he pours into the flame,
but the breath from his throat, the words of his mouth, the
movements of his limbs, the loves of his heart, the flower of his
thought, all his strength and every hour of his life. For only the
genuine sacrifice of the entire man can wrench grace from the
God of Truth.

He who sacrifices to Agni can no doubt obtain from the gods
all worldly good; but he who gives himself up to inner sacrifice
rejects worldly good, does without the gods and outdoes them.

Through fasting, an ascetic can become a threat even to the
gods, for maceration will infallibly give him the power to seize
their thrones, provided, of course, that he is willing to turn away
from his goal, which is to deliver himself from good and evil, as
indeed from all states, including that of divinity.

And so, while the Brahmins take wives and have homes and lay
sacrifices on altars in their homes and in temples, the strange and
numerous children of Shiv live alone or in bands in the forests and
caves and have no other temple than the body of man which they
destroy and rebuild during their lifetime.

The monk's robe blazes red: he is clad in the fire of Shiv.
Or else he goes naked, his body smeared with ash, 'clad in air'
like his master.

Sometimes his hair is reddened with henna and it flames round
his head, while in his ashy face his eyes glow like embers.

24

It required the cult of this ferocious, phallic god to introduce two
elements into the religious life of the Hindus: tender piety
and chastity.

There is nothing of either in the Vedic hymns that embody
the most ancient tradition. Their content is solemn glorification
of the great gods in their stormy or sun-like splendour; prayers

to these gods, when they are kindly disposed, for long life and
numerous offspring, for abundant harvests and flourishing
flocks: and when the gods are redoubtable, supplications to turn
their wrath against the enemy and spare those who glorify them.
They also contain dialogue to be chanted, the rudiments of drama,
philosophical riddles, charms for making hair grow or for lessen-
ing the resistance of a beauty.

Towards the sixth century of our era the Shivites of the south
became inspired with mystical fervour such as made the Blessed
Raymond Lull and Saint Francis of Assisi tremble, weep and
sing. It was at the feet of this god bristling with swords that, for
the first time, the hearts of the devout melted, not with terror,
but with tenderness, and that their hynm burst forth as a free
and intimate outpouring of the adorer's love to the adored one.

*

Celibacy was no more prized by the saints in Vedic times than by
the patriarchs and prophets in the Bible, but for the Yogis of
Shiv it is a strict rule. For the Shaktas also, I believe.

The Shaktas are the fanatics of Shakti, or Power. The power
of Shiv being nothing other than his wife, they adore the goddess,
since Shiv, through her, manifests himself to the world and works
on it. Shakti is not merely one of the goddesses who dwell in the
temple in the shape of wives of Shiv, each with her name and history, and all perhaps only different forms of a single wife: Shakti
is also all the female divinities, and even all women and all cows,
who without doubt are only the various forms of one great
Mother of gods and men and all created beings, so that the Shaktas end up by seeing divinity only in female and maternal form.
For them, God withdraws into an abstract heaven.

What the Shaktas want from Power is power, that is to say,
magic powers. They are distillers of love-potions, amulet-makers,
spell-casters, healers and miracle-makers.

Their holy books are the Tantra. Almost unanimously, orien-
talists affirm that the Shaktas give themselves up to ritual orgies.
I am inclined to think that these authorities have missed the point.

Even if we are told that when the master submits his disciples
to the trials of the Tantra, he offers for their contemplation the
organ of the sex which is not theirs, that he shows them an image

of it so lifelike as to disturb them, even if we are told that this organ is neither painted nor carved but of living flesh and presented as such, and that it is not only exposed to their sight but is stimulated to the height of excitement, and even if we are further told that the disciple stands there naked before the eyes of his master, it has still not been proved that we are dealing with an orgy.

The Bacchanalia, the Liberalia, the Saturnalia, the Phallophoria were all sacred orgies and their purpose seems clear—to honour the sources of generation and abundance.

The witches' sabbath was an orgy, and even a sacred orgy. The intention of the participators was clearly to satisfy in ceremonious revelry an instinct till then imprisoned, cursed and driven into secrecy, and at the same time to avenge that instinct on all those who had condemned it, by obscenely aping and ridiculing their rites. The practices of the Tantra, on the contrary, result in a domination of the same instinct, or rather show that this domination has already been achieved. Naked in the sight of his master, the disciple could not yield to the provocation of the spectacle presented to him without being betrayed (at least if he is a man) by the obvious and shameful reactions of his body.

Just as the howling or whirling dervishes, far from seeking to make themselves dizzy with their howling and dancing, achieve at the climax of noise and agitation the entire possession and enjoyment of inner silence and immobility, so do the Shaktas obtain purification by giving themselves up to what the uninitiated call orgies.

The basic principle of the Tantra may be summed up in this way: acts which are sins when they lead a man into attachment and ignorance, carried out solemnly under the watchful guidance of a master, lead the same man to deliverance and illumination.

Nothing could be more subtle or more profound than such a thought, nothing more dangerous or more efficient than such a method.

The Shakta seeks magic power. And magic power is nothing other than genital power, diverted from its natural outlet and used for seductive action on the substance of things. For the other monks, the rule of continence is strict and tolerates no exception.

*   *

Besides, nothing lends itself less to debauchery than phallic worship. For in so far as sex is sacred, it is vowed to sacrifice.

25

Lingam means *Sign* and Lingam means *Phallus*. It is the magic key, the key that opens the forms of all things.

26

The fire that leaps up the outer porches of the temple, those pyres of stone loaded with their pyramid where all the orders of creation, piled up row on row, mingle and burst into flame,

the fire that runs along the stone of the paved courtyards in the noonday blaze,

the fire that glides like a snake on the green lake,

the fire that flames in the robe of a wandering monk,

the fire that burns in the bronze of all these dancing figures,

the fire that whirls with its thousand limbs, its thousand heads, its thousand swords,

the fire stops in the heart of the sanctuary, stops in the cold, rigid, black lightning of the Lingam.

27

TIRIPARAKUNDRAM

The time came to leave Madurai. My faithful lazybones insisted on accompanying me to Tiriparakundram, where we visited the temple of Ganesh. The façade is like a long, flat architrave supported by a row of pillars that mask a forest of other pillars. Rearing stone horses frame the main porch.

The high priest himself did us the honours of the place and showed us the lakes and the gardens full of broad-leaved plants where at fixed dates the god is taken out 'for ventilation' as the priest explains in a loud, strident voice that rings out under the arcades.

More sacred than the temple itself, the mountain of Tiriparakundram, whether it be a rock miraculously sprung from the flat

earth or a block fallen from the sky, rises abruptly from the plain
of the rice-fields to the plain of the heavens.

The sun was setting as we paused at the foot of the mountain
to look at the little town, the scanty stubble and the scattered
cattle grazing it. Between the roofs one could see smoke coming
up, or trees.

My companion's gaze was fixed on some ruins. At last, turning
towards me, he said, 'There's my house.'

After a silence he went on, 'Yes, that's where I was born, and
that's where my father made me repeat the holy mantra and
where my mother, whose head used to loll from side to side,
so often comforted me for being lazy and not wanting to learn
anything. That's where my father gave me a wife. That's where
he died. And where I lived with my wife and believed I was happy.
That's where she died . . .'

The setting sun was lengthening our shadows. We started to
climb the path uphill. I, too, began to think of days that had been
happy and were gone, of people who had been dear to me, and
still were, but who were now gone. Whereupon the Brahmin
remarked, 'The only thing one does not lose, since it is always
there, since it is always, since it is, is what we lose more quickly
than anything else, yet we never weep over that loss.'

Then suddenly changing his tone and the subject, 'By the
way,' he said, 'since you're leaving tomorrow, I must give you
back your purse.' And he put the double-knotted handkerchief,
heavy with my fortune, into my hands. 'Take good care of it!'
he shouted. 'Don't let it out of your hands! It's all you have
left. If you lose that, you are sure to die!' Whereupon he burst
out laughing as he had done the first time, on the steps by the
water-tank.

Around us rose dark rocks and unknown trees strangely
twining, and behind him was the glow of sunset, and there he was,
roaring with laughter and slapping his thighs.

I waited patiently till he had finished. Then we went on
climbing, one behind the other.

The path twists up, raised now and then by steps cut out of
the living rock and bordered at each bend by small, carved
benches. Further on, it burrows into grass as tall as a man; grass
which, when you bruise it, smells of lemon. The bare rock

reappears, and engraved on it are the names of pilgrims who passed this way long ago. When they could not write, they outlined a foot on the rock. The summit is rounded, like a brown back on which the sunset-streaked sky rests.

But no sooner has one gone round the shoulder of the hill than one's sight plunges abruptly into the plain patched with rice-fields and pools of water and studded here and there with cone-shaped hills.

A white eagle turns in the air without the beat of a wing. Its movement signs the immensity of the visible space.

Here the path narrows and one must stoop to go through the porch of the sanctuary, cut out of the sheer mountainside.

On the other side of the short tunnel, one discovers the sanctuary itself, a roof borne on a few columns, deserted at this time of year when there are neither feasts nor pilgrimages.

A short flight of steps leads down into a natural courtyard, walled in on the left by rock and ending abruptly on the right in the vast space where the last streaks of sunset are fading.

At the foot of the wall of rock, an oblong cleft lies full of water so deep and of such a vibrant green that the gods have moved into it. Ganesh himself swells out of the rocky wall at the level of the water.

Dying flowers are fading on his belly and there is still a trace of saffron reddening his foot.

His worshippers can reach him only by swimming. They invoke him, their bodies stiff with the deathly chill of the water, and their legs dangling over the bottomless pit.

28

Night had come, so beautiful that I could not tear my sight away from the stars.

And I said to the Brahmin, 'Let us pass the night here and we shall also have dawn.'

'That's all right for me,' he said, 'but what about you?'

We had left our blankets down at the priest's where we were to have slept and were wearing only our cotton robes.

'What's all right for you is all right for me,' said I. 'Do you take me for a little girl?'

'Just as you like,' he replied. 'In any case, it's time to sleep.'

And without more ado he stretched out where he was on the rock, pulled a corner of his scarf over his head and started snoring.

I remained lost in my thoughts for an hour or two longer. In the meanwhile the wind had risen and fatigue had descended on me.

I looked for the shelter of some hollow, but the dome of the holy mountain was round and bare and the wind assailed it on all sides at once.

I lay down in my robe which was flapping like a flag in a gale and when I shut my eyes it felt as if my naked feet were flying away from me. The gritty dust scouring along at ground level forced its way into my nostrils and my mouth.

I got up several times and went to have a look at the sleeping Brahmin. His steadfastness in sleep was impressive.

Finally, I sat on my haunches with my arms tightly crossed, gripping my shoulders, and waited for the night to pass over me.

When at last the stars slipped aside to make way for dawn I was near exhaustion, but as the light increased, my tiredness fell away and I rose, upheld only by my second body, the one whose flesh and blood are made of light and whose resurrection on the Day of Judgement is promised us in the holy books.

At daybreak it was the third body that answered—the body which is of the size of a thumb and dwells in the top of the heart. My third body exulted at daybreak like a song-bird when his cage is hung outside.

The sun burst open the horizon, rose into the sky without a trace of mist and closed my eyes.

In the eye of every man there is a black point, and in this point stands a man, tiny but shining with life. That is why the point is called the 'pupil' of the eye.

But the friend who looks into the eye of his friend recognises the person standing in the black point; he recognises that the person is himself, tiny but whole and shining with life.

If we were pure enough to look the sun in the eye, we should see a door opening in the middle of its globe, and in the open doorway, the Person would appear.

The Brahmin below was reciting his morning prayer. I heard him intoning these verses from the Isha Upanishad:

'Protecting Sun, open your door
of golden clarity that hides
the Person of the God of Truth,
that I, a seeker after truth,
may look upon Him.

Protector, Eye of Justice, oh Almighty Sun,
Son of the Lord,
you who disperse and join your rays in righteousness
    and spread warmth according to your grace,
grant me to see your hallowing face,
yes, your face,
yes, the Person,
yes, the one I am.'

29

At the foot of the mountain we took our separate ways, the Brahmin the road to Madurai and I the road to the north.

'You have been a good friend to me,' I began. 'I shall think of you and I'll write to you now and then.'

'What for?' he said. 'When my father died, he never sent me a postcard. When my mother died, she didn't write to say that she was better off where she was. When my wife died, she didn't send me a view of the main entrance to the moon or a map of the Land of the South where the Dead are seated. Why should those who leave recall themselves to mind? When you are gone, I never want to think of you again lest I miss you. Regret is an evil that springs from attachment. Just think: one single regret at the moment of dying makes vain all hope of non-return to this world. Goodbye, and be sure to take care of that money!'

He made an attempt to laugh and opened his mouth to that purpose, but no laughter came and turning his back on me, he set off.

I watched from where I stood till he had disappeared round a bend in the path.

Goodbye, my friend!

We shall not see each other again in this world, at least, not in the raiment of our present bodies.

III

SHRIRINGAM

OR THE PHILOSOPHER ON THE ROOF

I reached Trichinopoli by train and asked my way to the temple. This temple is hollowed out of the rock which it also crowns, and dominates the town.

I was shown a small green bus drawn up at the edge of the pavement. I climbed into it and asked once again if it went to the temple. The other passengers assured me that it did.

When the bus was full, it started up, shot across the town and escaped into the countryside.

'Well, that settles Trichinopoli and its temple,' I thought, as the town and the hill disappeared on the horizon. 'Those good people didn't understand what I meant and now God knows where we are heading.'

But it is enough that God knows. And I am not in the habit of interfering with events when I notice that they intend to follow their course without taking my plans into account. When this happens, I let them explain themselves right to the end, so as to get the full benefit of what they have to teach me.

I have always found this method successful, but it has never been so profitable to me as it was that day, for I gained three things:

first, I visited Shriringam of which—I confess—I had never heard till then;

secondly, I made the acquaintance of Vishnu, the Supreme God to whom—I must confess—I had hitherto paid not the slightest attention;

and finally, I obtained my second deliverance, for I parted there with my 'purse' and all the money I had, a deliverance which—I again confess—I should not have sought unaided.

2

On its island in the arms of a wide river, framed rather than protected by seven belts of wall, stands Shriringam, the fortress of Vishnu, the greatest temple in the whole of India.

I do not know the length of the outside wall, but it seemed to me that it would take a good hour to walk round.

The vast enclosures make seven concentric squares on the ground. Four walls part from the centre and cut through the middle of the sides of each square. They are straight, and form a cross oriented with precision.

At the seven cardinal points, that is to say, across the opening of each walk, straddles a porch supporting a headless pyramid decorated with statues and geometrical designs.

From every meeting of a walk with a wall there results a porch, so that each arm of the cross carries seven porches.

Their arches are so skilfully contrived that the first ray of the first day of spring darts through the seven porches that open eastward and strikes the gold roof of the central sanctuary.

The Temple of Vishnu is planned like this because the Square is the symbol of matter, dense and limited, and the Cross is the natural support of the earth and is its connection with heaven.

There are seven walls round the temple of Vishnu because there are seven notes in the scale and seven colours in the rainbow. Whenever the Unity pleases to unfold on the terrestrial plane as a peacock spreads its tail, His accomplishment is sevenfold.

Four being the number of solid matter and Three that of Divine Power, the placing of three over four in the sum of seven is rightly the order of fulfilment.

The same interplay of similarity and correspondence has gone into the building of the sanctuary. The top, rounded, compact and mountain-like, rests on cubic foundations. The swellings that enfold the corners of the base only underline the material heaviness and inertia it symbolises, while the gold of the cupolas exalts the temple's solar and celestial significance.

Like all Hindu sanctuaries, Shriringam is modelled on the Mountain of Meru, the centre of the world and the source of the Ganges. Now a mountain is an effort made by the earth and all

the cumbrous burden it carries to thrust itself up into Heaven.
It is also the mark by which the Creator has signed matter.
Graces come to the earth from above by means of the mountain,
as a gift in the water of the sacred rivers, as treasure in the mines
guarded by the Nagas, as power in the accumulated merit of
the hermits who dwell on the mountain.

Thus caves in mountains were the first temples and are still
the most sacred. Those who made temples in the plain had
to begin by building a cave and then a hill to cover the cave.

Now, Vishnu is in Four and Vishnu is in Seven and Vishnu is
in the mountain, for Vishnu's name is The-Fulfilment-of-God-
in-Matter.

3

Who is the man over there whose head is the head of a pig? It
is not a man, and it is not a pig. Let there be no mistake: it's
God. God who fulfils himself in matter.

It is Vishnu in his incarnation of a boar.

To fulfil oneself in matter, one must dig into it and bury oneself in it. And for that burial God could choose no better tool
than the funnel of a snout.

No other creature in the world is so perfectly buried in its
own mass as the pig. No other is so stubbornly voracious. No
other grouting, grunting beast is so eager to dig itself ever more
deeply in.

Bore your flat snout in, pig! And work your jaws! Further
down, further still lies the root of substance and the truffle
of essence.

Now, in the time when the primordial waters covered the face
of the earth, the Boar of Vishnu plunged into them till they
came half up his body, and searching and snuffing he went
routing about until, grubbing in the mud with this tusks, he
brought to light the Earth, the divine Bhoomi. And Brahma,
bursting with the desire to create all beings, quickly peopled
her with them.

Here she is, gentle and pretty, the divine Bhoomi that you see
here in the arms of the man with a snout and a tiara on his head.
And to think that we were on the verge of pitying her for falling
into the hands of such a monster!

c

The fact is that the acts of God always seem monstrous to those who are not in the secret of things.

4

Once, while Manu, the first man, was bathing in the river, a little fish got caught in his hand.

Manu was going to put it back into the water, but the little fish cried, 'Keep me! otherwise the big fish will eat me.'

So Manu put him in a bowl and gave him three grains of rice.

Next day the fish had grown so much that Manu had to put him into a jar.

A few days later the lake was not big enough to contain his fish and he had to carry him to the sea.

And there the fish said to Manu, 'The flood is coming, but do not be afraid. I have prepared an ark for you and the six other Wise Men, and I shall bring it to you.'

Manu recognised that the fish was Vishnu and bowed down before him.

When the ocean overflowed, the Ark appeared, steered by a fish using its one and only horn. The Seven Wise Men embarked and voyaged to the Mountains of the North and still sail together on the waters of night, each seated at his place on the deck of the Great Bear.[1]

5

On the earth renewed and steaming, Manu made a great sacrifice to Vishnu.

At that time, the Ashvins came down on to the earth, being in love with Ila, the very beautiful.

But she would have nothing to do with them, saying, 'I belong only to him who made me.' And she went to Manu.

'Who are you, Blessed One?' asked Manu.

'Do you not know me?' she replied. 'I am your daughter. I was born of your sacrifice to Vishnu. When you were pouring melted butter into the fire, at that moment, I was born.'

Finding her beautiful, Manu desired her, but she hid. He had almost caught up with her when she changed into a cow. He made himself into a bull. She turned into a she-goat; he became a he-goat. She flew away, a hen. He turned himself into a cock. And the chase went on in this manner till it became a dust of insects, a seething of tiny worms.

And that is how animals came into being. They are born of Man out of his wits with desire or fleeing himself in fear. That is why it so easily happens that when the soul of a dead person remains entangled in the slightest snare of desire or fear, it slips aside and is reborn in an animal body. This delays its deliverance indefinitely, as well as the deliverance of the whole world.

As for Vishnu, he comes down only in order to take back with him to his home all those who recognise him.

He chooses the shape of a fish, because a fish can dive into the depths and come and go there at ease.

During the Flood and during this the universal disaster of Time, Vishnu guides the ark of the wise.

When the sea was being churned, he came down in the form of a tortoise. That he should choose to do so reveals once more his taste for depth.

The tortoise is a dome incrusted with gold; it is therefore the firmament. And it swims under water and applies itself to mud.

6

The gods and the demons were fighting each other for empire. Victory, as too often happens, went to the latter. The gods in their anxiety sought help from the wisest of men who was a dwarf and lived in the hills.

The dwarf agreed to speak on their behalf. He went to the Prince of the demons and said to the barbarian:

'Glory to you, great conqueror, the gods are ready to give themselves up. Deign to grant them the space I can cover with three of my steps: they will stay within these bounds and will leave you undisputed reign over all the rest.' The demon, with a sidelong glance at the wretched legs of this ambassador of the gods, swore to the bargain without more ado.

Whereupon the dwarf took one stride over the earth, a second over the sky and a third across hell. For such is the power of the dwarf whose name is intelligence, that in a flash he can bring victory to the gods over force.

The three steps of Manu are the law of the world and its peace.

7

In the struggle between the gods and the demons, Vishnu always gives the unexpected little tap of the thumb that makes the scale swing down on the side of light.

He is the Great Conciliator.

For instance, he was the one who advised the gods to join the demons in the churning of the sea, a great enterprise which neither would have been able to carry out alone and which was expected to have no less a result than the extraction of ambrosia, the elixir of endless life.

Again, when the demons refused to grip the serpent Vasuki's tail, which was the handle of the dasher, considering it ignoble and not a fit part for them to touch with their proud claws, Vishnu advised the gods to give up their place at the serpent's head and to put themselves at its scorned tail.

And when the dasher—the Mountain of Mandara too loosely held in the serpent's coils—began to sink, he hung on and saved it.

Lastly, when the cup of ambrosia floated up to the surface and the demons rushed at it to carry it off, he appeared in the ravishingly beautiful guise of Maya, Illusion, and made them lose their heads, the cup and immortality.

8

It is proper that this temple should be an island lying between the arms of a river, for Vishnu is 'He-Who-Reigns-Over-the-Waters',[2] upholds all creatures, rights them, washes them, lays them down to sleep in clear, deep waters.

Vishnu comes down like grace, like ambrosia or mercy; he

> 'droppeth as the gentle rain from heaven
> Upon the place beneath.'

9

The lingam of Shiv is by no means a symbol of Generation or of Pleasure. In him, the virile member, far from being an instrument for procreation, becomes a weapon. It pricks, pierces, burns and rapes, and that is why it is adored.

The Hindus associate the male principle with fire, see it as destructive and sterile like fire. And that is why they worship it; because it governs spiritual transformation, exalts burning light and leads to ecstasy.

For the same reason, in their written tradition, unlike other peoples, they refer to the sun as to a force that lays all waste. Burning seed, drying up springs, scorching green leaves, striking with barrenness the coupling that takes place under his sign, 'he takes all creatures up in his rage'.

It is the moon that makes the earth, the cow and woman bear fruit, and from the moon that comes the uneasy and deceptive sweetness of flowing into time through the wounds of birth.

The moon is the dam in which the waters are stored, and water is the unstable substance of life, where vision is blurred and distorted and happiness and hope shimmer as in a play of mirrors.

And Vishnu Narāyana reigns over the waters as he reigns over the fruits of the earth and the belly, and the pleasures of the flesh.

When Vishnu takes on the shape of a god, he usually has a kindly, smiling face. He stands upright; one of his hands makes a reassuring sign, another holds a disc which is a weapon, the sun-disc, but he holds it as if it were a flower. Another hand grips a club, but only so that he may lean on it.

Sometimes one sees him resting on the coils of the great snake he uses as a bed, lying under the canopy of its raised head and hood. And there he lies in an intemporal night between two creations.

For this world of ours, its peoples and animals and jungles throughout millions of years, is but an outgoing of his breath, after which he will breathe us in again.

Not that he cannot be fearsome at times. When Hiranya-Kashipu struck the pillar shouting, 'Since he is everywhere, let him come out of here', Vishnu leapt from the pillar with a roar; his head was a lion's and he had three pairs of arms with which he tore Hiranya-Kashipu to pieces playfully before making himself a garland with his entrails.

If a Hindu god could not dance or tear somebody to pieces now and then, he would end up by falling into meek and mild oblivion.

10

To a certain extent, that is what has happened to Brahma, the uncontested god of gods and Principle of Principles—in principle.

Brahma does not dance, and I have never heard of him tearing anybody to pieces. That is why everybody speaks of him with respect. But nobody prays to him, and nobody adores him.

11

Vishnu, on the contrary, is the living god. Something of him flows in every life. Sometimes his whole self has flowed into the life of a man, for on occasion he has taken flesh and been made man. Not just once. Every time justice goes astray on this earth, every time truth is in danger, he comes in the shape of a warrior or a wise man or a king.

So far he is known to have had ten complete incarnations. The eleventh is expected, for justice has indeed gone astray and truth is indeed in danger on this earth.

Among the ten incarnations of Vishnu, the Brahmins have at last included Buddha, Buddha conquered and taken over once and for all.[3]

This annexation remains purely nominal, however, for the Vishnuites do not know Buddha. He is not even contested: he has been forgotten.

Two of Vishnu's incarnations are still the subject of dreaming and raving among women, poets and the people, but only two. One is his incarnation in Krishna, the blue cowherd who stole the shepherdesses' gowns when they were bathing, and whose flute they followed by moonlight in the clearings of the forest of Brindaban, forgetting their husbands, their houses and their children. Krishna the stealer of souls, the beloved of cows and princesses. He had sixteen thousand wives, ruled over the city built in the middle of the sea and was great by his prowess in war.

The other is Rama, the Prince Charming, the pupil of the ascetics, whose adorable and faithful wife was carried off by demons. Rama killed them all in order to regain her, Rama whom the army of monkeys followed into battle and to whom trees bowed

as he passed. And when he entered a town, the women hurried to
the windows, and their joy at seeing the hero with the long arms
was so overflowing that 'tears welled up in their eyes and milk in
their breasts'.

12

There is a text which says, 'When one waters the root of a tree, all
the branches grow green; likewise the worship of Krishna gives
life and joy to all the gods.'

*   *   *

'Love of the young god grew in their hearts like a liana in the joyful
forest in spring.'

*

'So among tender glances and kisses, in the midst of play, dancing
and laughter, God who is the essence of joy enjoyed his joy with
the beautiful shepherd girls like a child revelling in his reflection
in the water.'

*

'It is good,' Krishna told the shepherdesses, 'to love those who
love us, but better still to love those who neglect us.'

*   *

'As for me, when I do not always show my love to those who love
me, it is in order to teach them the depth of divine love, so that,
driving out of their hearts everything that is not me, and forgetting
themselves, they may give themselves up to devotion and achieve
salvation.'[4]

13

Let us make no mistake: Vishnu is not a man and he is not a wild
pig; he is not a tortoise and he is not a tiny fish.

Neither is he a god among the gods.

How could he be, he who is the mediator between the gods and
the demons?

14

The first exploit of Rama was to pull on Shiv's bow until it broke.

*

Shiv, smeared with ashes, his eyes smouldering, leaps from the caverns of the Himalayas brandishing his weapons and throws himself upon Krishna. In vain.

Loyally, he prostrates himself at his conqueror's feet, recognising him as the Almighty and confessing his error and his sin. But the Lord helps him up. 'Art thou not another fashion of myself? Wherefore, I hear the prayers of all who worship thee.'

15

At that time no thing existed. Nothing did not exist either. And there was neither space nor the firmament beyond it. What was it? Where was it then? Guarded by whom?

What is this God, that we may serve him by our sacrifice?

There was neither death at that time, nor non-death. There was no day and no night. The One breathed without breath, moved by himself.

What is this God, that we may serve him by our sacrifice?

What was he when the great waters came carrying the Egg of Gold whence came the One, the beginning of life and of the Gods?

What is this God, that we may serve him by our sacrifice?

The gods came after the Egg hatched. Who knows the One before that?

What is this God, that we may serve him with our sacrifice?

Who knows truly, and who here can tell whence all these things have come? Were they fashioned or were they not? He who watches at the summit of the sky perhaps knows. Or perhaps does not know (Rig Veda x, 129, 121).

And the Upanishad repeats like a refrain,

'Nameless, faceless, ancient, inconceivable, and not the god that people worship.'

16

There is nothing of the stupefying profusion of Madurai at Shriringam. The geometrical ideogram of its plan, whose proportions correspond to the distances between the fixed stars and reflect the course of the planets, keeps a tight grip on the wealth of decoration and nowhere lets it get out of hand.

As leaves and flowers belong to a bough, so here the sculpture belongs to the structure. It is lithe and rounded, warm and alive.

When you go under a porch in the first wall and walk for ten or twenty paces in its shade, you see, through the light of the entrance on the other side, more and more of the height of the next porch and its tower. Sometimes the towers are high, sometimes low, sometimes embossed with gadroons or wreathed with intertwining tracery, and four times seven times, the astonishing marvel is renewed.

17

I was about to go through the fourth wall when I caught sight of the Mountain of Love.

Capping the porch was a squat tower, flesh-coloured and in some places reddened. Before my astonished eyes, it broke up into a mass of naked human bodies seething like maggots in the belly of a rotting carcase.

Linked in couples or copulating in heaps like goats or dogs or toads, lying down, or standing, or on all fours, or upside down, grabbing each other by a knee or the hair or by a breast, they tumble and lick each other, laugh, stick out their tongues, straddle, titillate and ride each other.

Love kneads this dough as it pleases, pulls it out and flings dollops of it up to the summit.

The stem of the phallus rises and sprouts and its branches burgeon with bodies that twist like great leaves or float like flowers or hang like fruit full of juicy ripeness.

And under it, the people come and go, children on the way to school, women who glance neither right nor left as they pass carrying on their heads the heavy load of their baskets; monks with shaven scalps and rose-coloured robes; all grave, their faces marked by the woe of the world. And they come and go through this gate as they came out of their mother's womb one day to enter the womb of death, while the passionate tower burns like a funeral pyre in the sun.

*　　　*

A Tamul version of the Rules for Sculptors and Painters says: 'The craftsman must understand the Atharvaveda, the thirty-two rules for craftsmen and the Vedic Mantra by which the deities are evoked.

'He must be one who wears the holy cordon and a necklace of holy beads; one who delights in the worship of God and is faithful to his wife; one who avoids strange women and piously acquires knowledge in the study of various sciences.'

The texts sometimes call the craftsman a *mantri*—that is to say, a priest, sometimes a *yogi* or wandering monk.

Two instruments are available to the artist who is preparing to conceive a work of art, the mantra and the yantra. The mantra is something halfway between a charm and a prayer: its effect is to evoke the deity. The yantra is a holy ideogram, a geometrical figure, an abstract emblem of the attributes of the god, a suitable support for meditation, the key that opens the passage to the Name, or *power*, and to the Form, or *the act*.

Living figures and their movements are constructed according to an abstract canon of consecrated lines and proportions and draw their life and grace from an act of piety.

'The lines in imagery,' says Shukracharya, 'are determined by the relationship between the adorer and the Adored One.'

The craftsman must, through meditation, purify himself from all desire, free himself from all attachment, fathom the emptiness of all things and then let Divinity take place in him and shine there with its own brilliance. 'This brilliant image will be the artist's model.'

Which, I think, is enough to show that the inspiration of the Mountain of Love can be attributed neither to imagination run riot nor to shameless lechery.

*

In the coach-house of every temple there is a chariot for the feast.

Its wheels stand higher than a man, starry wheels painted with colourful and significant scenes through which the cycles of creation turn.

Not oxen, not elephants, but the entire people singing psalms and harnessed to long ropes as thick as a thigh, drag this moving temple through the streets in triumph.

Many of these chariots are covered with paintings of naked bodies intertwined and writhing in the throes of frantic lust.

And often one of the worshippers, drunk with holy fervour, throws himself singing under the wheels and is crushed to death.

* *

Couples clasped in each other's arms, youths running after girls in the streets or paying compliments to ladies and singing under their windows, are never seen here.

The women are carefully guarded, not that their fathers or husbands hide them away as they do in Arab countries or in the south of Europe, but because no one presumes to tempt them, although they are sometimes beautiful and always gentle and refined.

Don Juan's exploits are impossible here and the tawdry glory that surrounds them inconceivable.

A lover hides more carefully than a murderer.

A hundred years ago, widows threw themselves on their husbands' funeral pyres, considering it indecent to survive them. They still do not marry again.

Many young men give themselves up to study and remain virgin till their twenty-fifth year. Others, in order to keep themselves whole for the selfless love of their fellow men, take a lifelong vow of chastity. There are also married couples who by mutual consent return to chastity and live as brother and sister under the same roof.

Every Indian is 'untouchable' for everyone else. The body of one's neighbour is sacred or impure and in both cases untouchable.

One is never brushed against or jostled in the street. People do not shake hands. Friends do not touch each other on the elbow or the shoulder. When a woman wants to go through a doorway where two men are in conversation, she claps her hands once and the men leap aside to let her pass.

There are no games or dances that mimic the play of love or offer an occasion for contact; there are not even any meals taken in common where men and women sit side by side.

Among the Indians I have known, I have never witnessed an indecent sight or heard an obscene joke.

The widespread belief that the climate in hot countries fosters licence is a mistaken one. As for me, since I set foot on this burning soil, I have felt myself delivered, as it were, by enchantment, and absolved from all fleshly desire. It is a fact that the further south one goes and the further east, the more love takes on a dangerous and sacred character. What is exhibited in the drawing-room and in the street in Berlin or New York, withdraws behind gates and studded doors in Spain and Sicily, and in this country, behind three temple walls. But here the veil is rent only by great spiritual bravery and the serenity of the illuminated intelligence.

No people is more modest or more pure than that of India; none is more peace-loving or gentle. Their reason for attributing to divinity the lascivious and bloodthirsty nature of which there is nearly nothing in themselves is that they know that the privilege of giving and taking life belongs to God alone.

18

The town has been built in the three outer enclosures no longer used by the temple. It consists of fruit-stalls, wretched mud or wooden huts that cling to the walls, and one-storeyed houses.

Nothing could be more touching than the humility of these homes men have built for themselves in a far corner of this great house of God.

Nothing could be more beautiful than the richness af the sanctuary's gold roofs and the jewels of the god; nothing more plentiful than the rice, the honey, the milk and butter that flow over the bellies of the statues while the people, emaciated and half naked, keep up their song and draw strength from it.

*

Orchards and palm-groves spread round the town. Women draped in red or dark blue pass through them along sandy tracks, and when they cross a patch of sunlight, the copper vases they carry on their heads flash or blaze.

A man and three children armed with slings are chasing the monkeys who have come to steal fruit. The stones skip in the thick greenery, while the leaps and bounds of the nimble band splash the tall palms with light.

19

High noon. With my foot I touch the shadow of my head. Man and beast have taken shelter and lie asleep. The palm-trees scarcely breathe, for the very air is drowsy.

I go down to the white beaches of the river and lie down naked in the water. It is warm and clear and shallow. My body has already lost its blanched-vegetable look, having returned to the elements. My legs, abandoned in the water, no longer terrify the fish. And there I swim and dream during the empty hours.

I put my clothes on again but, having picked my scarf up, I see to my astonishment that the knotted handkerchief has disappeared, and with it all my wealth.

20

I take stock on the beach of footprints that are not mine.

All the strangeness, all the enormousness of the earth I am on suddenly reveals itself to me. It lies all before me with its endless plains, its wild mountains, its jungles and rivers, its wild beasts, its unknown peoples. I feel myself small again, helpless and lonely just as when I got off the ship with nothing behind me but the sea, separated by it from everything that made me, from everything I loved, from everything I used to be; and now, nothing before me but a blank tomorrow.

In the very midst of these thoughts, the lazy Brahmin sprang into my memory like a jack-in-the-box.

'Ha! ha!' he roared. 'I see the joke! I see the joke all right!' And he hopped and slapped his thighs as he laughed uproariously. I saw the joke too. The fact was that it was really very funny, and I was forced to laugh myself.

I went up from the beach stepping absent-mindedly on the footprints of my robber.

There are times in our lives—rare and chosen moments—when God makes a point of showing us beyond all doubt that he is our only support. A man is a fool if he does not understand that the things that happen to him are signs, and makes no attempt to read them.

21

I returned to the town where I had left my goat-hair blanket, my other robe, my missal and my passport.

As I was passing under the tower of the second wall I caught sight of the philosopher.

We each looked at the other for some moments just as old friends, after long years of separation, are not sure at first and hesitate to make the first advance.

He had the large, dark, gentle eyes that horses have, and a short, greyish beard like rice-stubble. The noble forehead above his bushy eyebrows bore three long upward strokes and aslant his naked chest lay the holy cordon.

He took me to the house of his ancestors, built against the wall of the third enclosure, a small house, but the façade was adorned with ancient wood carvings. A steep flight of steps led up to the flat roof, and there we sat down cross-legged and facing each other.

From here I discovered a surprising view of the uneven towers, the last four rows of walls with their rounded battlements and beyond the last, like a pomegranate in a cluster of green, the golden sanctuary.

Small green parakeets with rose-coloured beaks were quarrelling for possession of the cracks in the wall opposite.

The man with the mark of Vishnu on his forehead began talking to me of God who is unique, personal and the creator of all visible and invisible things, who lives in the heart of every man, to whose will we must surrender and by whose grace we must hope for salvation, salvation that can be achieved by prayer and charity.

When speaking of the surrender of our own will, he used words which seemed to be taken from *The Imitation of Christ*. More than once, quotations from St Augustine sprang to my lips to confirm what he was saying about grace. His description of the Divine Person was in no way different from St Thomas's in the *Summa*. And to end with, unlike the ascetic sects, he maintained, just as the Fathers of the Church do unanimously, and as Ruysbroek the Admirable does in his *The Adornment of the Spiritual Marriage*, that there is a specific difference between the human soul and the nature of God, which persists even in union and ecstasy.

When I remarked on the Catholic orthodoxy of what he was saying, he replied that he was only following the teaching of Shri Ramanuja, the greatest of Vishnuite thinkers, who had revised and moderated the theories of Shankar, master of the Vedanta, especially that of the unreality of the whole of creation. 'We do not believe,' he confessed, 'in the unreality of the whole of creation.'

'That is another point we have in common,' I said.

'Yes, Shankar's is a somewhat excessive philosophy; only ascetics have a right to it.'

'What is this *philosophical right* you seem to be alluding to? Must one really be *entitled* to believe that such and such a thing is true or another untrue?'

'You know very well,' he said, 'that nothing is false or true by virtue of pure reason, since contrary statements can be defended with equally valid arguments. Logic can only judge the chain of reasoning at work but not the truth of principles which, by definition, are not linked to anything else, and that is why any theory is merely a futile puzzle, a boring pastime. The only thing that proves the truth of what a philosopher claims is how far he puts his philosophy into practice in every act of his life and how far his beneficial power reaches. He possesses truth in the same measure and degree as truth possesses him: that is the philosophical right I mean.'

'Very well. But why do you say that only ascetics have a right to the *excessive* truth of Shankar?'

'Once, when somebody asked the great Shankar what ecstasy was, he opened his mouth and his eyes went blank. He was rapt in ecstasy. That was his answer. It is the answer to all the questions that his doctrine leaves open. His doctrine is not the conclusion of a process of reasoning, nor a *Discours de la Méthode*. It is a conclusion drawn from ecstasy and a method of meditation leading to ecstasy. On the plane of reason, his reasoning is the shadow of a body moving on a higher level. His answers are riddles to those who remain on the plane of reason and seem absurd to those who drift below in the obscure regions of feeling. A philosophy is not a vat containing truth but a ladder leading to it. If it is too satisfying, one is in danger of staying on it, of never reaching one's goal. A doctrine is not knowledge but an instrument for attaining knowledge, provided that one handles it carefully and applies it correctly. Shankar teaches that One only is and the rest (that is to say the whole world and we too), all the rest is absolutely and substantially an illusion. We, on the contrary, maintain that there is duality in the Unity and that this world has relative reality. It is clear that the same man cannot profess each of these doctrines at the same time. Nevertheless, each proclaims itself orthodox. The one is a steep ladder, the other an easy, well-built staircase. One cannot perch on one and go up the other at the same time. But look at where they are leading: it is the same direction. Not the doctrine, but the direction is orthodox. Ours has a more perfect logical structure, more complete moral teaching, more moving human motives, which proves that it belongs to a lower plane. It is not addressed to sublime, disincarnate persons like the Shivites of the great Shankar, but to ordinary human beings, worked on, working and thinking, who have nothing to hope for unless it be from the grace and providence of the merciful Lord.'

'You are not one of those people, then,' I said, 'who thinks that man can save himself by his own means.'

'We are not so presumptuous as to assert that others cannot,' he said. 'We only know that we, at least, cannot.'

'And since you rely on God for everything, for you, naturally, it is faith and prayer that save and not just one's own achievements.'

'Action, whether good or bad, attaches man to the chain of causes. Every act leaves a deposit in the soul, a sort of dust that dulls it. That is what condemns it to turn on the wheel of rebirth. Ascetics break the chain, fight their way back upstream and keep themselves in stillness. But it is too hard a battle for the common man. So action becomes inevitable. And our problem is this: *How, through action, can a man be freed from action?* To this, God in person gives an answer in the Bhagavadgita, speaking through the mouth of the chariot driver: "Consider as equal: pleasure, pain, gain, loss, victory or defeat. Give yourself up wholeheartedly to the battle; in this way you will avoid sin. For whoever has cast out of himself desire for the fruit of his work remains in repose even while active. Whatever he may be doing, he is not bound by his activity. Doing the work only with his body, he does not contract sin." God is his sole aim: the accomplishment of the law is what he achieves and his work is a pure sacrifice. Whether his work is a charitable gift or a thrust of a sword, and whatever its results for him and for others, it delivers him.'

'Yes, action is not what one must renounce, but desire. Action does not enchain a man so much as passion. Passion is "the dark enemy with a thousand masks, the source of all evil" that must be overcome.

'Ascetics burn it out, tear it out. But for us, the problem presents itself in the same terms as the first: *"How, through passion, can man be freed from passion?"* This is how: all the frenzy, all the folly of first love, the trembling and the sighs, the swoons and the tears, the sweet words whispered and the solemn vows, the swimming eyes and the outbursts of joy, the songs, the frolics, the dancing and raving, the dreams by night and by day, nothing of all that should be missing from the love for him, the One, the Infinitely Lovable. Then passion, which is self-forgetfulness, saves the soul instead of soiling it. But it is impossible to love with that sort of love the One, Ineffable, and Inconceivable as such, or even a stone statue or the lingam of Shiv. With that sort of love, a man can only love what has human form, a living face, flesh and blood, a voice and looking eyes. So God in His infinite kindness deigned to share our manhood by incarnating Himself.'

I interrupted him eagerly, crying, 'I believe you! Oh yes, I believe you more than you can imagine. But for reasons which are probably not the same as yours. I believe, I do believe that God deigned to share our manhood, as you put it so well, that he came down from heaven, took flesh of the Virgin Mary by the action of the Holy Spirit, and was made man. For our sake too, under Pontius Pilate, he was crucified, suffered death, and was buried. And the third day he rose from the dead, as the Scriptures had foretold. And he ascended to Heaven, where he sits at the right hand of the Father. He is the One, the Unique One, that we love with sighs and tears.'

And in a loud voice that pierced me to the marrow, the other man said, 'I confess that Jesus Christ is the Son of God, God Himself incarnate.'

He got his breath back, then frowned and in an angry voice, as if he had been contradicted, shouted, 'And why not, I ask you? Why should the Almighty not become incarnate?'

I waited open-mouthed for the rest of this speech, and out it rang:

'He has done it so often.'

22

Not only the Philosophers here believe in a unique God.

The ordinary Hindu has more or less the same idea of God as the ordinary Christian: God is the Creator, the Provider, the Father, Law-giver and Avenger of Iniquities, whom they invoke daily by such names as 'The Lord' or abstract names such as 'Paramatma', the Supreme Soul, or Vedic names like Brahma, Ishvara, Pradjapati. They submit to His Will, attribute to Him the way fate works, impose certain renunciations on themselves and practise charity in His name, as we do.

This is not because of the already ancient influence of Islam, as one might think, or because of the more recent but much stronger and more seductive influence of the Christian gospel. The sacred texts of the Hindus nobly affirm that God is unique, and distinguish Him from 'the God that people worship'. Their definition of Him in negative terms is reminiscent of one given by Saint Denys the Areopagite in his *Mystical Theology*.

Now, even though Western critics underestimate the fabulous antiquity of the Hindu scriptures, they nevertheless attribute them to biblical or even older epochs. A new sect, the Arya-Samaj, even go so far as to affirm that the Upanishads are the original source of belief in the One God, and that the great religions— Jewish, Persian, Moslem or Christian—which flaunt it on their banners took it from that source.

It may be that these great religions all sprang thousands of years earlier from an oral tradition of which the traces are lost. Or it may be that here and there, wise men and saints discovered truth within themselves and did not borrow their creed from anyone. Or else that it was revealed from above, at various times and in various places. God knows; we do not. What is certain is that the Hindus know God as we know Him. But it is not to Him that they raise temples or address prayers.

23

It is surely the most astounding fact in the whole history of religions that Parabrahma, the Supreme Brahma, the Great Swan that swims above all other things on the eternal waters, Paramatma, the Supreme Soul, Ishvara, Living Order, whose emblem is the starry sky, Hiranyagarbha, the Golden Embryo that God invisible placed on the original waters so as to emerge from them visible, Pradjapati, the Master of all creatures, God—yes, God Himself—has no temple.

Do travellers point this out in their accounts? Do books on Hindu religion mention it? I have not read enough books to know. But it astonishes me that so few persons are astonished or even know that there is not one Hindu temple to God.

Indeed, although these pre-eminently religious people have known Him for centuries or more, they have not yet begun to pray to God.

For no one here offers up prayer or gifts to what dwells beyond words and things.

'What these people worship' is Power made perceptible: the power of transfiguration, transmutation and death in Shiv, the power of the Law and joy in Vishnu, the power made manifest in the Great Gods and the Goddess; in the heroes Rama and Krishna; in human form in the Guru for the disciple; in the father and mother for their children; in the husband for his wife; in the wandering monk for those who keep house; in the wise man in meditation for all, in semi-animal form in Ganesh and Hanuman and in natural form in the Ganges, the Banyan-tree, Fire, the Moon, the Sun and the Cow.

And this explains the multiplicity of gods within God and the multiplication of idols within the worship of the One.

24

The feature proper to the Hindu religion is the *Assimilation of its Object*. This is what defines it and distinguishes it from all others. All over the world, the gods are the object of religion: prayers, hymns and sacrifice its instruments.

But with the Hindus—already in their most ancient texts—the substance, the immensity and the power has passed from the gods to the instrument of worship, and the cult—prayers, hymns and sacrifice—has itself become the object of worship.

The gods, like men and beasts, are reduced to dependence on it. 'The priest must chant and hope that by his chant the gods will obtain immortality, the spirits of the dead oblation, men hope, and animals water' (Chandog. ii, 22, 2).

That is how Agni, the Fire of Sacrifice, the mouth with which the gods eat, has become a god among the gods and even the god of gods.

And how Soma, the liquor of sacrifice, has become a god and dwells in the moon.

But above all, that is how Brahma the Creator has been created.

Brahma (neuter) as the sound of the word indicates—it is pronounced Brumme—is the vibration of the voice in hymn and prayer, the impulse that makes the chant swell, and, by extension, the impulse that makes everything grow. Brahma (neuter) became τό θεού: divinity, the quality common to all the gods.

Brahma (masculine) became a god among the gods and even one of the first three. Finally, Brahma has become God, the unique being after whom there is no second.

He is the 'I am that I am', the Swayam Bhoo, the non-manifest.

But the assimilation has not stopped there. Worship having been assimilated to the gods, the priest was assimilated to worship, and the Brahmin to Brahma: 'You walk like gods on the earth', say the texts.

At the same time, parallel with this religion of priests, the religion of the monks developed. It was, in fact, the completion of the religion of the Brahmins, since, during the high epoch, only a Brahmin who had fulfilled his family duties in this world could attain to the dignity of becoming a begging monk.

And this second religion took the last step in the process of assimilation.

Worship, instead of being public and ceremonial, became secret, perpetual and intimate.

Far from invoking the gods, far from pleasing them, the monk alarms them.

In the Ramayana we see the gods deeply disturbed and consulting each other about how to hinder such and such an ascetic in his maceration. For the maceration of ascetics puts the gods in danger of losing their precedence.

The monk does not go to the temple. He has nothing to obtain from the gods. He adores God only. He adores God who lives inside everything, who is Being, who *is* therefore everything—God that man can *become* if, through meditation and exercise, he succeeds in recognising that he *is* already God, since God is no other than one's innermost Self.

The horse immolated in Vedic sacrifice, whose 'head is the dawn, whose eye is the sun, whose breath is the wind, whose open mouth is fire, whose soul is the year . . . the horse whose bones are the constellations and whose flesh is the clouds'—that sacrificed horse is replaced in the second religion by the ascetic's own body.

The victim is the link which binds man to his god. His body prevented the ascetic from uniting himself with God, from recognising that he himself was God. He will, therefore, make his own body the victim of the sacrifice.

The space enclosed in a sealed vase is no different from the space that surrounds it or from space anywhere. If you want proof of this, break the vase and you will see that the two spaces were only one, as they now are.

'*So aham asmi*'—'I am He'—cries the ascetic who has broken his body like a vase and who, delivered from his limits, has achieved union: Yog. Assimilation of the Object is thus made complete.

25

'Dearer than a son, dearer than wealth, more than all and more intimate, is the Self.'

'If one were to say of a man who speaks of another as being dearer to him than himself, "he will lose what he loves too much", one would be telling the truth.'

'One must hold dear only the Self' (Brahad. 1, 4–8).

'It is not for love of his son that a man cherishes his son, it is for love of the Self that a man cherishes his son.'

'It is not for love of God that one cherishes God, it is for love of the Self' (Ib. 11, 4, 2).

The litany goes on page after page, and is often taken up in the Upanishad.

One might think a doctrine like this a glorification of selfishness. But the *one* who might think so neither knows what he is nor what he is saying when he speaks of *self*.

In practice, this doctrine leads to total self-forgetfulness and self-abolishment.

'I am God himself,' says the Yogi.

'The Being in the celestial regions, among the constellations and in the moon, I am that Being, I am that very Being . . .'

'The Being—wind, space, sky, lightning—that one sees in the flash of lightning, I am that Being, that very Being' (Chandog. VI, 12, 1).

'*Tat twam asi*': '*And you yourself, Oh Svetaketou, you are That*': you are God (Ib. VI) is what the Sage teaches his son and disciple.

And Shandilya speaks of 'This myself, smaller in my heart than the germ in a grain of millet, greater than all these worlds . . .'

One might think this doctrine a glorification of pride, for reason here has become delirious and blasphemous.

It leads, on the contrary, to the renunciation of all self-love and to the depths of humility.

26

As for the association of Brahma, Shiv and Vishnu which the Occident names the 'Hindu Trinity', while the Hindus more properly call it the 'Triple Form', it has nothing in common with the Holy Trinity of Catholic dogma.

The uniting of the three gods seems to be the result of a compromise between equally powerful sects, each of which placed its god at the summit and described the other two as inferior forms of that same god. Confusion has consequently arisen as to their essence and their prerogatives, which are attributed now to one, now to another. At times, the three gods also lend their forms to one another, or serve, all three, as forms for the hidden God who has no form.

As Indian thought branches off easily into contraries, and proliferates rather than crystallises, it has accepted this intermingling of the gods without any difficulty.

The diamond-clear gnosis of the Holy Trinity in Catholic dogma, which preserves Distinction even in supreme Unity and Relation in the Absolute, has no equivalent in any other religion, since some religions affirm that there is one unique God who is absolutely different from all else; and the others, that there is a whole people of gods mixed up with things.

Hindu religion has the peculiarity of going to both of these extremes. Nevertheless, it contains truth for sages of all times and all tongues, for truth, as St Augustine says, 'dwells in the interior of man'.

The fact remains that Hindu tradition has preserved a formula which has no relation to Hindu cults or mythology and which transposes on to an abstract plane, in perfectly correct terms, the definition of the Divine Persons and their correlation.

God, according to this formula, is *Sat*, that is to say, Truth and Being; *Chit*, Knowledge, or, rather, Wisdom; *Ānanda*, Beatitude. Now God the Father is indeed the Truth of Being (*Sum qui Sum*). Wisdom is indeed the Word, the Logos of the books of Wisdom.

Beatitude is indeed the gift of the Holy Ghost who, according to the theologians, is Fruition, Gift, Eternal and perfect love of the Father and of the Son. And to make it clear that *Sat*, *Chit*, and *Ānanda* are one in God, the Brahmins link them together in one word, Satchidānanda, whose meanings are condensed in the three letters of the monosyllable *Aum*. To say this word the voice goes from the most open of vowels to the most closed of consonants and ranges through the whole cycle of sound, or, rather, occupies its centre. It is the natural conclusion of all hymns, the fixed point of contemplation of the Saints: *Aum*.

'Whoever knows it, knows the whole of the Veda,' says the Law of Manu.

27

God is one: yes, in God and for God. He is not one for the great number. He is one for the man who is one with God, for the man who is one, for the man who is, as God is, as God is one.

The great number, and the vulgar man who can only find the great number in himself, always arrive at the heathen idolatry of Force and Number, by whatever name they call it.

28

The Hindu monk, freed from all worldly obligations and from the practices of worship, fixes his thought on an image of the unique God. When he has succeeded in giving life to that image, he rejects it and fixes himself on God Himself, God without limits and without any image, absolutely inward and absolutely one.

So that the Hindu monk is the only man of religion in the world who succeeds in avoiding every kind and every appearance of idolatry.

29

Night was falling on the roof-top where we had been talking. At the first star, the philosopher stood up and invited me to share his meal.

I could not help noting inwardly that the invitation was well timed.

Things right themselves if one is careful to let them take their course.

How does a man who cannot swim manage to drown?

His body is lighter than water and floats naturally; how does he manage to drown it? He takes fright, thinking that he is going to sink; struggles, and sinks.

The man who falls into the sea of destitution need only stretch out on it with a blissful smile. And he will find himself floating.

*

My host began by pouring a few basinfuls of water over his head, for a Brahmin cannot set his hand to the rites of cooking without first having purified himself.

After which he carried the trivets on to the terrace and lit the fire under the pots.

'In the north I got into the habit of cooking rice in the morning only, so I shall give you bread tonight, provided that is to your taste.'

'Whatever you care to offer me will be to my taste,' I said.

'Are you equally polite to our universal host—I mean the Lord —and is everything that happens to you equally to your taste?'

'Nothing has happened to me so far that hasn't brought me joy or taught me a lesson, so I haven't had to make any effort to be consistently polite.'

He asked me what my plans were for the future. I told him I was thinking them over anew in the light of my changed circumstances, and I told him how the change had come about a few hours earlier. I even requested his advice on how to continue my journey.

'I have tried my hand at different trades on my travels,' I said. 'I do finicky work skilfully and patiently, and even when it comes to hard work, I don't tire quickly. I don't need much to live on. There's no vehicle I prefer to my legs, and they've always taken me where I wanted to go. In a familiar country, I should have no difficulty. But here I know neither the language nor the customs. And over and above all that, I shall have to reckon with a different climate, great distances, fever, animals and other obstacles.'

'Don't worry, you won't meet any obstacles. You won't need to waste time earning a living. Pilgrims are crossing India all the time, in their thousands, in all directions. The road is prepared for them. Hospitality is a communal institution here. In every village there is a shelter for travellers and rice is handed out to them free. But you will not be allowed to have recourse to it, because the notables of the village will vie with each other for the honour of welcoming you into their own homes.

'You will have nothing to fear in the jungle since you are worthy, I think, to be called a true solitary. Our hermits live there, and always on good terms with the wild beasts. And if you accidentally tread on a snake and it bites you, its venom will do you no harm.'

'But what makes you think I am safe?'

'Poison,' he explained to me without hesitation, 'has no power over a man who is chaste.'

The sauces were ready. He poured a little of each on to the edge of the terrace for the gods and the spirits of the dead, then offered me the ewer for ceremonial washing and poured water on the floor. I sat down on a rug in front of a round copper tray while my host, seated on his heels, set about cooking the bread.

This consists of round pancakes the size of a hand, which are flattened between the palms and then heated, dry, in a pan without a handle. When they have become firmer, they are laid on the red cinders or propped against the legs of the trivet. They are served hot and limp.

Then whoever is eating must tear a strip of this bread with his right hand (touching a dish or one's mouth with the left hand would be a gesture of such indecency that one shudders to think of it) and with the strip of bread wipe the plate containing the spicy sauce and some vegetable or other.

I complained that he was neglecting himself in order to serve me.

'Aren't you going to eat too?' I asked.

It must be admitted that it was almost impossible to keep the fire going, serve the bread and eat, all at the same time, and bread that has been allowed to go cold is only fit for dogs.

'Do not think,' he said, 'that I am trying to avoid eating with you. The Old Law expressly forbids us to eat with anyone who does not belong to our own caste. But since I became a disciple of Mahatma Gandhi I have given up obeying any rule that might be a hindrance to friendship between people.

'When you know what a hold our Law has on us, dinned into us from childhood by our venerable fathers and teachers for hundreds of generations, and when you know the fear and trembling the very thought of breaking it caused us at first, and when you know what punishment breaking it exposes us to, when you know that we could be disowned by our families and thrown out with an irrevocable curse on us, and we and our children reduced to the rank of pariahs and stray dogs, then you will understand, from the mere fact that a Brahmin is willing to dine with you, just how much courage the holy man requires and how great his power is over our souls.'

And he told me more about Gandhi and how, from the very first, he himself had followed him with fervour.

He described the events in Bombay in which he had taken part.

'They kept advancing in great numbers, their arms stiff by their sides and singing under the blows. Wherever a man was struck down, two others rushed up to be struck down in his place. It was a heartbreaking sight, and even the police shed tears.

'I remember the Sikhs going into combat in full uniform, their heads held high and their swords by their sides, and not one of them drawing his weapon.

'I remember a young man in front of me that a soldier was threatening with his raised rifle-butt, while shouting, "Get back or I'll hit you!"

' "Hit me then!" answered the young man. "I shall imagine that you are my father and that you are doing it for my good."

'Such a spirit of grace spread among the rioters that it was almost tangible. I felt it on the nape of my neck like a warm breath.

'When it was my turn to pass under the blows, I received them without feeling anything. I even think that I have never been so close to happiness.'

'Everything you tell me about Gandhi touches me deeply,' I said at last. 'Do you know why I have come to India? To give myself to him.'

'Oh?' said the philosopher, and then, almost in a whisper, 'Thank you.'

We looked each other in the eye for some moments.

30

The following morning, when the first ray of dawn had shot through the gates and awakened the gold on the cupola of Shriringam, I waited till my host had come to the end of his morning prayers and then took leave of him.

He put into my hands a handkerchief tied with two knots, like the one I had lost the day before, and said to me, 'This money was waiting as if on purpose to make your journey easier. Take it, you have no time to lose on the way. Go straight to your destination first: go to our Master. You will travel without any money later on if you feel like it.'

I protested vehemently. I had no need at all of the money; he himself knew I had no need of it.

He pointed out to me that it was not very friendly of me to prevent him from acquiring merit by doing something honourable.

'In any case,' he said, 'what has been given cannot be taken back. If this money weighs on you, you need only throw it into the river.'

I saw that it would be unseemly to persist in my refusal.

And although new to the country, I also saw that it would be just as unseemly to thank him.

Holding myself straight, my head high and my hands pressed
palm to palm against my lips, I looked into his eyes.

He stood in front of me in the same attitude. Neither of us
spoke.

And that was our farewell.

31

TIRUVANNAMALAI, *January 1937*, Ramana Hermitage

'He was sixteen years old when the thing happened. He had gone
up to the temple. There, nobody knows what took place between
God and him.

'Whatever it was, he came out of the holy place without sight in
his eyes or voice in his throat.

'He went down into the baths for purification and came out and
left his clothes lying on the steps.

'Then he came out of the temple stark naked and squatted at
the foot of the outer walls and stayed there several days without
moving.

'People shook him, thinking he was asleep, but he had kept his
eyes open. Others brought him food that he left to dry up at his
feet. So then some devout women poured into his mouth a little of
the milk that runs into the gutters of the temple after flowing over
the gods.

'At last he stood up, walked and ate, but still did not speak.
When he was hungry, he would clap his hands at the door of some
house, throw into his mouth whatever was brought to him and go
his way.

'After a few months of this, everyone took him for a madman
and the children began to throw stones at him.

'As he didn't like noise, he withdrew to this mountain. That was
thirty years ago and he has stayed here ever since. When he came
here, it was covered with woodland and inhabited by wild beasts.

'Out of curiosity, some people came to look for him. They found
him sitting in a damp cave surrounded by scorpions.

'The reputation of the Blessed One grew and the cave became a
place of pilgrimage.

'That was when I heard his name and left my village, feeling
myself called.

'Carrying a basket of fruit for him, I went up by the paths that are torrents in the rainy season.

'As soon as I saw him seated on a staircase of rocks, I dropped my basket, and with my face on the ground I wept uncontrollably. When I raised my head, he had come down and was leaning over me. He spoke. He had not spoken for five years and I was the one he spoke to, because of my tears. He said, "My son, weep no more. Or, rather, weep now that your tears are innocent of bitterness and rebellion. You once wept tears of despair, but these are tears of salvation."

'Indeed, I had lost, one after the other, my wife, my son and my daughter, and I had said to my senseless heart, "So there is no God."

'He spoke to me again, and said, "When a man thrashes his robe on the stone in the river and wrings it, it is not because he wants to hurt it, but because he wants it to be clean for the feast-day. In the same way, when God strikes a man and washes him in tears, it is because He wants to be clad in him.

' "You know very well that a family is simply a meeting of travellers. You know that it is sinful to become attached and to pour oneself out, and quite vain to flood our near ones with our affection. We ought to live as if we were alone, for we are truly alone: we see this on the day of our death. When a man cannot learn the truth through wisdom, he has to be taught it by suffering.

' "You lost your wife and children and you wept in despair, but you had lost something much nearer to you than your next of kin, and you didn't even think of weeping for it: you had lost yourself. And now you are going to seek, and you will find yourself. Weep no more, my son."

'I have not left the Blessed One since that day. I saw him come down from the top of the mountain to the foot of the mountain where he lives now. I have seen the huts of the hermitage going up round his seat one after the other over the years and pilgrims from all countries coming to ask for peace.'

The Disciple ended the story of his own and his master's life. He had a fine, dark, shining face, close-shaven like his head; his nose was straight and delicately shaped, and his eyes looked at one straight and clear. He was wearing the gladiola-red gown of a monk.

From where we stood on the hillside, we could see the plain
dotted with sanctuaries and water-tanks surrounded by steps, and
rice-fields spread like patchwork up to the flat and meagre town of
Tiruvannamalai and the carved pyramids of its temple.

Away below, the hermitage roofs of tressed palm-leaves huddled
together. A humble place, but holier and more frequented than
the temple.

'Let us return,' said the Disciple, 'and you, too, bow down
before him, for he is God Himself.'

We began walking again, and he went on, 'I am God too, but I
do not know it.'

'Since you do not know it,' I said, 'why do you say that you are
God?'

He answered, 'I know it from hearsay, I know it in words, I
believe it. I do not know it as he knows it.'

A few steps further on, he continued, 'You also are Shiv.' But
I cut him short, crying, 'Oh no! *I* know that I am not God.'

He was dumbfounded by such an out-and-out statement of my
own ignorance.

32

'Perhaps you don't know what knowing is,' said the Disciple on
another occasion. 'Listen to this story and you will find out.

'A king one day called for the Queen who had hitherto been his
one and only wife, and told her that he intended to take a second
wife.

' "Since the law allows you to do so," said the Queen, "what else
can I do but give in to your whim?"

' "Whim indeed," said the King, highly peeved. "In everything
I do, I follow the teaching of my spiritual guide."

' "And may I know who the happy Princess is that you have
chosen?"

' "You know her already," said the King. "She is my sister."

' "I must be dreaming," said the Queen. "Or else you are joking
perhaps."

' "It's easy to see that you are only a woman and don't understand the first thing about philosophy," remarked the King. "I
shall try to explain. Everything is in everything; everything is the

same as everything else. That is what my Master has taught me. A man who makes the slightest distinction between one being and another lives in a world of illusion and ignorance. I no longer do so: I will make no distinctions. Since I was a child, I have had a tender inclination towards my sister. The thought that she was my sister always hindered me from telling her so. But at present I am so well able to master my thought that I can look on her as a stranger I have met for the first time. Consequently, nothing stands in the way of our marriage. Indeed, I am in some haste to make it known, so that my subjects may become aware that through my knowledge I have reached a different state from that of ordinary man."

' "I am, indeed, only an ignorant woman," said the Queen, "and have no word in the matter, but I beg of you to consult your master before taking the step." The King, sure he was in the right, thought that quite unnecessary, but she insisted.

' "It is already a lack of respect for your master not to have spoken to him before telling me about it. Should he not be the first informed of everything that concerns you?"

'So the King sent for his spiritual adviser and told him of his intention. The holy man replied with severity:

' "The man who knows that everything is in everything and that everything is the same as everything else can make no mistake. He is above sin and no one has the right to judge him.

' "If you know, oh King, that everything is the same as everything, you can do anything you wish and not sin. But is it true that you know it, my noble disciple?"

' "I know it," the King declared. "May I be reborn in the belly of a jackal or in the body of a pariah if I am telling a lie."

' "Get yourself a sword, then, and you will be able to prove to me right away that you are telling the truth."

'The sword was brought. "Take a good grip of it," said the Wise Man to the King. "Good! and now, cut down this young banana-tree."

'Without hesitation, the King struck the soft trunk and the tree fell to the ground.

' "Good!" said the Wise Man. "Now you are going to be able to prove that your faith is as sure as your hand and your intellect as keen as your blade.

' "Raise your left arm. Fine! And now, cut it off just as you have cut down the tree. Do not hesitate one second! Since everything is like everything else, since you know it and felt no pain when you cut down the banana-tree, you should feel none when you cut off your arm—since you know.

' "Oh, if only you did know, my noble disciple, and knew what it is to know!

' "Oh, when you know it, oh King, you will be able to marry your sister without it being a sin.

' "But when you know, you will marry neither your sister nor anyone else. You will keep yourself from all desire, whether good or evil. Your spirit will be one-pointed, and you will have entered bliss!" '

33

For three days now I have been living in the Hermitage of Maharshi Ramana. He is the one who knows. He is the one who dwells in the Self. Such as we are, though without knowing it, in the deepest sleep, untied, free, absolute, all-powerful, such is he able to be at all times by the strength of his thought and will.

This, at least, is what I am told. Actually, he is a little man who goes about half naked and remains perfectly simple in the midst of the great honours done to him. His hoary head trembles and he looks twice his age. His chin is as heavy as a clod with its tuft of withered grass and his mouth hangs open; the grey eyes in his dark face are mild and vacant.

He has been laid on a small sofa styled in the worst taste, and on each side of it, incense-burners have been lit and smoke rises from them. In the evening the Brahmins meet round his bed and recite the Vedic mantras in droning chorus, then sing some old hymn and then some new one, in honour of the Blessed One.

All day long, the disciples remain seated on the floor in silence round the Blessed One. From time to time, some newcomer enters the large room where he puts down his bundle and his sunshade, then he comes back and kneels in front of the Blessed One, joins his palms above his head, stretches out full-length, face downwards, raises himself, touches the earth with his brow, his nose and chin, stands up again and goes to sit among the others in the silence of the Blessed One. The disciples look at Him who Is and think of what they are. Or, rather, they think of what they are not. They are not this arm or this leg, this head or this heart, they are not this body, they are not this anxiety or this joy, this hope or this remorse, this anger or this love, nor any of these changing emotions. They are not their thought, since their thought ceases when they sleep, whereas they do not cease to be. They are not the I that names itself.

'What is this God, that we may serve him with our sacrifice?'

'Who is the Self?'

He is above sin, above error, above death, the man who knows; who knows this and knows what it is to know.

The incense smokes and one after the other they prostrate themselves. The Blessed One sees none of it. The Blessed One waves a fly off the end of his nose. Then he gropes in a little box and takes a leaf out of it; he is chewing betel and nutmeg. God is chewing betel and nutmeg. Sometimes he opens his mouth wide and belches.

God is belching.[5]

34

The Blessed One asked about me. He wanted to know who I was and on three occasions gave me some friendly nods and a wave of the hand, by which I felt that he was bestowing a remarkable honour upon me.

My neighbours told me that if I wanted to ask him a question about doctrine he would answer it. I asked nothing.

In any case I knew what I wanted to know: that the air of the place was not what my lungs required. There is a Christian restlessness in me that prefers itself, imperfect as it is, to the perfect serenity of which I see the model here. If I had the rare courage and the power to dedicate myself to godliness, I should seek it, not so much in the peace of absolute sleep as in the frenzy of the enamoured soul. If I had the rare courage and the power to do so, I should still not think I had the right to seek salvation by myself and for myself. I should have to reach my own good through the good of others, and I maintain that charity is greater than wisdom.

For these reasons, I decided to join Gandhi at Wardha.

Yes, in order to learn how to be a better Christian.

D

35

This people reveals itself to be incapable of anger, irony or vulgarity, in which it differs vastly from ours.

It occurs to me that there are animal peoples, greedy and fever-ish, and vegetable peoples. This one is like a great tree in its peace-ful majesty, its contained aliveness, its unaggressive strength. It is evangelical by nature. Everyday life here is made up of simplicity, humility, chastity, friendliness elevated by a certain feminine delicacy, hospitality, the respect of all life, resignation to the Divine Will, and this much more than in Christian countries. Those who come here to preach Christian truth must be slightly em-barrassed at the outset.

Not that these people have no faults. They are riddled with them. But their faults harm only themselves, whereas the whole earth can rightly complain of ours.

As our own faults are those we have the least patience with in others, nothing is easier for us than to look on theirs with indul-gence. That is why the beings the most different from us are the easiest to understand and also those who have the most to teach us, provided that we cease to think ourselves superior. Otherwise we shall have to be content with our self-deceptive superiority and give up all hope of learning from others.

The Western person who has never left the West is like a boy who has never left boarding-school and has only known boys. The day comes at last when he wakes up from childhood, comes home to his family and the world, and woman is revealed to him.

It is a similar experience that awaits us in India. We find hu-man beings there who are just as much our opposites as they are similar to us: indeed, we find something like another sex.

The rapturous astonishment, the wonder and delight, the dis-appointments, the mistakes, the pity and the tenderness that en-rich lovers—India offers us all this, and the discovery of ourselves as well.

36

As I was hurrying along the crowded station platform, a boy tried to take my bundle out of my hands, and when I clung to it, said gently, 'It's not for money, sir.' Then he ran to keep a seat for me in the train.

When I had settled in, he asked me what country I came from and I told him.

'And you are wearing the Dhoti of Kaddar?' he said with some surprise.

Now, it is by their hand-spun robes that one can tell Gandhi's followers.

'Gandhi-Jee?' he asked.

'Yes, Gandhi-Jee.'

'Thank you!' said the boy, blushing with pleasure. And he disappeared.

1. The Hindus call this constellation 'The Seven Wise Men'.
2. Narāyana
3. It is interesting to note that Brahmanic tradition presents Buddha as an incarnation of Vishnu who has taken on the shape of Buddha for the purpose of deceiving mankind. Only today, and probably because of Western influence, are the Hindus beginning to accept the saintliness of Buddha.
4. These quotations are taken from the Purana.
5. It has never been my intention to make fun of a wise man who incarnates one of the oldest and deepest spititual traditions. I am simply giving my first impressions as a traveller and newcomer and am aware that the ridicule may rebound upon myself. For all that, the fact remains that however wise a man may be, the Hindu custom of seeing him as God and worshipping him as God will always be shocking to a Christian.

IV

WARDHA

OR THREE MONTHS WITH GANDHI

Dawn already streaks the sky, but our path still twists and turns in the dark countryside. We meet a group of disciples returning from the ashram and greet them by joining our hands against our closed lips. The Mahatma has already spoken to them. We are among the last to arrive.

Daylight has come by the time we reach the little close. In the middle of the parched field is a small clay hut, open and so low that it makes no break in the countryside.

In the doorway under the slope of the thatched roof, a little, half-naked old man is seated on the ground. It's he!

He waves to me—yes, to me!—makes me sit down beside him and smiles to me. He speaks—and speaks of nothing else but me—asking me who I am, what I do and what I want.

And no sooner has he asked than I discover that I am nothing, have never done anything and want nothing except to stay like this in his shadow.

Here he is before my eyes, the only man who has shown us a green shoot in the desert of this century.

A man who knows the hard law of love, hard and clear like a diamond.

The captain of the unarmed, the father of the pariahs, the king who reigns by the divine right of sainthood.

He has come to show us the power over this earth of absolute innocence. He has come to prove that it can stop machines, hold its own against guns and defy an empire.

He has come into the world to bring us this news from beyond, where nothing changes, to teach us the truth that we have always known, being Christians. Truth so ill-assorted with us, so strangely contradictory to everything that the world and men had taught us, that we did not know what to do with it. We kept it between the four walls of the church and in the dark of our hearts. He, the Hindu, had to come for us to learn what we had always known.

While the old man questions me and smiles, I am silent, trying not to weep.

*

It is seven o'clock in the morning and time for his first walk. I may accompany him if I wish, but I must excuse him if he devotes himself entirely to the young disciple who has made the journey from Travancore for the purpose of bringing him news from the village there and receiving instructions. The three of us set off. He keeps me on his right hand but turns towards the other man.

He walks with a very lively step along the sandy path, carrying a long bamboo stick. His bare head is shaven, he is naked to the waist and wears no holy cordon, his legs are bare and his loin-cloth is tucked up between them.

That was more or less how he was dressed when he entered Buckingham Palace to shake hands with the late King of England.

His thinness is not dry and bony but resembles youthful slenderness, being slight and supple.

His skin is the colour of old ivory. To tell the truth, he is far from handsome. His shaven skull has great wings of ears, his nose dips over his toothless mouth and sometimes, when he ponders, his lower lip hangs down over his short chin; but there is something touching in his ugliness, rather like that of the newly-born child when it opens its mouth wider than its whole face.

His black, almond-shaped eyes hide behind small metal-framed spectacles; faint, mischievous lines prolong their upward slant.

He is at all times friendly and cheerful. But there is no beating about the bush when he gives an order (or advice, which is the same thing) or makes a rebuke. (God keep us from ever deserving one.)

Energetically articulated but even, his speech flows without the leaps and bounds of elision. On the contrary, his sentences are carefully linked and introduced by 'that is why' or 'so'. He avoids ellipses, which can be violence done to logic and a form of self-conceit.

Every statement he makes is illuminated by different approaches to the same point, so that the humblest intelligence has access to it and the keenest is riveted. Not even the most trifling detail is beneath his dignity, just as in his eyes every man has his worth and nothing is without its importance.

We turn back. The day is beginning to burn. I wander through the house.

Ba, the Mahatma's wife, is scouring a copper pot with earth and wet grass.

Mira-Behn, Admiral Slade's daughter, who came to Gandhi a long time ago and has never left him since, is washing her linen on a stone by the well. Her shorn head is covered with a coarse veil.

A white-bearded personage, a former minister of state, squats behind the kitchen peeling vegetables with great dignity. A princess of the house of Kapurtala shakes out the rug of the one and only room.

A tall man with a profile like an axe greets me. He is Abdul Gaffer Khan, one of the Moslem chiefs of the north-western tribes famous for their warlike virtues. He has given himself and his men to non-violence with all the loyalty and intransigence that distinguish warriors. He speaks to me in affectionate terms of Bapu-Jee, the name given to Gandhi by the people in this house as well as by all his followers and intimate friends. It means something between 'Father' and 'Your Lordship'. He gives me a lump of cane-sugar to chew.

After we have recited the mantra together at table, or, rather, on the ground, since there is no table, I find myself beside Bapu-Jee who puts into my bowl a portion of bitter herbs, rice, brown sugar, wholemeal bread and fresh butter. Each guest holds out his bowl in turn, for the Master insists on serving everyone himself.

The food is light and fresh and contains no spice.

He himself dips his bread and vegetables into a bowl of goat's milk.

He refuses to touch any food that the Indian peasant—the poorest and worst-fed on earth—could not afford, nor will he give any such food to his guests. But by a careful combination of the same ingredients and quantities he composes healthy, nourishing meals which he tries out on his own household before introducing them first in his schools then in the thousands of villages run by his disciples. This ascetic who is known the world over for his fasts shows, of all men I have known, the most concern for the health and well-being of others.

The hot hours go by. People keep entering or leaving his room through the doorless doorway. He goes through his papers, dictates letters, and gives advice to those who have come to seek it. Sometimes a bird hops into the middle of the room through the door on the left, nods and flies away through the door on the right.

Framed in the dazzling doorway, the great plain flies away too in the sun and turns into dust that is swept off by gusts of wind.

Women in white pass in the foreground; a white ox grazes, seeking the shade of the trees. The women's spinning-wheels hum.

When work is done and care put away, the Mahatma makes a sign, and his flat, fiddle-like spinning-wheel is brought to him. And until night falls, he draws from it an even, strong thread, while the sound of the wheel nurses thought.

2

'I strongly advise you,' he said to me at the start, 'to put all clerical work aside and busy yourself with your hands.'

The work of the hands is indeed the apprenticeship to honesty.

Honesty is a certain equality one establishes between what one takes and what one gives.

No man is dispensed by nature from working with his hands. Even the man who devotes himself to the incomparably superior activities of the mind is not dispensed from hard work unless he gives up everything that has cost labour in this world below. If he dispenses himself from it and does not give up what costs labour, he is putting his burden on others and remains in their debt. Mental work entitles him only to mental satisfaction, which is, moreover, incomparably superior.

Honesty requires that every problem shall be solved in its own sphere. Jumping from one sphere to another at the moment of settlement is cheating. Paying one's debt of labour with money is perhaps cheating too, for money in the hands of someone who has never worked with his hands is a meaningless token. The debtor may be satisfied with it, but honesty cannot be.

One must first earn the right to give. Whoever has not paid his debt has no right to give.

Desires should be reduced to needs. Manual labour will soon satisfy these: man will then find himself free. Good can only come from free men, and first and foremost from men free from debts and desires.

3

Even if you have another and higher way of sharing the common task, never give up manual work completely.

Beware of being sublime without depth, great without foundations, and perfect in the air. Touch and feel through action the truth that your intelligence has seen.

Let the work of your hands be an act of gratitude for the human state and homage to it. One stoops in order to bow: bow to every man by stooping to work. Think, 'I refuse to consider myself superior to common man.' Actually, nothing is more common than to think oneself superior. It is true that humility is not a virtue one can set about acquiring. It is a grace that descends on the best of us. Make yourself worthy to receive it.

4

I am, therefore, being put to the spinning-wheel and the carpenter's bench. I am entering the school at Wardha this very day. My new life is beginning. With my talents that are luxuries and my futile knowledge, I feel as naked as a new-born babe.

There is no likelihood of my feeling superior to common man today. I can think of nothing but my debt. How could I have failed to see how great and how flagrant it is! It will take me some hundreds of years to pay: I have not a minute to waste.

5

Wardha is a dusty little town. It spreads because of the wasteland and parched meadows that cut across it. It has neither shape nor purpose. The countryside around it is a huge doormat bleached by the fury of the great winter sun.

The school is called Maganvadi. It stands at the end of the town
in a grove of orange-trees. Its low buildings are scattered among
the trees on each side of the road: dormitories, kitchens, the refec-
tory, offices, stables, workshops, the presshouse and the wide
deep well where I wash my morning linen and myself, and into
which I dive with a great splash when the heat of the day is too
strong.

Then, lying in abandonment on my back in the black, bubbling
water, I watch through the gaping well-mouth a swallow diving
into the blue of heaven.

6

My companions are aged between eighteen and twenty-five. They
come from every province and every caste. Most of them are clean,
strong, smiling, friendly fellows who have given themselves body
and soul to the good cause.

Apprenticeship to a craft goes hand in hand with the learning of
the doctrine. Everyone must be able to card and spin and must at
least spin his own robe; it is possible to learn another craft as well:
carpentry or making leather or paper.

All must eat together, which seems a natural thing for work-
mates to do—outside India—but which for a Brahmin's son is the
most horrible thing that can be forced on him.

Each in turn must sweep the premises and empty the latrines.
(A Brahmin's son bathes three times a day but prefers living on a
heap of filth to 'soiling' himself by cleaning the ground, a task
which belongs by birth to the Untouchable.)

They must support, teach and exhort each other and exercise
themselves in the eleven virtues that constitute the Rule.

Once they are ready, they will be given charge of some poverty-
stricken village. They will have to win it over to the common cause
by their teaching, their way of life and profitable work.

It will be their duty to support the ancient village industries or
to revive them and create new ones. They will have to develop
cotton-spinning everywhere, for the raw material is at hand and
the equipment costs little.

They will have to see that roads, streets and water are kept clean;
prevent epidemics; distribute simple medicines; keep an eye on

nutrition; see that children and all animals are protected, and not just cows and snakes; co-ordinate the various trades and the rotation of crops so that the village becomes self-sufficient; and send the excess produce and products to the distribution centres of the Association of Village Industries, from which they will be sent to shops in towns and sold at fixed prices.

National independence must be prepared by economic independence.

One and all must be taught the duty and the power of non-violence.

7

Let every man be self-sufficient, let every man think of himself and his own family first; that is charity well ordered. Provided he is content with what he produces himself. That is the principle of Swadeshi (self-reliance), the kernel and gauge of independence.

Whenever a man cannot be self-sufficient, let his family be so; if his family cannot, let the village be so; if the village cannot, let the district and, lastly, the country be so.

Self-government is the best of systems, the only dignified and the only stable one. But self-government cannot begin and end with the State.

Let the vital foodstuffs be produced everywhere and travel as little as possible. Let spices, precious stones, luxuries and works of art circulate as freely and as widely as before, even beyond the frontiers. But keep the hands of brokers, speculators, native and foreign politicians off the products on which the people's life depends. It is not right that a few should play ball with the fruit of somebody else's work. The stimulation of trade, which is a risk, the creation of needs, which are deficiencies, the enforcing of haste, which is a disorder, can only lead to catastrophic upheavals.

Irreducible needs should be satisfied in the simplest and surest way; labour and exchange should be regulated; agitation and anxiety eliminated; and men should be rid of complicated and vulnerable artificial systems; they should be contented, and, above all, set free.

*

Let man always remain greater than what he makes and more precious than what he has.

*   *

Let us get rid of squalor and cultivate poverty.

8

If people today are not convinced of the unsatisfactory character of a system which has led them from crisis to crash, from bankruptcy to revolt and from revolution to conflagration; which spoils peace and makes it busy and full of care; which makes war a universal cataclysm, almost as disastrous for the conqueror as for the conquered; which takes the sense out of life and the value out of effort; which consummates the disfigurement of the world and the debasement of its inhabitants; if people today blame no matter whom for the great evils that are overwhelming them and attribute the cause of them to all and everything except the development of the machine, then one can only conclude that no one is deafer than the man who will not hear.

Their childish admiration for the shiny toys they play with, their fanatical exaltation of the idol they have forged and to which they are ready to sacrifice their children, have turned their heads and blinded them to the obvious, since they continue to believe that the unlimited progress of the machine will usher in an age of gold.

Leaving aside the upheavals that the progress of the machine is constantly inflicting on human institutions, let us consider only the advantages by which it tempts the fool: it saves time and labour, it produces abundance, it multiplies exchanges between the peoples and brings them into closer contact, it will eventually ensure perpetual leisure for all.

If it is true that it saves time, how is it that in countries where the machine is master one sees only people who are pressed for time? Whereas in countries where men do everything with their hands, they find time to do everything, as well as time to do nothing, to their hearts' content?

If it is true that it saves labour, how is it that wherever it reigns, people are busy, harnessed to unrewarding, fragmentary, boring tasks, hustled by the rhythm of the machine into doing jobs that wear a human being out, warp him, bewilder and weary him? Is this saving of trouble worth the trouble?

If it is true that it produces abundance, how is it that wherever it reigns, there also reigns in some well-hidden slum the strangest, the most atrocious misery? How is it that if it produces abundance it cannot produce contentment? Over-production and unemployment have been the logical accompaniment of the machine whenever it has been impossible to thorw the surplus into some hole or devour it in some war.

If it is true that it has increased exchange and brought people into closer touch, it is little wonder that the people in question feel unprecedented irritation with each other. There is nothing calculated to make me hate my neighbour and him hate me like forcing me upon him in spite of his will and mine. This may be regrettable, but it is only human. Forced contact does not engender union. It is a great pity, but that is the way of nature.

Finally, even if it were possible to avoid all these disasters, God knows how, and relieve man of all hard work and ensure perpetual leisure for him, then all the damage that the progress of the machine has caused by ruin, revolution and war, would become insignificant compared with the ultimate scourge: humanity deprived of all bodily toil.

The truth is that man needs work even more than he needs a wage. Those who seek the welfare of the workers should be less anxious to obtain good pay, good holidays and good pensions for them than good work, which is the first of their goods.

For the object of work is not so much to make objects as to make men. A man makes himself by making something. Work creates a direct contact with matter and ensures him precise knowledge of it as well as direct contact and daily collaboration with other men; it imprints the form of man on matter and offers itself to him as a means of expression; it concentrates his attention and his abilities on one point or at least on a continuous line; it bridles the passions by strengthening the will. Work, bodily work, is for nine-tenths of humanity their only chance to show their worth in this world.

But in order that work itself, and not just payment for it, shall profit a man, it must be human work, work in which the whole man is engaged: his body, his heart, his brain, his taste. The craftsman who fashions an object, polishes it, decorates it, sells it, and fits it for the requirements of the person he intends it for, is carrying out human work. The countryman who gives life to his fields and makes his flocks prosper by work attuned to the seasons is successfully accomplishing the task of a free man.

But the worker enslaved in serial production, who from one second to another repeats the same movement at the speed dictated by the machine, fritters himself away in work which has no purpose for him, no end, no taste, no sense. The time he spends there is time lost, time sold: he is not selling his creation, but his very lifetime. He is selling what a free man does not sell: his life. He is a slave.

The problem is not how to sweeten the lot of the proletarian so as to make it acceptable to him, but how to get rid of the proletariate, just as we got rid of slavery, since the proletariate is indeed slavery.

As for the whole peoples who are doomed to idleness, what is to be done with them, what will they do with themselves?

In reply to which people will tell you that the State (and if you don't know what the State is, I shall tell you: it is mechanised Providence), which will have solved the problem of work by complete industrialisation, will then only have to solve the problems of leisure and education. It will plan games and entertainment and will distribute learning to all.

But the pleasures of men without work have always been drunkenness and mischief. The State can offer them educational pleasures for all it is worth, they will still prefer drunkenness and mischief. The games will then have to become compulsory and for many will cease to be games and turn into discipline and duties, falsifications of work from which no good can come. It would have been better to plan work.

But there is a pleasure dearer to man than work, dearer than drunkenness and mischief, that of shouting 'Down with—!' and setting fire to everything. That is a game which will quickly replace all others in the mechanised Paradise.

If the misfortunes that overwhelm even civilised people today finally prove to them, by *reductio ad absurdum*, that they must turn their hopes elsewhere, they will have been of some use after all.

9

In Europe, in America and even in Japan, techniques are continuing their progress, but the Religion of Progress, thank God, is
beginning to recede.

One no longer hears the paeans and chants of glory that accompanied the rising of coal-smoke and balloons in the nineteenth
century.

There is no sign of any serious attempt at deliverance in any of
these countries, but there are at least some glimpses of clear-
sightedness, and grave doubts about tomorrow.

Men are carried along now, not by the initial impulse of their
faith in progress, but by its continuing course and their submission
to fatality. 'Whatever you may say,' they tell you, 'you can't go
against the laws of history and economy. There is no turning back
now.'

And here you see how strong-minded people who have rebelled
against all belief, and claim to be guided in all they do by their sole
courage and intelligence, lose their critical faculties and let themselves be led by the nose when superstition is artificial and learned
and bears the name of history or economy, and resign themselves
to a fatality which is nothing other than their own stupidity and
obstinacy.

Drought, floods, earthquakes, pain, old age and death are fatali-
ties against which it is senseless to protest. History and economy,
being man-made, are done and undone with equal ease. The only
thing that makes them ineluctable is to believe them to be so. It is
senseless to resign oneself to them instead of working to change
them.

10

To turn back is *not* Gandhi's intention. No one is less given than
he to historical revivals or to harking back to the good old days.
He professes neither hatred of the West nor a horror of civilisation
nor contempt for economy. On the contrary, his revolution looks
forward with sound and sober hope. He is the first wise man in the
East to prescribe work as a duty for every man and a road to
salvation.

He has laid the foundations of a new civil constitution, of new economic development and of a new culture.

But for him, the sole interest of economy is what the great economists have never taken into consideration (and Karl Marx in this respect is just as oblivious as the others): the sole interest of economy is not to develop economy but to develop the human being, give him peace, raise him and set him free.

11

'You're not going to tell us,' people object, 'that reasonable, limited use of the machine and control of its progress could not contribute to man's good and his deliverance without exposing him to the apocalyptic cataclysms you like to foresee.'

If machines could be used reasonably, within limits, and their progress controlled, there would indeed be no drawback to putting them to work. One can very well use machines provided one can do without them. Gandhi himself makes no bones about climbing into a train when he has to confer with the Viceroy about the country's affairs. But 'If railways were abolished,' he sometimes says with a smile, 'we should not weep over their loss.'

If a machine is useful, then use it; if it becomes necessary, then it is your urgent duty to throw it away, for it will inevitably catch you up in its wheels and enslave you.

Provided that neither its making nor its use involve any abuse or fanatical exaltation, provided there is no inevitability in its progress, we are free to use it, just as the king in the fable was free to marry his sister—on condition that he cut his arm off without turning a hair.

Remember it is the same kind of proof that the Master of all things expects of us before granting us permission to play with fire.

*

The machine enslaves, the hand sets free.

12

It has been proved that the Byzantines knew the principle of the steam engine. Wiser than we, they were careful to keep their admirable craftsmen's guilds safe from such deadly competition.[1]

For centuries, the Chinese kept the secret of gunpowder. More intelligent than we, they contented themselves with making fireworks and crackers.

Writings of Vespasian have been discovered in which it is forbidden 'to use machines that deprive the people of their work and their means of living'.

The first reaction of the weavers of Manchester and Lyons, when mechanical looms had reduced them to unemployment and hunger, was to attack the factories and break up their enemy, the machine.

But the machine has taken devilish revenge. Man has been conquered. Twice conquered: convinced. He no longer protests, not even inwardly.

And now we are like the beggar who exhibits a flourishing sore, a source of profit for himself and an object of envy for his colleagues.

13

The machine conquered man. Man has become a machine; he functions and no longer lives.

His movements have been mechanised and so have his desires, his fears, his loves and his hates. His tastes and his opinions, the education of his children, his productive activity, his sport and entertainment, the application of law, the police and administration, the army and the government all tend towards the inhuman perfection of the machine.

When the State has been turned into a machine, how can we prevent some madman from snatching the steering-wheel and driving the machine over the edge of the precipice?

When you have turned the State into a machine, you yourself will have to be its fuel.

14

To a civilisation of which the characteristic feature is the struggle between the proletariate and the upper middle classes, Gandhi wants to oppose a culture based on harmony between farmers and craftsmen.

For a divided civilisation like ours to subsist, the State must impose its domination more and more strongly, either by letting the struggle between the classes go on, and keeping the seesaw of political parties, or by abolishing one of the extremes, subduing the other and bringing about unity for its own profit.

But the chief aim of a government such as Gandhi conceives it is to make itself less and less necessary, to create the conditions which enable the people to do without it. 'The best government,' said Goethe, 'is the one that best teaches us how to govern ourselves.' It is clear that the less capable men are of obeying the law of their own free will, the more powerful will the State become. Meanwhile, the habit of giving in to force destroys the critical faculties and self-control, and aggravates the evil. In the Gandhian régime, on the contrary, the greatest possible administrative autonomy would everywhere strengthen economic self-rule, so that the authorities of each village would acquire almost sovereign rights.

The system is one that prevailed in India for thousands of years. It was the same system that prevailed for over a thousand years in China and Egypt, throughout all the lasting empires. Thanks to that system the great thinking and peaceful peoples were able to set up unshakable institutions, preserve their fundamental traditions and bring their culture to maturity so that for other nations they became the true sources of all culture.

We, the ephemeral, the intermittent, the accidental, we must not forget that we possess nothing good that was not conceived, known, and practised centuries ago by those peoples, even though the intermediaries through whom it came to us claimed the honour of inventing it.

Without doubt, these empires upheld powerful theocratic and military dynasties, waged wars and underwent devastating invasions. But neither the course of war nor the form of government concerned the practical and spiritual life of the village, which, in spite of all outward change, remained unchanging in its essence. When he had paid tribute to whomever it was due, the farmer was quit, and a mere onlooker at the quarrels of the princes and even at the successive arrivals of the conquerors.

Even the Moslem Mongols, bloodthirsty and hateful masters, respected this order of things and contented themselves with taking advantage of it. It was the coming of the English—much less inhuman and much less tyrannical—that corrupted the country from top to bottom. It was not the burden, heavy as it was, of the Imperial Government, nor the army with its guns that made its ruin complete, but the cheap-jack with his attaché case.

15

The régime of Gandhi has three points in common with those that are warring for supremacy in the West.

With the liberal régime: political liberty as the liberals see it. Respect for the antagonist's opinion. The feeling that even people's own good cannot be imposed on them by force.

With the communist régime: the primacy of work. The duty for all to do manual work. Equality of duties and rights for workers of every kind, whatever the inequality of their abilities.

With the nazi-fascist régime: self-government. The replacement of the principle of commercial competition by that of solidarity between the corporations. The affirmation of the human will as being something that does not depend on economic conditions. Recourse to the individual and his authority. The formation of administrators and leaders.

But there is one aspect of Gandhi's régime which has nothing in common with those of the West, present or past, and that is its truly Hindu and Christian character.

16

This characteristic may be summed up in one word: Ahimsa, the doctrine and practice of non-violence.

Etymologically, Ahimsa means 'refraining from harming'. Negative in meaning, the word and the virtue it denotes are characteristically Hindu. Ahimsa has been cultivated by the sages and the people of India since her beginnings.

Horror of killing is as widespread here as it is rare elsewhere. Horror, not only of killing a man or a calf, but of killing a rat, a fly, a mosquito or a louse. The Old Law prescribes special penitence and purification for the *involuntary* murder of tiny creatures in the house—woodlice or ants accidentally squashed when one has moved a jar, or been sweeping, or has stepped on one of them. Meat is strictly forbidden to Brahmins and they do not even know what it tastes like. Generally speaking, no self-respecting Hindu, whatever his caste, has the profane and disgusting habit of feasting on corpses.

Nevertheless, traditional Ahimsa remains a negative virtue, of the order of abstinence and observance. Genuine pity, that impulse of the heart that makes one rush to the help of any suffering creature, is perhaps weaker here than in our carnivorous and bloodthirsty West: indifference, and even fear of killing, sometimes lead to greater cruelties than do natural ferocity and greed of gain. The prolonged agony of stray dogs, which is one of the scandals of India, is an instance of this. 'Kill them!' I have sometimes shouted to the consternation of villagers. 'For God's sake, kill them!'

In its positive meaning, and as Gandhi defines and practises it, Ahimsa is a Christian virtue in no way different from charity. First of all, it is marvelling and merciful goodwill towards everything that lives.

It is the first of the commandments, and sums up all the others. It is perpetual wakefulness of the spirit, an unremitting effort of the heart, an ever-flowing spring of action. It is order arising from freedom, since whoever loves has only to do what he wants to do, in order to carry out the commandments. It is liberation from desire and attachment, our shadows; it is the effacement of our ignorance and the ignorance of others; it is the righting of our wrongs and the redress of injustice. It is the abolition of barriers and limits, perpetual giving without loss, total sacrifice without suffering, and thus makes our nature the same as the nature of light. It is the only door into the Kingdom, for God is truth and truth is the goal, but love is the way. That is why love of God which does not show itself through service to mankind is a snare and a delusion.

A revolutionary method and a weapon, Ahimsa is a revelation almost without precedent, and the most singular event even in this age so troubled and full of unheard-of adventures.

17

The policy of Gandhi is incomprehensible if one does not know that its aim is not political but spiritual victory.

Whoever saves his own soul does not only serve himself. Although bodies are separate, souls are not. Whoever saves his own soul saves the Soul and accumulates riches that belong to all. Others have only to perceive the treasure to partake of it.

Some may set out from the other end of the road and by serving others, save their own souls. The Hindus call this sort of man a karma-yogi, an ascetic of action. They depict him as a sage seated in the pose of meditation with a sword in his fist. To rule may be a way of serving others and saving one's own soul. Ridding India of the English would be a mean and trivial ambition indeed for such a great sage as Gandhi. His purpose is to deliver his people from their evils (of which foreign rule is one of the least). His aim is to deliver his soul from ignorance, to live, that is to say, to try out truth.

18

Gandhi has told the story of his life in a book of great human interest, even if lacking in literary beauty. He entitled it *The Story of my Experiments with Truth*. The modesty and the assurance implied in this title are admirable. Nobody is less pedantic than this great teacher of a great doctrine, nobody more wary of abstract statements or claims that cannot be verified. No one is more devoid of dogmatic obstinacy or blind fanaticism than this great religious leader. No visions, no prophecies, no miracles adorn the legend of this saint. His saintliness shines out in the simplicity of his everyday work and in the timeliness of his public action.

Like very great men, he has only one idea. Like very great ideas, his is simple and of the nature of obvious mathematical truth. He has taken it to its ultimate conclusions and immediately applied them with that lucidity of mind, purity of heart and rightness of action that sweep away obstacles and disarm the foe. He is unique. Yet, 'Anybody could do the same thing in my stead,' he says artlessly.

19

'Passive resistance' is the common way of naming Gandhi's policy. To give it such a name is to predispose oneself to misunderstanding it completely. One has only to give 'passive' the meaning of 'inert' and then people will imagine some 'force of inertia' or other, no doubt some new form of the famous 'oriental laziness', or else they will connect it with the equally famous 'oriental fatalism' and see in it resignation to injustice as a misfortune sent by God.

The non-violent resistance that Gandhi exemplifies shows itself to be more active than violent resistance. It requires more daring, a greater spirit of sacrifice, more discipline and more hope. It obtains its results on the plane of tangible reality as well as on the plane of conscience. It brings about a profound transformation in those who practise it, and sometimes a surprising conversion of those against whom it is carried out.

20

Gandhi-Jee says, 'It is a noble thing to defend your rights, your honour and religion at the point of the sword. It is still more noble to defend them without trying to harm the wrongdoer. But it is abject, unnatural and disgraceful to abandon your post in order to save your skin, and to leave your rights, your honour and religion at the mercy of the wrongdoer.

'I see how I can teach non-violence to those who know how to die: to those who are afraid of death, I cannot.'

*

'The ability to inflict injury is a premise of non-violence. Non-violence is conscious and deliberate restraint of the desire for revenge. Taking revenge is no doubt better than giving in feebly, passively and effeminately, but the desire for revenge is also weakness, because the desire for revenge is born of fear.

'When a man is afraid of nobody, he finds it trying to have to be angry with someone who is vainly attempting to harm him.'

*

'The clemency of a sheep or a rabbit means nothing. One must possess power in order to renounce it. One must possess courage in order to renounce violence. One must show one's courage by refusing to be violent.
   'Pardon is the array of the warrior.'

*   *

One can be sure of non-violent victory when one has conquered fear in oneself.

*

Non-violent combat does not seek to win victory over the enemy, but to conquer enmity and win peace.
   'The non-violent fighter is not trying to escape the effects of violence, but to resist violence without violence, and conquer.
   'His problem is this: How to fight violence without harming the violent.'

*

It is not the enemy you have to fight, but the enemy's error: the error your neighbour commits when he happens to think himself your enemy. Make yourself an ally of your enemy against his mistake.

*   *

Enmity is a result of ignorance. For between every man and every other, there remains a fraternal link forgotten by whoever practises enmity. It is up to the non-violent person to remind him of it. The fraternal link was forgotten because the other man was thinking only of himself. You can only recall it to him by forgetting yourself.

*

Every game is a sham combat and every combat is a game. It is the balance of contrasts. The give-and-take of attack and defence creates excitement which, in the player, takes the form of pleasure, and in the fighter, of anger, fury, frenzied obstinacy and a lust for blood and devastation. In the game of fighting, the violent person refuses to recognise that the blows given are wrongs, and murders. The innocence of gallantry is one of the delusions from which one must free the violent, one of the points where the make-believe of the game turns into a lie.

*   *

It takes two to make a fight. They must agree to fight. The resistance that the object of the attack puts up is necessary to the attacker; that is what he is attacking. Either of the combatants can therefore put an end to the combat whenever he wishes. All he has to do is to refuse the support of his resistance.

'I disappoint the expectation of the bully and his attack falls wide, to his astonishment. He is even more astonished to meet in me with resistance that comes from my soul, and on which he has no hold. This resistance will at first blind him and without fail he will become twice as furious with me as before, but in the end it will force him to give in.

'And the fact of his giving in will not humiliate the aggressor, but elevate him.'

*

If I smite you on the right cheek and you retaliate with a blow, your blow seals our agreement to fight. We can now let fly! But if you turn to me the other cheek and say, 'You may smite this one too, my friend: I shall gladly take this trouble to show you that you are wrong', then I am flabbergasted and my rage gives way to stupefaction, and stupefaction to reflection.

*   *

To flee is also to play the game and sign the agreement to fight. Flight is the most widespread weapon of defence, a display of strength and cunning which is bound to provoke the aggressor into pursuit and slaughter. This is not refusing violence, but giving in to it. It is withdrawing from victory without withdrawing from the fight.

In the last resort, one can raise one's arm and ask for mercy; it is no doubt one way of bringing the struggle to an end and perhaps escaping the consequences of violence. But this is not refusing violence, it is doing homage to it. It is choosing between blows and shame, and preferring shame: choosing between death and slavery, and preferring slavery. 'If the choice were only between violence and cowardice,' says Gandhi-Jee, 'I should not hesitate to recommend violence.'

*   *

Injustice is something that demands that one should oppose it wherever it appears. The non-violent person does not always wait to be attacked with weapons. It is often he who takes the first step and goes forward to meet violence. Not only does he bear blows, he provokes them. He seizes the throat of the iniquitous law in which injustice is latent and makes it spew up its venom, until those whose duty it is to enforce it feel shame. 'The most constant goodwill towards all, together with the firmest resistance to evil.'

21

Solitary non-violence is the dignity of the person who, even in contact with the aggressor, keeps himself intact from the contagion of anger. It is the mark of absolute self-possession, the outward sign of faith in the victory and peace of the other world.

Collective non-violence takes on a different character. Since the people has a chance of surviving ordeal, it can reasonably entertain some hope for this world. The people who, as Mirabeau said, 'has only to fold its arms to become formidable', can make non-violent resistance an invincible weapon. This is the way (a way along which, for lack of trying, humanity has made no progress for centuries), and perhaps the only way, that the Kingdom of God will come and His Will be done on earth as it is in heaven.

Collective non-violence differs from solitary non-violence in that it can become contagious. The ordinary mortal will admire a saint in so far as he believes himself incapable of adopting the saint's conduct. But the example of a whole people will sweep him along with it almost against his will. The first to undergo the contagion will be the enemy, on whom the daring patience of a great number has a paralysing effect.

Every honest man is willing to fight, but no warrior will consent to becoming a butcher or a hangman. So long as armies and police forces are not solely composed of monsters, devils and lunatics, and are for the most part made up of decent fellows anxious to carry out their duty without questioning the orders they are given, non-violent resistance will act with sovereign efficiency. And Gandhi's experiments with truth have shown that in a group of defenceless men who expose themselves to violence and of their own will hasten to meet death, there are fewer victims than in a troop of well-armed soldiers fighting for their lives.

The fact is that both in South Africa and in India, Gandhi has not once applied his tactics in vain. From a prison cell, half-dead through fasting, he has always in the end succeeded—he the disarmed—in dictating his conditions to the powerful.

Several heads of Congress, including Nehru, who do not attach to non-violence any of the religious significance it possesses for Gandhi, have notwithstanding adopted his method because experience has shown them how efficient it is: 'Because it works.'

*

In a lengthy treatise an American author named Greg has studied the psychological and practical effects of *The Power of Non-Violence*. He compares its defensive value to that of ju-jitsu (a Japanese discipline of Yoga origin, by the way) in which one uses the enemy's own limbs as levers, slightly displacing his centre of balance so that even the most furious development of his force miscarries, making him the victim of his own reactions and rendering him helpless at the very instant of striking his decisive blow.

But the comparison only serves to make practical people understand the aspect of non-violence that they can comprehend. Non-violence is not a trick, an ingenious discovery in the style of making an egg stand on its end, the sort of cleverness that everyone feels silly not to have thought of sooner. The trick, alas! the trick of putting an end to bloodshed and iniquity, is a trick of great worth, and of great cost too, alas! In Gandhi-Jee's own words:

'Non-violence is not a thing that can be achieved mechanically. It is the highest quality of the heart; nevertheless it develops through practice.

'Walking on the razor's edge of non-violence is not easy in this world of fraud and hatred. Wealth is of no help, rage is an obstacle, pride devours it, sensual pleasure obscures it, lies empty it of its substance, unjustified haste compromises it . . .

'Non-violence and truth are so intimately part of each other that it is impossible to separate them. They are the face and the reverse of the same thin disc. Nevertheless, truth is the goal: non-violence the way.

'Certainty of achieving our aim depends entirely on the purity of our ways.'

Therein lies the whole secret.

*   *

'The toughest fibre must melt in the fire of love. If it does not melt, the fire is not strong enough.'

Therein lies the whole secret.

22

'I used to say, "God is truth."

'But some men deny God. Some are forced by their passion for truth to say that there is no God, and in their own way they are right.

'So I now say, "Truth is God". No one can say, "Truth does not exist" without removing all truth from his statement. Therefore I prefer to say "Truth is God".

'It has taken me fifty years of persevering meditation to prefer this way of putting it to the other.'

That, I think, is the only metaphysical statement Gandhi has ever made. Even so, it is a principle of his faith rather than the result of speculation.

Another of his remarks should be added to it. 'God is love. For us, God is love. In Himself, He is truth.' (*Sat* means *truth, substance,* and *being*—all in one.)

What he means is love of truth, love from which all sentimental attachment is excluded, just as severely as all desire for the things of this world. Exactly as in Christian love.

*   *

Ardent, tender words of love rise to Gandhi's lips when he speaks of truth. 'Truth is as hard as lightning[2] and delicate like peach-blossom.'

*

Truth is the first of the virtues. Without it, the others have no substance.

23

Gandhi is a great politician. Everyone who has had to deal with him admires his skill.

Just as violence must always be countered with gentleness if wrongs are to be righted, so bad faith must always be countered with sincerity. The simple truth is always the surest of defences, the most piercing of swords, the straightest road to an end.

Therein lies the whole secret.

*   *

'I myself have always believed in the honesty of my enemies,' he says. 'And if one believes in it hard enough, one finds it. My enemies took advantage of my trust in them and deceived me. They deceived me eleven times running; and with stupid obstinacy, I went on believing in their honesty. With the result that, the twelfth time, they couldn't help keeping their word. Discovering their own honesty was a happy surprise for them and for me too. That is why my enemies and I have always parted very pleased with each other.'

24

'Bapu-Jee,' I said to him shortly after my arrival, 'they have already come and checked my papers and questioned me. My companions have warned me that I must soon expect to be shadowed by an informer. Now, there is nothing I have such a horror of as a policeman, unless it be a spy. But having both of these rolled into one, constantly at my heels, will make me sick. If this does happen, how should I behave?'

'It is indeed humiliating,' he answered, 'very humiliating, to think that for a little money a man can resign himself to such a profession. You must avoid tiring and worrying him needlessly.

You must give him all the information he wants to discover and keep him informed of all your comings and goings; show him your letters and tell him your secret thoughts. I urge my own people to reject any thought that they would not like their enemies to know of. It is a good way for us of making sure that we only have good thoughts.'

25

It sometimes happens that some foreign visitor, with the praise-worthy intention of being agreeable to the great rebel, launches into an attack upon the English, seasoning his tirade with sarcasm and embellishing it with eloquence.

This is followed by the embarrassed silence of the listeners.

Each of them looks at the ground in front of him. Then Gandhi speaks. At first his voice is stifled but it grows in warmth and clarity as he goes on.

'Their system is bad. They are the first to suffer from it. Doubly so because they do not know that it is bad and that they are suffering from it. As for them, they are men, that is to say, like ourselves, a mixture of good and bad with more good than bad.

'I know only too well how inclined we are by our nature to see only evil in our enemies and to stuff evil into them at any cost and all amiss. And so we think they are deceitful when we have been mistaken about them; when they are not thinking about us at all, we find them disdainful; when their presence harms us in some way, we believe them to be full of hatred towards us; when they are wicked, we call them stupid too; when they are ignorant, we think they are cruel.

'The evil we see in them more often than not depends on the mean and hasty way we have of seeing others.

'The evil or the good that shows in them always depends on which side of ourselves we turn towards them; if it is the best in ourselves that we present to them, the best in them will be brought out in spite of themselves, for like attracts like.

'But whatever our enemies may be, I cannot judge them; for one cannot be judge and party in the same lawsuit.

'The tyrant we are cursing is perhaps the right arm of God, the arm of God that is righting us.

'It is a fearful thought that we may be cursing God made manifest in his right arm.'

26

I have never heard any patriotic talk from Gandhi-Jee or his followers. Good manners which I appreciate.

27

If you think a thing good enough to do, do it with good grace: as befits the dignity of a free man.

If your task is troublesome, consider that the trouble is your business only. Remember that a task carried out bravely and with good grace is never vain, and brings its own rewards.

If you think an act is bad, simply refuse to do it and submit with good grace to the consequences of your refusal.

But never put yourself into the degrading attitude of the unwilling servant or the ridiculous one of the protesting citizen. For shirkers and the underhand there is no place in the ranks of men.

Respect your masters, even if they are bad, for power comes from God. And it is better to have a bad master than to have none. Respect the law, even if it is unjust, for it is better to have an unjust law than no law.

But if your master or the law force you to do wrong, then disobey deliberately after giving them proper warning of your decision and explaining your reasons for it. Expose yourself without anger to your master's anger and with good grace to the penalties of the law, for you owe them that homage.

Do not try to bring your master round to indulgence. On the contrary, offer yourselves up in great numbers and demand that the law be enforced on you in its utmost severity.

It will not be in vain. The law that is founded on fear is undermined and soon overthrown when its victims ask for punishment instead of trying to escape.

You have no other legal means of getting an unjust law abolished and forcing your masters, whoever they may be, to respect justice.

28

Serve the oppressor diligently: force his respect by your work done well and willingly, and your good manners. When a slave is a constant grumbler, he is whipped into working, and if he refuses to work, he is killed. But when a tried and devoted worker who has never spared himself, and whose worth is known, one day says 'No, sir', it makes his master think and compels him to reckon with him.

*   *

My very love of absolute truth has taught me the beauty of compromise.

29

Life feeds on destruction. Life is nevertheless the stronger. Love is stronger in the end than hate. Such, God be praised, is the law of the world.

I have brought this law into my own life in a rudimentary way. I will not say that it has solved all my problems. But it seems to me to be a more expedient method than opposing an evil by adding one more.

30

One of the least appreciated, but no doubt one of the most precious, benefits of the method of non-violence is slowness.

Gandhi is careful not to speak of it to his followers. They would not listen to him. They are hasty, being less aware than he of the greatness of the realities and the values that are at stake, just as they are less aware of the dangers ahead.

A revolution as profound as his, which required not so much a change in the social régime as the transmutation of the human substance, can only be achieved with the passing of time. Nothing is more contrary to wisdom than plucking the fruit before it is ripe.

To India, with forty centuries behind her, ten years is as nothing.

That some twenty thousands of soldiers and traders should hold in their power and freely exploit three hundred and fifty million people who are their equals in some respects and their superiors in others is a riddle that the reason of guns cannot wholly explain.

The domination of the British is an evil for India, but it is even more a symptom of her evil. Gandhi knows this and it is the evil, not the symptom, that he wants to attack.

Her ailment is her dividedness. For although nature has defined the country with such precision and moulded it in a single block between the highest mountains and the widest oceans in the world, its peoples have not fused. The fact is that it has never been united, except under the yoke of the British. The greatest empires in the north of India, the Buddhist empire of Ashok in the second century B.C. and the Moslem empire of Akbar in the sixteenth century, never went beyond the frontier of the Deccan. Even the early conquest of India by the Aryans (provided there is some basis for this scientific legend) stopped short of the black peoples of the south. The Brahmins settled among the latter by peaceful infiltration. They converted and policed them, imposed their rites, their thought and their ways on them, behaved like masters, but not like conquerors or sovereigns. Indeed, the Brahmins never attempted to subjugate them to their own Aryan rulers since the head of the law is the Brahmin and not the ruler, who is only its arm. Despite the proliferation of its gods, its practices and its contradictory philosophies, the Brahmic religion has been the only unifying element between the Himalayas and Cape Comorin. Ramified though it may be, its unity is none the less strong and green. It was the only religion that could attract into the sphere of its orthodoxy beings so immutably unequal and unlike each other, from those who are drawn only to fetishism and sorcery, to those who have given themselves up to the most subtle metaphysical speculation. And one can only wonder at the depth of the common imprint with which Brahmism has marked such widely differing people.

But this spiritual empire does not include all the Indians either. It must also reckon with the heretic sects: that of Buddha, which almost supplanted it; that of the Jains, which is still flourishing, and the foreign religions—the Zoroastrian communities, few in number but powerful because of their wealth, and the Christian religion, which gains numbers daily and forms a favourable element for European domination. But it must above all reckon with Islam, whose presence cuts Hindustan in half.

Actually, Hindus and Moslems are two peoples who are more than strangers. Between them, there is no guarded frontier. They are everywhere face to face and side by side, which makes their hostility all the more constant and marked. They pass each other daily in the streets, they come face to face, alone, on the forest path. Whereupon one turns his head this way and the other that. They exchange neither a sign nor a word. Between neighbouring nations, even when they are hostile, relationships are formed through trade, hospitality, personal friendship and marriage. But between Moslem and Hindu there has been nothing of the kind for ten centuries. Moreover, in spite of all the aversion and contempt they feel for each other, they rarely come to blows. Because in order to fight, one has to touch one's enemy, and even that fills them with horror. They are more than strangers, as I have said.

The Indian Moslems are distinguished from the Hindus by a certain savage roughness. They are in the sorry situation of the domesticated wild beast. Not one of the great spiritual movements that have occurred in India during the last century has originated with them. They have no great man today who can be put on the same plane as the Hindu thinkers. It is they, along with the Gurkhas of Nepal, who provide the British Army with the best soldiers in India. They are a minority of some seventy-five million. If some day the British leave, the Hindus have every reason to fear that this warlike minority, remembering Tamberlane, will attempt to undertake the conquest of the whole country. This is a threat which suffices to make them look upon the King of England as a heaven-sent protector.

Although the Moslems bear the British a grudge for having snatched their empire from them, they are only too willing to strike a blow for them when they have occasion to bully the Hindus. And the British find it easy to envenom this dissension, which strengthens their own power.

Following Akbar, enlightened leaders, poets and mystics have time and time again attempted to reconcile the two Indias. They have met with nothing but deafness and mistrust on both sides.

Gandhi alone has succeeded in moving the people and bringing them into contact. There is no lack of Moslems among his followers. Once, he successfully urged the Hindus to make common cause with their hereditary enemies in the matter of the

Caliphate, which concerned only the latter. He has never lost an opportunity of deserving their friendship.

But this brotherhood is of difficult and slow birth.

It is a far cry from the paradise of Mahomet, opened by the point of the sword, to the terrestrial and celestial glory of non-violence.

The religious fervour of Gandhi beats against the wall of the mosque without rousing much echo.

31

But even among themselves, the Hindus are as separate, or nearly so, as they are from the Moslems, their society being chopped into castes, as everyone knows. And each caste has come in the end to form people shut in by invisible and impassable frontiers.

There were four original castes. Strange to say, the first is not the caste of the princes.

The first is that of the Brahmins, the caste of those who sacrifice, pray and know. The second is that of nobles, kings and warriors. The third that of traders, townsmen or breeders of flocks. The fourth is the menial caste, that of labourers, craftsmen, farmers and shepherds.

In this aged trunk the sap no longer circulates. Marriage between persons of different castes which, with certain reserves, used to be tolerated, has become strictly impossible today. Texts prove that it used to be possible for a person or a family to move into a higher caste through merit or successive marriages. Today, the differences between the castes cannot be broken down. There are provinces where one caste or another has disappeared. The lowest caste has been subdivided into as many castes again as there are trades, with a proportionate increase of taboos concerning marriage, food and contact.

Caste implies a family cult of the gods and the spirits of ancestors, alimentary and sexual taboos, and rules that are all the more numerous and severe as the caste is high. Caste does not entail any privilege of wealth or power.

In the West, it may happen that the son of a good family who has suffered misfortune becomes a taxi-driver or a dish-washer. But this is considered as a great come-down and exceptional. In India, it is the rule that persons of the highest caste are to be found

E

in the most diverse, and above all, in the most wretched conditions and are yet in no way thought degraded. One meets with Brahmins who are priests in temples (strangely enough, this is not considered an honourable profession) or who are humble clerks in some commercial firm; others become ploughmen, cooks or beggars and I have even known some who were policemen.

As no distinguished person can bear to be approached or touched by someone who does not belong to his caste, a Brahmin can inevitably have only Brahmins for servants, just as a noble can only employ nobles. It follows that there are more Brahmins and nobles who are servants than Brahmins and nobles who are masters.

The class struggle does not, and cannot, exist in India. Not hatred but fear of contact keeps her people apart. The lot of the upper castes arouses no envy in others. Ambition and pretension have no object there. There is not the slightest trace of contempt in the care that the higher castes take not to be touched by the lower, but terror of being supernaturally defiled and losing their caste. For although caste is a prerogative that cannot be acquired by deserving works, it can be lost at any moment by even an involuntary fault. And to lose caste is to be outcast like a leper.

Caste therefore plays no role in public office. It gives those who belong to it no privileges. It has become merely a hindrance to human contact between human beings.

It is a superstition in the proper meaning of the word, that is to say, a left-over. It is the remains of a social pyramid which had its purpose, its greatness and its beauty, but from the very start that purpose, that greatness and that beauty carried with them their counterpart of shame.

That counterpart is the abjection of the pariah.

32

Round every Indian village, on the heap of filth, alone or in packs, the trembling dogs prowl—creatures one need not feed and that one disdains to kill.

Their tails tucked in, they shiver in the burning sun. Their backbones are saws, their ribs pierce their mangy skin, a collar of vermin crawls round their necks.

In spite of their fear of sticks and stones, they watch the ever-open doors of the wretched huts, live on what they can steal and what is thrown to them, feast on the carcasses of rats or reptiles.

At night they swarm round the bitches on heat and celebrate their yelping orgy. Misery alone limits their proliferation and wears away their carcasses with such atrocious slowness that they linger day after day between life, death and decomposition.

A population of several tens of millions of souls undergoes a fate similar in all points to that of the dogs, unless it be that suffering and degradation have their limits in the animal and none in the privileged nature of man.

Such is the people of pariahs whose cause Gandhi has taken in hand.

33

A whole school of erudition traces the origin of the pariahs back to the aboriginal tribes in the peninsula who were subjugated or repulsed by the Aryans.

The same learned persons see the caste system as a method of self-preservation adopted by the ancient white conquering race against the more or less black races of the conquered.

No ancient text supports such a theory or explains any of the facts.

Even a superficial observer can see that the three great races known in ancient times met and mingled. In the plains of the north, one can see Hindus of every caste who are as white as southern Europeans and who look like them.

In the counterforts of the Himalayas and on the Burmese frontier, there are others, also of every caste, rajahs as well as Brahmins, who have yellow skins and slit eyes, like Mongols.

There are Hindus in the south, Brahmins as well as others, who are black and have long high heads and delicately carved noses like the Abyssinians. It has never occurred to a Brahmin to deem himself superior to any other Brahmin because of the colour of his skin. It is clear that caste is founded on rite, not race.

What is the point of concocting theories concerning the origin of the pariahs when the Code of Manu explains it clearly: 'Illicit marriage between persons of distinct castes, marriages contrary to the rules, and the omission of prescribed ceremonies are the origin of the impure classes' (x, 24).

And now, here are the crimes which, as well as ill-assorted marriage, unfortunate birth or the parents' omission to invest a child with the holy cordon, may lead to degradation. One cannot but find it an odd list.

'Harming a Brahmin, smelling things one should not smell, drinking alcohol, deceiving, committing sodomy, entail loss of caste.

'Killing an ass, a horse, a camel, a stag, an elephant, a he-goat, a ram, a fish, a serpent, or a buffalo is declared an act which reduces a person to a mixed caste.

'Receiving gifts from contemptible persons, carrying out an illicit trade, serving a master of menial caste, and lying, must be considered as reasons for exclusion' (x, 67, 68, 69).

The crimes also include consorting with a man of vile class and 'drinking the foam from the lips of a woman of a low kind'.

Proof enough that the company of the pariahs, constantly enriched with new recruits, is of the same blood as the other Hindus. And here is proof that blood has nothing to do with the question:

The son of a nobleman and a Brahmin woman has the very best blood there is, and can boast of the most illustrious of ancestors on both sides of the family: yet he is a pariah of the most abject species, untouchable even for the Untouchables.

It would be a mistake to think that common misfortune puts them on an equal footing:

'From the marriage of a nobleman with a Brahmin's daughter, a Soot is born; from the marriage of a townsman and a nobleman's or a Brahmin's daughter, a Magadh or a Vaideh is born. From the marriage of a rustic with women of military or priestly caste come impure mixtures which are the Ayogava, the Kshattri, and the Chandal who is the lowest of mortals.

'Just as a rustic engenders with a noblewoman a son more vile than himself, so one of these vile beings engenders with a woman from one of the four castes a son more vile than himself.

'The six abject classes, by marrying between themselves engender fifteen classes even more abject' (x, 11, 12, 29, 31).

There follows the list of the fifteen classes recognised by the legislator. But the outlawed themselves immediately set about subdividing the degrees of the hierarchy of abjection and observing its distinctions with inhumanly punctilious severity.

Here is the law inflicted on the Chandals, the lowest of mortals:

'They are to live outside the village and their possessions shall be limited to dogs and asses.

'They shall have no other clothing than that of the dead, their dishes shall be broken pots, their ornaments shall be of iron. They are to keep wandering from place to place. Let no duty-loving man have anything to do with them.

'They are to keep out of villages and towns at night. They are to enter them by day to do their chores, with the prescribed signs. Such is the law' (x, 51).

Chandals stick crows' feathers in their hair and advance with shouts that empty the street. They go into the houses by a hidden door and remove the garbage. They carry away the corpses of those who die without relatives. They remove rotting carcasses, and sometimes eat them.

34

Some distance from the village of mud and thatch, their huts, poorer still if possible, squat beside the stagnant pond in which they quench their thirst. Rags of meat hanging from the straw of the roof dry in the sun and stink far and wide. By this stench and by the black swine rolling, grouting and grunting in the surrounding dust one can tell where the Untouchables live. In rags, and grey with dirt, sometimes covered with scabs, hard-featured and with hoarse, grating voices, the Untouchables come and go. And sometimes they move in nightmarish silence.

35

In the course of the centuries, numerous varieties of Untouchables have been formed, sedentary as well as nomadic.

Some have settled in the outskirts of towns where they serve as scavengers, sweepers, porters, factory workers or stone-breakers.

Others are agricultural labourers and help to carry dung, and water for irrigation. If they manage to till some plot of ground, the neighbouring peasants can take it from them before the harvest, since they are not allowed to possess anything.

Others bake bricks, which, in this climate, kills.

Others dig wells, camp on the work-site, and when they have received their pay let themselves be moved on without protest.

Some make alcohol from palm-juice, drink part of it and sell the rest, and after drinking, sleep like the dead.

Some, in Mysore, men and women alike, live stark naked.

Some have taken refuge in the jungle where they fight for their food and their lives with wild beasts. At the approach of a stranger, they leave their huts and flee. They throw the bodies of their old, their sick and their dying to the beasts; the next-of-kin carry out these anticipated funerals with hand-clapping and jeering songs.

Some wander in bands, choose leaders, have their own laws and take the punishment of transgressors into their own hands. Ostensibly selling seeds, salt, herbs or talismans, they travel up and down the country looting all they can.

There is also that colourful people of jugglers, actors of obscene farces, bear-tamers and fortune-tellers, of which our gipsies are no doubt a tribe who for centuries have forgotten the place of their origin. But traces of that origin persist in their language, their customs and ornaments as well as in the pride and superb bearing of their unwashed daughters.

36

Says the law: 'One should recognise by his behaviour a man who belongs to a base class.'

'A lack of noble feeling, roughness of speech, cruelty and neglect of duty are the marks of the man who owes his birth to a worthless mother' (x, 57, 58).

Oh! the power of the law! The pariahs do their best to justify these definitions and make themselves as contemptible as they are held in contempt. The Christian missionaries who have devoted themselves to them in a spirit of charity maintain that their cruelty surpasses their wretchedness and their corruption their filth. Pariahs beat and prostitute their wives and their children and there is no shameful traffic they do not carry on. Their customs have nothing in common with those of savages, but are the dregs and leprosy of a civilisation whose day is done.

37

Although it is forbidden to reveal to them the secrets of science and religion, which are the possessions of respectable persons, and although they are even not allowed to write from left to right, a smattering of the culture of their fathers has come down to them, and the spirit 'that bloweth where it listeth' has sometimes visited them.

Instead of priests they have sorcerers and these invoke demons rather than gods. Their weddings are limited to brief ceremonies followed by abominable orgies. Their evil spells are greatly feared. Some tribes who go in for medicine have a knowledge of herbs and bring about almost miraculous cures.

They have traditional songs in the local language, for work, travelling and love. They tell wry fables that end with a twisted moral. They play satirical comedies which send simple people wild with delight. These productions sometimes have a vigour of style too often lacking in the classical Sanskrit or Prakrit works, whose beauty has its insipid side—oily and over-sweet and tediously long.

And lastly, from the pariahs of the Coromandel coast came a great poet who was also a great saint: Tiruvalluva, whom the Brahmins themselves call the Divine Pariah Priest. He wrote a rejoinder to the Law of Manu: *The Book of Duties*,[3] which the Brahmins have adopted after cutting out such passages as this:

'Woe to them who have forbidden the pariah the earth, the sun, water, rice and fire! Woe to them who have cursed him! Woe to them who have forced him to shelter the old age of his parents and the cradle of his children in the wild beast's den! Woe to them who have cast the pariah out into the caste of yellow-clawed vultures and filthy jackals! For the pariah is a man!'

When Untouchable girls are weaving their baskets at the edge of the marshes, they still sing Tiruvalluva's lament:

'Where are the springs of pure water that can quench our thirst? The water that falls from the troughs of the cattle into their hoofprints is our only drink. Heaven and earth, look on what we are! Enchantment of the eyes, treasure of the heavenly regions, Oh India! thou whom men adore, we may not implore thee, our prayer would sully thy hearing. Heaven and earth, look on what we are!

'In vain have I braved death, seeking to surprise the mantra that evoke the gods; in vain, hiding in the secret depths of the forest, have I made libations to them for their favour. The gods flee at my approach. Heaven and earth, look on what we are!'

38

That which is refused to the pariah—the earth, water, fire, salt, bread and rice, the pity of the faithful, the company of good people, the sacraments—is exactly what the Church in the old days refused to the excommunicated by a condemnation which fell upon them for eternity as well as for life.

There can be no doubt about it, the pariahs have been excommunicated and have proliferated in malediction.

39

They proliferated to such an extent during the periods when some slight leniency was shown to them, that by their very number they became a danger to those who had banished them. To get rid of them, new edicts and new interdictions of almost inconceivable harshness were inflicted upon them time and time again.

It is difficult to understand how a people as wise and gentle and as kind as the Hindus can have acquired the habit of turning a face of stone to such revolting misery: the misery of the dogs that nothing on earth could induce them to kill, and which they leave to rot alive, out of a horror of hitting them, or for fear of defilement, or through prudery; for their non-violence does not spring from the spirit of justice, or from faith, or from kindness of heart, and is, as Gandhi has so well taught, worth nothing.

'One is always brave enough to put up with other people's ills,' says Chamfort. We know that, of course. But how much more wisely one resigns oneself to them when one knows the law of Karma and believes in reincarnation!

Every Hindu not only believes, but knows with certain knowledge that at death he will come back into this world in a higher or lower form than the human one, or in a happier or sadder human

form according to his Karma, that is to say, the measure of his
merits and sins, and that when he has burnt out this form through
suffering proportioned to his wrongdoing, he will weave himself
another form, and yet another, until step by step he reaches union
with the one, the One-in-Self, the Self. He knows that he wove his
fate with his own hands before birth and that he is now fore-
shaping the life he will live tomorrow.

This philosophy justifies pain and evil less inadequately than
others and is the only one that explains non-human suffering. It is
seductive in the extreme.

It has only one defect: it explains really everything as if we knew
everything, and it over-satisfies those who feed on it.

When one knows everything, there is nothing more to be done.

Pity for one's neighbour becomes puerile when one knows with
absolute certainty that his suffering is perfectly justified. Helping
him and relieving his pain is like making a hole in water, since the
pain will return to him and he must suffer it sooner or later. Charity
is foolishness when one knows all.

That is why the Hindu looks on at the calamities that befall his
neighbour, and sometimes at those that befall himself, not with indifference, as is said, but with tormented and reflective serenity
fraught with self-searching.

The Code of the Law of Manu is not the work of proud and cruel
self-styled priests.

It reveals great knowledge, a sovereign, contained dignity and in
certain passages poetic grandeur and delicacy of feeling rare in a
juridical text.

Here are a few quotations of which the solemn beauty is such
that some of it may survive even in this inadequate translation:

> 'Let man build up his goodness act by act
> as the white ants their dwelling,
> taking care to afflict no living creature,
> lest he go alone into the other world,
> for his father and mother and his son and his wife
> and his kinsmen will not go with him.
> Only his righteousness will stay.
> He is born alone, dies alone, alone eats his merit or
> his crime.

Leaving the body in the earth
Like a log of wood or like a lump of mud
His kinsmen will turn aside from him
And go their ways.
Only his righteousness will stay.
Let man act by act build up his righteousness
Lest he enter the other world alone
for led by his righteousness he will walk through
The impassable valley of darkness
And washed by fire of his evil he will reach the heights
Carried up in the hub of his celestial body' (IV, 236).

And this remark on lying:

'The word has fixed all things.
It is the substance of all things and from it all things
    come.
The deceiver by stealing it steals all things' (IV, 256).

The honour of Manu is his abhorrence of impurity. Evil to him
is filth. He teaches man to wash himself with water, fire, a sharp
iron blade or a ray of absolute knowledge, since the Veda washes
clean of sin 'like a great lake into which a clod falls'. He teaches
man how to wash himself. Yes, himself. The honour of Manu is to
have faith in the free man, the twice-born as he calls him, and to
make man's will to be purified the mainstay of his law.

The honour of this law is that its authority does not depend on
a sergeant, a judge or an executioner. A man should inflict punishment on himself of his own free will, just as he bathes and dresses
all by himself.

He must chastise himself for his own good so as to go clad in
justice into the other world and return from it radiant in a higher
form, or go back perfect into the bosom of his Creator.

The benefit of the law is granted him as an instrument, a support, a key, a way to this.

It is not a soft law; it does not enable a man to fall asleep in his
comfortable habits. It is vigilant and severe; present in all the acts
of a man's life as the skeleton is present in his flesh. It keeps him
in its grip even when he is in bed; holds him while he sleeps, serves

him at his meals, does not turn its eyes away when he crouches to empty his belly on to the earth. It prescribes penitence for every sin, venial or serious, voluntary or involuntary. Even mortal sins have their atonement.

> 'He who defiles the wife of his father
> Shall cry out his crime in a loud voice,
> On a bed of red iron he shall stretch himself out
> That death may purify him.
>
> Or else he shall cut off his testicles and penis,
> And holding them in his hand
> Shall walk with a firm step towards the south-west
> Until death overcome him' (XI, 103).

There are some cases, however, where one must give oneself over to the civil authorities:

> 'He who hath stolen gold
> Shall go to the King and declare his sin.
> He shall carry on his shoulder an iron sledge-hammer.
> The King shall strike him with it. Dead or left for dead
> The criminal is purged of his crime.
> But if the King striketh not,
> Let the sin of the thief be on the King's head' (VIII, 314, 315).

40

Far from becoming more lenient during the long course of the centuries, the Law of Manu has become even more strict and punctilious. It has taught the Brahmin how to govern himself. It has taught him the Five Great Sacrifices: to the saints, to the gods, to the spirits, to men and to the shades of the dead. But it has also taught him that the sacrifice of the greatest worth is that of his five senses; the perpetual gift of his breath, that of his words and gestures, that of his sex, his heart, his thoughts; the oblation of his whole person to uprightness and knowledge.

It has taught the Brahmin to govern other men without resorting to force. First by his example. By giving to each person the part of truth that is his due. By administering the sacraments of propitiation, protection and liberation. By seeing that at every hour, in every house, the rites are performed ardently and the observances kept; and that all keep themselves pure and cleanse themselves if they are defiled.

Now the priestly caste is the first in the hierarchy; the only one whose authority remains indisputable, traditional, legitimate, based on human worth and knowledge as well as on divine power. This is not always true of civil power. Civil power has never been anything other for the Brahmin than an arm to second and enforce the law in exceptional cases. It is a means.

But if the king is a usurper, this means becomes impure and even impracticable. If he does not even belong to the noble caste, the king is only 'a butcher exploiting a thousand butcheries'. To approach him, says the law, is a horrible thing. And if the king is not even a Hindu, if he is a Mongol Moslem who despises the law, who knows nothing of the Veda and whose touch defiles, who among us would have recourse to the judgement of such a man? Who would stoop to ask for his help?

So if we have guilty men in our numbers, we shall take good care not to deliver them up to him. Our honour is at stake. But which of us could take it upon himself to seize the body of the law-breaker? Who will execute him if he stubbornly refuses to execute himself? If he refuses to throw himself head first into the fire, for example, whereas that is exactly what the law prescribes in his case? If his ignorance is such that he scoffs at the misfortunes that are waiting for him in his next life, if his nature is so perverse that he has no desire for his own good and his purification?

Against the obstinate rebel, the priest has only one arm—excommunication. 'You will not submit to our law. You are free, then. Go! There shall be nothing more between you and us.'

The noblest side of the Law of Manu, the horror of bloodshed that distinguishes this people, and its love of purity are therefore the cause of this hell of suffering, this great blot on the face of the earth: the abjection of the Untouchable.

41

'I do not wish to be born again,' Gandhi has said, 'but if I must be reborn, I wish it to be in the body of an Untouchable and among those who are called the lowest of mortals, so as to save myself, and save them from their wretched plight.'

He says: 'It is an insult to humanity to affirm that the very presence of a man, whoever he is, defiles us. It is a sin that every Hindu must expiate. It is up to you, my friends, to do so, by approaching the Untouchables in a spirit of love and service. That is how you can purify yourselves.'

He says: 'So long as we ourselves are inhuman, with what heart can we ask of God to deliver us from the inhumanity of others?'

42

In his book on the pariah, Louis Jacolliot notes: 'England can only reign peacefully over India because of the separations of caste which do not allow two men of different caste to sleep under the same roof or eat together, which makes any unitary revolution impossible. A caste may rebel as happened in 1857, but just as then, all the others will let it be crushed without raising a hand to help, because religious prejudice forbids them to fight alongside people who are not of their own tribe . . .

'. . . England will do nothing for the pariahs because a law abolishing caste and setting the pariahs free by letting them have possessions would be the signal for the fall of her domination. She would either have to repress the insurrection of two hundred million men who refused to recognise her law, or else, if they accepted it, faced with the Hundus united and demanding their independence, she would have no other choice but to withdraw.'

The man who towards 1875 was writing these prophetic words had no idea that already, in Gujarat (a country inhabited by the most humane of men, so that neither deer nor birds take fright at their approach) a boy was growing up—a boy like all other little Indians, a boy with beautiful, tender, burning eyes, and a thoughtful, full-lipped mouth, the boy who, grown to manhood, was to undertake the work of uniting all the Hindus, a union which would

be the pledge and beginning of the union of all men of goodwill—
the boy Mohandas-Karmachand Gandhi.

43

If the pariahs were the excommunicated, the first thing they
needed back was the benefit of the sacraments. The temples they
had hitherto been forbidden to enter had to be opened to them.
But to achieve this, Gandhi had to overcome the resistance of the
Brahmins of strict observance, the most stubborn kind there is, the
Brahmins who have the law on their side, the Brahmins who have
the law and the temples in their keeping.

Day by day, Gandhi gains ground from them and knocks down
another barrier in defence of the pariahs.

To those who have been waiting on the threshold for ten,
twenty or thirty centuries, the door is at last opening. Every day
one hears of a new victory—at Delhi, or at Poona, or in Orissa or
in Malabar, another temple opens its doors to the Untouchables.

Each of these occasions is a solemn feast which the Mahatma
attends so that he may lead his strange flock by the hand into the
heart of the sanctuary. He has given them a new name: Men-of-
the-Lord, Harijans.

Schools have been founded for them as well as hospitals and
dispensaries.

A whole army of non-violent volunteers is taking part in this
civilising crusade. Attempts have been made to get the nomads to
settle, and to cultivate in the sedentary tribes a taste for study and
cleanliness and a more orderly, hard-working life. Hindus, Christians and Moslems, men and women of the four castes, especially
the highest, have assumed this great task of redemption in a spirit
of friendly collaboration.

44

In the course of the last century, a Brahmin came to the door of a
pariah's hut. He was holding a broom in his hand and asked if he
might sweep the house.

The Brahmin was no other than Shri Rama Krishna, the Great
Swan.[4]

The pariah, his blood running cold with fear and horror, threw himself on his knees and cried out to him not to come near an Untouchable, not to enter an Untouchable's house: heaven and earth would collapse at such blasphemy. For the pariahs are the first to believe in the curse that has fallen upon them.

So Shri Rama Krishna, the Great Swan, withdrew. But he came back at night and swept the pariah's house with his own hair.

One day when he was teaching in the midst of his disciples, he said, 'Since the whole world is in the Lord's house, we must have pity on all his creatures . . .'

As he spoke the last words, his voice failed him and he fell into ecstasy. His disciples, who had often seen him pass out of life, waited for him to return to them.

After some time, he did in fact return and continued, 'Pity on all creatures! Wretched worms that we are, what right have we to take pity on others? We must approach them with infinitely humble love, with profound respect and serve them, rather than pity them, as we should serve God himself.'

*   *

'Whoever does not understand,' he said one day, 'that the first man he sees passing in the street is God himself, will not find God in the temple, nor in his heart, or in this world or in another.'

Rama Krishna is the first Hindu saint whose disciples, like the Christians, have spread over the continents to announce the good news. They have not taken advantage of this, however, to found a new religion but to urge everyone to become converted to his own religion so as to find truth, which is one, and through it to become united with God who is one.

In his visions, Rama Krishna was visited by our Lord and by the Virgin Mary. I have no doubt that it was from this meeting with the majesty of Christ that he drew the fervent and active charity that distinguishes him from other contemplatives of Asia and brings him so near to us.

The fact is that the monasteries in which his discipline is followed are at the same time hospitals, schools, alms-giving centres and the starting point of missions.

45

In Gandhi, it is a quickening of the Christian spirit that has re-awakened the Hindu virtues. Tolstoy's evangelical dreams gave him the first impulse and led him to formulate his social doctrine. Careful reading of the New Testament confirmed him in his vocation. He considered having himself baptised. But his relations with Christians gave him no desire to be one of them. The various arrangements they have come to with heaven were not of a nature to satisfy his thirst for the absolute and for action. But some of the truth that Christianity makes clear struck him and marked him. Moreover, his promptness to act, his sense of historical opportunity, his organising abilities are purely Western qualities. All this contributes to make him a supremely universal person. His teaching is addressed to all, and his success concerns us all for reasons not at all political.

The future cannot be foreseen, and success cannot be our goal in any action that surpasses us. But if God pleases, the action will have success for its result. It is man's duty to fulfil his task by pure means and to hope in God. The ploughman turns the earth over and sows seed in it. He does not make the wheat grow. The crop is therefore not due to him. So when he has sown, he must pray, and if he reaps he must give thanks.

It is highly probable that the movement will deviate in India. I can see no one among Gandhi's lieutenants worthy of succeeding him. It may all degenerate some day into a violent revolution or just one more national emancipation. But the wheat has been sown. A new truth has entered the human heritage. Perhaps the wheat will rise elsewhere.

46

Segaon, where Gandhi lives, is about six miles from the school at Wardha.

I spend Sundays there and I may come back whenever my need to see him again and to ask him some question becomes urgent.

To reach Segaon we must cross a rolling wilderness patched with scrub. On the horizon lie the blue streak of a hill and the black bar of the jungle.

The path winds through sand and sometimes gets lost. Often, we pass Segaon without seeing it. The thatched roof blends into the parched grass around it and the dried mud of its walls fades into the earth.

Such is the palace of the man who reigns, more than king, over two hundred million men.

47

I am beginning to draw out a more even thread—it does not snap at each turn of the wheel. I shall soon have spun my pilgrim's robe. The fact is that I want to set out in April for the source of the sacred rivers, a pilgrimage that every pious Hindu achieves at least once in his life. I want to prepare myself for it, and take with me only objects that are pure.

*   *

Mira-Behn is teaching me to card with a bow, an art at which she is past master. For this operation, we shut ourselves into a room which has no window, but walls made of reed wattling. The bow hangs at one end of a rope over a beam in the ceiling and its counterweight hangs at the other. The bow is strung with a tough gut like the low note of a guitar and is sometimes decorated like a musical instrument. With a wooden ball on the handle, we beat time on the twanging bow-string and at each blow, the bow descends to the heap of raw cotton lying on the ground. The vibration of the string whips up the top, and little by little froths up the bulk of the heap. But it is tiring music. We gasp for breath and breathe in flock. Some of it goes down our throats. At the slightest wrong note, the cotton fibre twists itself round the string and stops the game. We then have to untwist it and pick it off with our finger-nails, a trying, finicky job that needs a great deal of patience.

Mira-Behn's close-cropped hair is going grey. There is something slightly mannish in her noble, commanding features and the way she carries her strong frame. From time to time we rest and talk. Her pure English is a relief to me from oriental turns of speech and intonation. I like talking about London, Paris, Rome and the world we have both left without regret and without any thought of return. Because I feel I shall never go back again, even

though it is not long since I left it, it seems to me that I am cut off
from my country by a great gulf of time.

I remember someone I left there four months ago as I remember
those whose death I wept for when I was a child. 'And yet,' I
said, 'if there were a meadow here of fine green grass covered with
daisies, and a chilly breeze blew the scent of it into our faces, own
up, Mira-Behn! the tears would come into your eyes just as they
would into mine.'

'No,' she replied, 'none of it touches me now. My childhood has
grown misty, and the life I led as a girl was futile. The restlessness
of the search spoiled everything, even the smell of the grass. Only
one thing can make the tears come and that is the thought that
Bapu-Jee will be leaving us some day, perhaps soon, for his heart
is weakening. Even though he scolds me and tells me that attachment is a very ugly sin and pure folly, I can find no cure for it. He
had a hut built for me a mile from here, behind the hill, so as to
give me a foothold in a life that is not filled with his presence. But
life wasn't worth living and I fell ill immediately. I had to be brought
back here, and now I am well again. That is how the body takes
advantage of the exaltation of the spirit to show who is master.'

48

It is not surprising that our folk-song died out with spinning. The
spinning-wheel is the nearest thing to the hurdy-gurdy. The
thread spun is a measure of time, like music. It calls for a tune as
a tune calls for words. Many songs are returning to me from my
childhood. New ones are coming to me too, and words for them,
but I make them up only to supply the lack of old ones. So I sing
all day long for my companions and myself while we work.

49

At the same time, I have become an apprentice to carpentry and I
spend every other day at it. The most difficult thing I am learning
is how to saw a plank while squatting on it and gripping it with my
toes.

There is a small tool here which is used for practically everything. It is a kind of short-handled, wide but shallow mattock, axe

on one side, hammer on the other. In the middle of the blade is a sort of keyhole for pulling out nails. Holding it either by the handle or the iron part, one uses it to cut, hollow out, shape, pierce, groove, scrape, plane, polish and even chisel planks and pieces of wood of all sizes.

As I watch him, the master, with one turn of the hand, ploughs a thin peg out, tapers it off, cuts out the grooves and rounds the head. His swift, tranquil hands turn the object round; they are the hands of a princess or a musician. I admire and envy this obscure workman.

The perfection of tools replaces man's skill and finally kills it. This explains why, the more our civilisation spreads and grows, the more man becomes small and helpless and dull. From the Stone Age, all we have left is a few flint axe-heads and arrow-heads. On this we forge an image of extreme savagery, perhaps rightly. But it is also possible that because of the very crudeness of these instruments, man at that moment had reached the highest degree of bodily and spiritual perfection. This surmise is not contradicted by the beauty of the earliest cave-paintings known.

50

It would be wrong to think that the care Gandhi takes to put manual work first and foremost rules out all mechanical progress.

There are machines whose efficiency depends on effort and which are in no danger of replacing it, such as the spinning-wheel, the lathe, the bicycle and the sewing-machine. That is the direction in which invention should be encouraged.

It is noteworthy that since Gandhi has taken in hand the development of hand-spinning, the output of an ordinary workman has doubled or tripled thanks to improvement of his methods and tools.

*

Winter turns out to be the gentlest season here. From half past ten in the morning till four o'clock in the afternoon, the sun blazes powerfully but remains bearable provided one keeps moving.

The nights are cool. We sleep on the roof terrace in the middle of an orange-grove whose fragrance rises to the stars.

The mornings are of silk and the evenings of velvet.

51

A potful of rice and vegetables, two whole pancakes, a bowl of sour milk and some brown sugar; that's lunch. For supper you get the same, the same tomorrow and every day of life, the same in the north and in the south of India and for everybody, or almost, and it is very well thus. Gluttony is held in check. The body is safeguarded from surprise and excess as well as from need. After the long sweat of the day and the bath in the well, these meals are not of the kind one turns up one's nose at. In any case, Lent has begun. I have taken advantage of it to skip both meals, twice a week to begin with, then three times a week. This gives singular savour to the meals I do have. Pleasure itself teaches us, without any help from morality or religion, that she is not what we must seek, for as soon as we seek her, she flees. But as soon as we drive her away, she pursues us and seizes us with unexpected force.

52

Despite Bapu-Jee's advice, I have been unable 'to put aside all clerical work'.

The school library is a temptation I cannot resist. From time to time I take a book from it and hurry to devour it under the mango-tree during the siesta. I finish it at night on the roof by dim lantern light. There is no lack of Sanskrit texts with commentaries, translations into various languages, grammars and dictionaries.

I am picking up a few rudiments of this primordial tongue, but only incidentally. It is the quick of the text I want to get at. Words and turns of speech settle by themselves in the memory. Besides, the only way of learning a so-called dead language is to make it live. And the life of a language is the meaning of what it says.

The study of Hindi is part of the school programme. A stout man comes and teaches us at fixed times. It is one of the northern dialects. Gandhi and his followers have had it adopted as the national language. I am learning it in the company of some Indians from the south, to whom it is just as foreign as to me. There are about forty languages spoken in India, each with its alphabet and its literary and poetic tradition. They can be divided into three main groups, the first containing those derived from Sanskrit, which consequently have the same roots as ours and are spoken in the north and in the centre. The second group contains those derived from Persian and Afghan, the languages of the Moslem provinces. Urdu is the chief of these. The third group contains Dravidian languages of the Tamil kind. There are four to the south of the Deccan without counting Cingalese.

They have no connection with the others. In these conditions, English remains the most convenient form of communication between one province and another.

The advantage of Hindi is that it has kept the Sanskrit alphabet intact. This is enough for all Hindus to grant it primacy. Hindi is to Sanskrit roughly what Italian is to Latin. But unlike Italian which, by dint of deforming a very beautiful language has ended up by substituting an even more beautiful one, Hindi is devoid of music and structure and is as jarring to the ear as to the intelligence. It is an idiom without verbs, or rather, it only has one, the verb 'to be' which is the only one conjugated. The others consist merely in invariable roots which are used with the verb 'to be'. The forms of the verb 'to be', of which the most common are *heh*, *hong*, *hota-hong*, *hoti-heh*, form the compulsory endings of all sentences and all parts of sentences, rendering speech heavy, flat and extremely monotonous. Nasal and aspirated sounds abound. Otherwise, the pronunciation of the syllables remains the same as in Sanskrit.

Do not be surprised if you see Sanskrit and Indian words spelt in a completely new way in these pages. I have tried to transcribe them as I heard them pronounced. The Brahmins recite Sanskrit every day aloud and clearly, and use the language in their philosophical discussions—so one needs only have recourse to their teaching. The teachers of dead languages have, of course, preferred to fabricate a new, inhuman gibberish as if it were not enough that they croak Latin and Greek and twang them through their noses. The Geneva Convention, by fixing the written word, has contributed to diversifying pronunciation.

Let nobody say that pronunciation is a thing of secondary importance or that only meaning matters. The Brahmins have it that a single wrong accent in the recital of a prayer suffices to make the efficacy of the prayer turn against the speaker. This is an indication of the care they have taken to fix the manner of pronouncing and speaking it and transmitting it intact from father to son. There is every reason to believe that the value of the syllables has not altered one iota for thirty centuries or more. So our learned men have no excuse for trampling it all underfoot at the outset. It is simply another mark of their lack of respect for the traditions on which they exercise their curiosity, as well as for the authority of those who remain its rightful heirs.

One of the difficulties of transcription arises from the fact that a certain number of consonants are missing from our alphabet, and the sound of them can only be learnt on the spot. One can only put a dot on the letter in our alphabet that most resembles the sound. But the habit of transcribing the sound 'sh' by *s* or *c* or *ç* is senseless, just as it is senseless to write *ca* instead of *cha*. This is nothing, however, compared with the stupidity of making Indian words run about on a multitude of *a*'s like so many centipedes. Have the transcribers never noticed that the short *a* never has the sound of *a* in 'apple'? Yet this is the first and most important thing taught here about Sanskrit spelling. The short *a* is pronounced like the *u* in 'butter' and sometimes like nothing—in other words, like the *e* in 'fame'.

The short *a* is the first letter in the alphabet and the vowel that turns up most frequently. It is just a colourless sound made by the voice like the '. . . er . . .' of someone who is searching for a word. In recitation it becomes a loud hum. It is the primordial sound, the sound in the name of the supreme God, Brahma, which is pronounced *Brumme*.[5]

This is what gives the language its unique character. Mingled with the strong vibration of the *r*'s and the powerful gasp of the *h*'s, it turns the recitation of prose into the rolling of a holy drum or contained thunder.

*   *

I asked Bapu-Jee to give me a new name. He did so: I am now called Shantidas, that is to say, Servant of Peace.

53

Spring has come. The heat grows from day to day. The wind thunders past over the countryside, sweeps a storm of dust along and drops.

Only heat makes the air move. The black earth cracks. Every clod has turned into a stone.

Clumps of trees turn yellow and lose their hard, clinking leaves.

And lo! far away in the plain, the tree that was black and seemed dead has put forth great red flowers. The crows perch on it screaming and clutch them as if they were meat.

Fever goes the rounds of the mud hovels.

Spring has come.

54

Fasting is going down and coming up the whole scale of our powers again. It is burying ourselves in our roots, getting to know our limits by touching them.

One can fast almost indefinitely provided one drinks enough, water being the true essence of all food; in the same way, a flower keeps its freshness in a vase of water almost as long as on the branch.

Fasting is a game which consists in not thinking about fasting. The rule of the game is that one keeps one's mind sufficiently occupied all day long to prevent it from wandering. So one must be more active, more tense, more ardent than usual. That is what one wins from the game itself.

If one undergoes a fast instead of mastering it, one droops, languishes, breaks into cold sweats, breathing becomes slower, the heart feels tight, the voice becomes blank, the head empty. But if one keeps the upper hand, in the end one discovers an inexhaustible spring of strength beyond the limits of one's own strength. And this spring is no doubt celestial, since the strength comes upon us like music, fills us with serenity, takes our weight from us and raises us up from ourselves.

55

The mangoes are in bloom. These trees are sometimes taller than
our tallest oaks. Their blond blossom foams in the light and their
heavy, penetrating scent is like the smell of flowering privet.

56

It is going to rain presently. People are busy everywhere preparing
for the event. Men's dwellings are as frail as barks threatened by
the squall.

A few drops lost in the face of the wind.

Me lying on my back, my eyes cast up at the great, stormy sky.

The women on the road make haste, pitchers on their heads,
rags of dust torn from under their feet and their blue and red veils
flapping round their raised elbows.

The setting sun comes out of a hole and its breath fills the dark
sky and the abysmal earth.

And the thought comes to me that I shall not be able to keep
this moment between my teeth—nor my teeth—nor myself. And
this moment is precious to me because I shall never find it again.

And am I precious to someone because I shall soon no longer be?

Yes, the Eternal seems to cherish in us what differs from Him.

Lasting, we should perhaps be to him what stones are to us:
indifferent.

57

Easter will soon be here. Some water-spouts and sudden showers
have marked the entrance of the burning season.

I have finished spinning my robe. I went to Segaon this Sunday
to show my skeins of cotton. I talked about my plan to make a
pilgrimage to the Source. Alas! my plan was not well received.

'Your health and your life have been entrusted to you for safe
keeping, or so I have heard. You have no right to expose them
without a valid reason. Last year, one of our men, a European, set
out for the Source and never came back. He caught a chill and died.
The roads are long and hard, food is coarse and poor and the nights

in the mountains are of ice. One reaches plateaux where the air is so thin that one falls down breathless with no strength left. Not to mention the forests and the wild beasts.

'Besides, you have no money. Now, you will have to be at the foot of the Himalayas at the beginning of May if you don't want to miss the season for pilgrimage. You can't get there on foot by that date. I should supply you with the necessary means if I thought your journey opportune, but that is not the case.

'On the other hand, I don't intend to keep you here. It is too hot and this is your first year in this climate. After Easter, I shall send you into the Nilgiris for two months' rest.'

To this I answered: 'If you are giving me an order, Shantidas must accept it without more ado, but I am hoping to make you change your mind. You know very well, Bapu-Jee, that thousands of pilgrims go to the Source every year and come back again. I shall come back too. I have put my body to various tests: it has never failed to respond or been unequal to the task or refused to follow me where I wanted to go.

'But if I must not go to the Source, there is no need to send me to the hills. I have not worked enough to deserve such rest, nor produced anything to justify such expense. It will be better to leave me in the job I am doing; the heat is in no way a hindrance.'

58

Shri Rama Krishna one day told this story of an ascetic's mis-adventure: 'There was an ascetic famed for his austerity. One day, when he was in front of a statue of Shiv, he invoked him saying, "There is nothing, Lord, that I am not capable of doing out of devotion to you. Impose any trial whatever on me, and you will see that I am speaking the truth." Thus he prayed, as one flings a challenge.

'At that moment, the statue came to life and from its bronze lips came these words, "Take a bowl and fill it to the brim with oil. Place it on your head. Go through the market, go through the city, street by street, and come back; let not a drop be lost."

'The ascetic filled the bowl, placed it on his head and set off, balancing himself with his arms, repeating at every step he took, "Let not a drop be lost". It was market day. He went through the crowd, and through the town, street by street, and not a drop was lost. Satisfied, he put the bowl down at the feet of the statue, sure that he had earned the Grace of God.

'He appealed to the statue to witness his victory, but the bronze statue maintained a bronze silence. He prayed, shouted and invoked it without obtaining any answer. The statue went on smiling disdainfully. Stupefied, the man wondered if God had deceived him.

'In the days that followed, Shiv continued to remain silent, so that at last, the devout man, having tried every approach to him, could no longer bear it. With his head between his knees, he wept bitterly and kept repeating through his tears, "and yet not a drop, not a drop of oil was lost".

'Whereupon the statue came to life, bursting with anger. "What does your oil matter to me, you fool? What have I, God, to do with a bowl of oil? How often, while you were carrying the oil on your head, how often, tell me, you fool, did you think of me?"

'And the man knew not what to answer, for he saw that he had thought all the time of the oil and the drop he must not lose.

' "It would have been better," said Shiv, "to spill the whole bowl through remembering me just once in rapture.

' "It would have been better, my friend, to leave aside all the austerity that makes an illustrious ascetic of you, and love God, even if only a little and in secret." '

A misfortune of the same nature awaited me on the road to Nagpur where I went to great trouble all for nothing. On that Good Friday I set out from Wardha in order to attend the resurrection mass at Nagpur.

Nagpur is forty-eight miles from Wardha. I had decided to cover the distance in one day, on foot, as was fitting, barefoot, as was fitting, and without eating or drinking, as was fitting on a day of great penitence.

I had been preparing this trip all through Lent, ardently, feverishly. I had decided that I was going to meet with something astonishing on the road that day; the astonishing thing I had been hoping for all these years, and that I had been seeking for years on every road.

I set out, then, a little before dawn, shivering with delight in the fresh air after bathing, and skipping from one foot to the other, light in body and baggage. I had rolled a spare robe and a new scarf for my head into the narrow rug that serves me as a bed wherever I may be. The green plumage of the margosa-trees hid white plumes from which the scent widened into the surrounding air. My heart rejoiced, for leaving is in some degree being reborn.[6]

But I pulled myself together and repented of my thoughtless excitement. This was not how a day of great penitence should begin.

I therefore walked a few miles accompanied by austere thoughts.

Morning was radiant on the river when I reached its side. The bank went down by ledges on to broad tables of black rock like a gallop of wild elephants. On the other side lay the outskirts of the jungle.

I ran over the bridge and the road plunged into shade. As I went in, I raised a flock of brightly coloured birds which flew chattering into the ceiling of branches and liana. Naturally, the wounds and nails in the flesh of the Lord also winged their way out of sight. I was almost aware of this when a family of mountebanks crossed the road and made me 'come-hither' signs: they were monkeys wearing black masks and fringed coats of grey silk. Their sinuous, slashing tails were longer than they by half. Oh! what a pity my approach had broken up their conversation! They hid behind the tree-trunks to defy and mock me, which amused me in spite of their anxious, aged look and the busy seriousness with which they capered and played naughty tricks. I had already seen their little ones playing and dancing on the edge of woods, halfway up trees, hanging on to invisible twigs. Their fur was of a reddish fawn colour which made them look like the honey-coloured flies that hang in mobile clusters from a sunbeam. I moved on, thinking, 'Ape that you are yourself, since your thought gets out of hand all the time and runs after everything it sees!' It was about the time when the Son of Man stumbles and falls on his way to Calvary and I, the pilgrim, was watching monkeys frolic.

Clutching my rosary, I entered the heat of the day. I tucked my robe up between my legs, and bareheaded and naked to the waist, I walked in the sun. I was not feeling my fast. Vigorous walking had shrunk my entrails to nothing.

Soon, thirst made me forget hunger, the strain on my calves thirst, the blisters on my feet fatigue, the thickness of my thoughts

my prayers. My tongue encumbered my mouth to the point of
choking me. I wetted my scarf in a pond and threw it over my
forehead and shoulders. With a finger, I wetted the insides of my
ears. Light had eaten up the plain, was pinching my eyes and
twisting my face. Everything around me seemed glassy and dark
like steel. At that moment, some trees flamed up from the embank-
ment, one half in leaf and the other half covered with flowers
shaped like fingernails and coloured like gladioli.

I observed—but this time without being able to do anything
about it—that my mind was entirely taken up with the milestones
and was becoming entangled with the addition and subtraction of
the miles I had covered and those I had yet to cover.

Towards the thirtieth mile, I saw a shallow, yellow river nearby.
I went down into it and lay in midstream, rolling from cool into
warmer currents and back again. With cruel, voluptuous slowness,
I let the level of the water rise to the corners of my closed lips and
rolled from side to side in the river without quenching the burning
inside me.

As I stood up again, I saw my reflection in the yellow water,
my scalp shaven like a monk's, a prism of bone gilded by the sun,
the vertical ridges of the forehead shining. 'You hypocrite!' I
shouted at it. 'You sanctimonious sinner! Who do you think you
are taking in?'

I started walking again. My feet, softened by my dip in the
river, now became raw and fiery. The tarred road was melting in
patches.

I kept my eyes on the road, made my mind a blank and quick-
ened my step for about ten miles. A gust of hot wind, stinging with
dust, knocked my head back. I wondered whether I were not dizzy,
for the sky, the earth and everything before my eyes was black.
But I was not dreaming: the horizon was fuming like the back of
an oven. Rolling banks of clouds were rapidly encumbering what
blue remained.

Twilight fell. On the outskirts of the villages, water-jars were
scraping the mouths of wells, a sound that made me shudder to the
bone. I hurried even more.

Behind me I heard the galloping of a horse come to a stop on my
left. It was two men in a gig; one was pulling on the reins, the
other was signing to me to climb in. I shook my head. The man

jumped from the step of the gig and ran up to me with excited gestures, speaking urgently and pointing to the threatening sky. Again I refused and thanked him politely. The man jumped back into his seat and lashed the horse into a gallop. Whereupon, night fell. A whip cracked in the heights and the chariot of thunder rolled over the rocky slopes of the firmament.

'All right, then!' I said to myself. 'Let it rain! What of it!' And my whole body, panting in the hell of thirst, howled to the sky, 'Split then! All right, pour! Fall down if you must!'

But all that had nothing to do with Jesus Christ.

I had passed the fortieth milestone. 'I shall reach Nagpur after ten o'clock,' I reckoned, 'too late to go and look up friends I don't know well. But I'm sure to find some sort of lean-to in town, perhaps a covered market or a station where I can spend the night sheltered from the rain.'

But these calculations had nothing to do with Jesus Christ.

That night, neither the road nor the landscape were extinguished for a second. Continually ripped out of the darkness by flashes of lightning, things flared into light, now in fleeting colour, now livid like plaster, now in their elemental rawness as if they had been skinned.

Membranes veined with split lightning had wrapped space up in pockets. Seven separate thunderstorms were giving each other chase in the boiling vat of the sky. Crashes of thunder, now rumbling, now roaring, now cracking, now mewing, came one after the other, one on top of the other without respite. I felt the counter-shock of these detonations in my heart, in the hollows of my palms and the soles of my feet.

After two gusts of wind, the air fell and lay asleep upon me like a warm beast.

Suddenly, for no apparent reason, two huge mango-trees by the side of the road went wild with fear and their branches flailed as if in distress. At the same time, I could hear behind me the sound of rushing and falling; it was the rain, writhing forward and livid. It caught up with me and at the same instant slapped me on the face, lashed me with stinging rods, shoved me by the shoulders beyond a ditch and pitched me headlong into a muddy field.

I covered my head and shoulders with my rolled-up rug. Shards of hail were hashing everything up and rebounding from the stones. I dragged my legs under me but they were already bleeding.

The clay into which I was sinking, clinging with both hands to my improvised roof, my nose on a level with the mud, was thick enough to prevent my being washed away as in deep sea water. The wind hurtled against the two mangoes opposite and tore off great branches, which I saw coming upon me, bouncing on their legs like monstrous spiders, when suddenly they were whipped aside and out of sight like straws.

And hopefully I said to myself, 'Now the world is being torn to pieces, something has to happen.'

My teeth started to chatter, shuddering seized me and cramp nailed me down as if to a cross.

When he cried, 'Lord, Lord, why hast thou abandoned me?' he had almost reached deliverance.

But still I saw only the mighty wrath of things.

The wind stopped howling an hour or two later. The rain was twisting in regular curtains. I set off again, limping. I was beaten. The amplitude of the disaster lay before me: nothing had happened, nothing was going to happen. I am a beast of burden that cannot see the hand that is flogging me. I am the muddy rag hanging round my loins. I am the mud by feet are squelching in.

Away over the fields, a light trembled. I stumbled through the mire towards it. I stood in front of the door. There were four or five thin, black men in the house. I could see them dimly in the feeble lantern light. I did not speak. Neither did they. They took me in, dried me and lit a fire of brushwood in the middle of the room. Then they rolled me in a woollen blanket and laid me on a bed made of string netting stretched on a frame. They beat time on me and sat on me, after which they inquired whether I was feeling better. I nodded. They offered me food and drink. I shook my head. So they left me and lay down where they could. I spent the night with fever buzzing in my head and thought sadly, 'It is useless fever.' The restless buffaloes in the yard, thrashed by the downpour, kept trying to get into the house even if it meant knocking down the doorposts and my hosts kept getting up to drive them away with shouting and sticks.

In the morning they again offered me some food, and milk, but I refused because I had to stick to my fast until after the great

Easter Mass. However, I had granted myself permission to start drinking again on the Saturday. I asked for water and poured several jugfuls into my mouth one after the other, until my hosts' jaws dropped. The water ran into my mouth as it might have run over a stone, for I felt not the slightest quenching of my thirst. The water was flowing into my body as into a void.

On the ravaged, puddle-holed plain, day was shining fresh and clear. Birds were singing in the leaves and the roads were strewn with branches and green mangoes.

It was the feast of Holi, a kind of Hindu carnival at which people joyfully sling mud at each other. As I was going through a village, a gang of boys surrounded me and threw some lumps of mud at my eyes, my mouth and neck. 'What does it matter?' I thought, 'since nothing has happened.'

*

I reached Nagpur towards ten o'clock and spent the rest of the day in the house of my friends there. Alone in my room, I lay on the flagstones drinking endless jugfuls of water, water the substance of life. I was like a convalescent coming listlessly back to living.

Next day, High Mass was a glory of electric bulbs among artificial flowers and plaster Virgins. The English ladies, wearing their frilly finery, had taken all the chairs and were busy whispering to each other. The Indians had decked themselves out in white or khaki trousers and were holding sun-helmets in their hands. The priest, an Italian priest with a goatee, gave a sermon, or, rather, a speech on Hell with a hellish accent. At the Agnus, a woman with a shrill voice screeched her utmost.

And leaning against a pillar, I wept for joy. In the fountain of my heart the light was now shining, the light of which, step by step on the road, I had abandoned all hope.

59

A few days later, I went to Segaon. Gandhi was working alone in the room, his head wrapped in a wet cloth because of the heat.

'Bapu-Jee,' I said to him, 'I want to obey you always.'

He looked up from his papers.

'But I want to go to the Source . . .'

He waited for the rest of a speech which had begun so well. So I went on:

'It is right, I believe—and your doctrine teaches us—that in cases of doubt one should leave the decision to the Almighty and wait for proof that the thing we want is the thing He wants . . .'

'Oh! my dear Shantidas, if you have received a formal order from the Almighty to go to the Source, I can only give in to it,' he said, smiling.

'Not an order, but at least a sign that the thing is acceptable.'

'And what is it?'

I opened my hand and let its contents fall out—a scatter of rupees.

'I didn't have this money yesterday,' I explained. 'I didn't even have any hope of it. I haven't done anything to make it come. It has just dropped from the sky. Before I left Europe, I sent a manuscript to the publisher. I never had any news of it and had forgotten it. Well, in this morning's mail there was a contract and the advance I had asked for should a contract be given me. One might think it pure chance, but it should be noted that the sum is within two rupees of what I need to reach the foot of the Himalayas in a day or two. So it *is* a sign.'

'There can be no doubt about that,' he agreed emphatically and laughed. 'There is nothing left for me to do but submit, which I do all the more willingly as I have been contemplating, since yesterday, sending you to the Source as you want me to.

'I've had some echoes of your outing to Nagpur. At least it proves that your health can do without the coddling we thought it needed.

'As a matter of fact,' he added with sudden enthusiasm, 'I'm glad you're going. Yes, Shantidas, I envy you this journey to the Source. I've never done it, and the life of a Hindu is not complete if he hasn't made the pilgrimage. But for me, the time is past.

'Can you imagine what a pilgrimage would mean for me with journalists, photographers, the crowd, flowers and speeches at every turn in the path? But you, Shantidas, take the chance, take advantage while you may of not being famous and a Mahatma!'

He threw his papers aside. He was preparing for a meeting of the Congress at which he was to preside and was leaving for Delhi next day.

And he told me about the thoughts of his youth, his spiritual exercises, his fasts, his personal and bodily experiments with truth.

'But nowadays I don't do anything for myself. I don't even fast for my own sake; I fast for reasons of State.'

He was silent and sighed. It seemed to me that in the silence and the sigh I heard the question: Is it the way to salvation?

'In any case,' he said after a while, 'I have not chosen my way because I wanted it, but because it pleased the Lord to push me along it. But let us rather talk about you.'

He then prepared my journey for me down to its last detail. He told me at which towns to stop, what things to see, what people to visit, who would help me in case of need or danger; planned my equipment for me from my sandals to my cooking-pan, drew up a diet for me, and gave me the cures for any ailments that might befall me on the way.

The time came for supper and for his evening walk. He made it the occasion for accompanying me over a long stretch of the road towards Wardha, followed by four or five of the intimate friends who never leave his side. Twilight deepened and he had to turn back.

I stooped to touch his feet with my fingertips. He put his hand on my shoulder. As I was straightening myself, he looked into my eyes.

I moved off. But when I had taken ten steps or so, I shouted to him over the bushes, 'Bapu-Jee, I am not leaving you. I am going in your stead. You are coming with me. I am taking your dear eyes with me, and through mine you will see the holy Source of the Ganges.'

1. On this subject; the two works of Gina Lombroso make profitable reading, especially *The Progress of Machinism*. They are standard works in the Ashram of Gandhi.

2. In Sanskrit, 'lightning' and 'diamond' are the same word.

3. There is a complete translation of this book into French by Louis Jacolliot in his study *Le Pariah dans le Monde*, Paris, 1876, a sound piece of work.

4. *Paramhanse*: the title given to Shri Rama Krishna, means the Great Swan. If a swan is given a mixture of water and milk, it will, according to the legend, drink the milk and leave the water. This world is reality mixed with illusion. Whoever drinks the milk of reality and lets the water of illusion flow unheeded is a Great Swan, that is to say, a wise man and a saint.

F

5. I have adopted the ordinary transcription of names that have become part of our everyday speech. English people have sometimes transcribed the short *a* by a *u* as in 'jungle', which corresponds exactly to the Sanskrit word *jangal*. It would be more appropriate to transcribe the name of Krishna as *Krshn*, since the flattened vowel one is forced to squeeze in is all that is needed. Short *i*'s and *a*'s are sometimes so short that they become inaudible. On the other hand, the long ones are two or three times longer than our vowels. The sound *ee* in a very insistent 'Please!' corresponds to one Indian *i*, and a very prolonged 'Ah!' corresponds to an Indian *a*.

The distinction between short and long vowels is the basis of recitation and prosody. In India, for the first time, I understood the metrics of Latin and Greek poets, which had been a puzzle to me throughout my student days. For even if one pronounces Latin in the Roman way—the best since it is Roman and consecrated by the Church—and even if one pronounces Greek like the Greeks of today, a line from Virgil or Homer upheld only by the tonic accents sounds more like fine, rhythmical prose than a line with the regular measure needed for singing, which suggests that the pronunciation of the classic languages was very close to that of Sanskrit, the only one of them that has survived, and that the hammering beat of accentuated syllables in Italian and Greek of today is perhaps of barbaric origin. As for the pronunciation of Latin and Greek usually taught in French and English schools, it turns the line of verse into an overcooked noodle and brings poetry into derision.

6. The author gives his own twist to '*Partir c'est mourir un peu*', a quotation from Haraucourt which has become a commonplace of the French language, and means 'leaving is dying a little'.

V

PILGRIMAGE

TO THE SOURCES OF THE GANGES
AND THE JAMNA

AGRA, *22nd April 1937*, The Taj Mahal

They called her Mumtaz Mahal, 'The Ornament of the Palace', and for her the Emperor had this tomb built, like a church and like a mirage, so that he could sleep there by her side until the end of time.

Away from the twisted streets of Agra and the seething crowd, far from the purple sandstone fort, beyond the wide yellow river cratered with whirlpools, above the gardens, the tomb rises with its crenellated walls, its domes and minarets, like a fortress.

I cross the bridge and go into it through one of the city gates guarded by towers built of huge red blocks of stone. A path lying alongside a cloister hewn from red granite leads me to a kind of great red mosque.

The façade is adorned with green and white marble over which runs a pattern of branches. They are alive like the surrounding greenery and the foil of the arches, which is supple and fresh like the edge of a leaf.

This façade is only the frame for a red, ogival-shaped apse which hollows it out and splits it right up to the top. At the back and the bottom of the apse, a flight of steps leads up into a porch on the other side of which you walk about twenty yards under a red, arched roof to find yourself in another porch, which this time opens on to shining space. On each side of the vaulted passage, there is a walled courtyard with fountains; the fountain on the right, struck by a ray of sunlight, looks like a vat of blood, the one on the left, bathed in shadow, looks like the bottom of the sea where dark corals are growing.

As I near the porch at the end, I see that the first building was only a gateway into the inner marvel. The marvel is gliding towards me on a path of water, white and doubled by the water; white with the whiteness of a fair-weather cloud. On a table of gardens, artificial lakes and terraces, this ivory casket as big as a cathedral lies under the blue sky. It is capped by three cupolas guarded by four minarets.

The avenue of water is bordered on each side by a marble pavement beside which runs a strip of smooth lawn, patterned with marble tracery. Pruned cypresses, boxwood, domes of greenery with broad leaves, trees of rare species, choice flowers and perfumes and precious cries of birds make the garden a skilfully devised paradise.

This marriage of plants and marble brings back to my memory the wide, green lawns round the Dome of Pisa; so does the calm of the place, and its frame of crenellated walls. The façade of the building itself recalls the façade of the Dome of Pisa, a stone harp on which the arpeggios of perfection play all day long. And this marriage of marble and water reminds me of Venice, and for a moment the memory of the Palace of the Doges veils the present whiteness with rose.

The geometry of greenery and stone, of regulated fountains and trained plants, has the royal serenity of the gardens at Versailles.

Baghdad comes to mind, and the Thousand and One Nights, and castles in Spain, and the palaces of petal and plume we dwelt in high up in the clouds.

But looking at this thing that has neither parentage nor peer, I want to think of nothing else. To think, to compare, is to disperse attention. I only want to behold.

And now, having crossed the garden and climbed up the slow steps to the terraces, I have entered. My feet, burnt by the paving of the terraces, bathe in the cool of the flagstones inside. The shade under the high, vaulted roof has a taste of spring-water.

In the middle of the great hall, openwork alabaster screens both hide and reveal two bare tombs lying side by side. A steep staircase leads down into the crypt, and there again are two bare tombs lying side by side. The bodies rest in the lower tombs.

It is as if the King had said, 'I died twice; once for you, once for myself. Even as I was married before your eyes but loved for myself; and even as I was King for you but alone for myself.'

The tomb has no inscription and no ornament. A diamond of unique size and brilliance is entombed with the King.

At Sikandra and on the outskirts of Delhi, I had seen more than one tomb built on similar lines, for it was the desire of all the princes of this race to make their death an object of delight for the living. But none desired as this king did to make his tomb a poem of love.

All have used red sandstone, which is the local stone, and all have ornamented it with white marble brought from afar. But none give, as this one does, their full meaning to the shock between the two colours and the marriage of the two kinds of stone.

The whiteness of the central palace with its taut ridges, its cupolas rounded like the breast of a dove, is a block of virgin crystal, a jewel-case with steel hinges; breast and belly and neck of lily, gentle breath and grace in its upward rising, and its smooth ogives are the female cave in whose shelter lie the peace of shade and water, a mystery of beauty and death. A jewel by day, flesh in the evening, moon and mist by night.

But the red of the warlike walls and jealous porches that surround it enfold and uphold this whiteness, exalt and protect it, clasp it in their arms.

The red gives the white its whiteness.

2

The Indian towns I have seen so far are just a string of shanties or bungalows straggling along four or five avenues which intersect in fields. Agra and Delhi are quite another thing. They are real towns and not merely because of the new quarters in them that have been copied from European capitals.

They are real towns where the centuries have heaped up their relics: a girdle of battlements; fountains and towers, palaces and hovels intermingled; sculptured porches opening into crooked alleys; then raised on a broad pedestal and framed by four tides of steps rising to placid pools of water, some mosque with a dome rounded like a breast, amidst springing minarets. Their citadels of purple sandstone are among the most beautiful buildings that the earth carries.

*

The dromedaries go one after the other under the walls of the fort. The colour of threadbare doormats, they swagger along awkwardly, but their lips curl in the disdainful manner that becomes the elegant. Each has a nail planted in its nose: a string is tied to the nail, and when it is tugged to make the dromedary kneel and sit, the creature grimaces with its lower lip and cries out like a man.

*   *

As I was going into the Moslem quarter, I came upon ten men shouting and beating a horse. They had done such a wonderful job that the rein—a rope—had passed under one of his hind legs and was skinning his belly. The more they belaboured it, the more the horse backed and struggled. I can never be present at a scene of this sort without seeing red. 'There are instances,' says Gandhi, 'where force is the only possible expression of non-violence.' I threw myself on the scoundrels with such fury that they turned their sticks and their cries against me; but no doubt the blue of my eyes struck them, for as soon as I looked them in the face, their arms fell to their sides. I caught the bridle of the horse, which was foaming and shuddering on its hooves, stroked his neck and brought him gently forward. I left him to his fate after having made the occupants of the cart throw their staves away.

A little further on, I found an old man dying in the dust. People were passing by without turning their heads. His only clothing was a loin-cloth. I picked him up in my arms; he weighed no more than a child of twelve. I carried him to the hospital.

Often, some Moslem seated on his doorstep signs to me as I pass. He pats the rug beside him, which means, 'Sit down and let us talk.' I sit down and he smiles to me. In a little while, he asks me, 'Are you a Moslem?' I reply that I am not. His face clouds and he turns his eyes away. We stay silent for some time. Finally, I say 'Salaam', and go.

Poor Gandhi! This brotherhood is difficult indeed.

*

Not that it does not exist. Personally, I feel the brotherhood is there all the more essentially because it does not show.

For over ten centuries, my forefathers fought the Moslems on land and sea, on the coast of Europe and the coast opposite. So they are quite familiar to me. When people have fought so constantly and loyally, they feel no need to hate or to despise each other.

And Islam looks the same everywhere, like the sea. From Morocco to the Pacific Islands, it raises the same face everywhere. White, or brown or yellow or black, it is always the same face. Is it a fire that changes into its own substance everything it touches?

Oh, noble among all men, brothers of the horse and the greyhound!

I love the desert they come from, the rose-coloured rubble of Happy Arabia, and I love everything that comes from them.

Four notes of their music with its taut intervals, sudden falls and poignant repetitions are enough to throw me into ecstasy.

I love their architecture, the vertical lake of the beautiful, flat walls, the celestial spheres of the cupolas, the minarets raised like the finger of the dying to testify to God.

I feel almost bodily love for their buildings. The squareness and plumbness of their façades please my thin shoulders; the leap of their arches pleases my bare feet, the hard and ardent purity they have translated so truly into stone touch me to the bone.

I love their brightly coloured robes, their jewels so rich in work, their turbans and coats, their weapons, their saddles and trappings, their gestures, the style of their beards which are works of the goldsmith's art, and a dignified conclusion to faces finely chiselled out of sterling metal.

I love their generous pomp and their wealth which is sister to holy poverty and like her in two features: grandeur and detachment.

I love their public testimony of God who is no other than God; their solid mystical theology, their faith that does not stink of philosophical platitudes and trite morality.

And I love your praise of wine, O fervent drinkers of pure water!

3

HARDWAR, HOLY CITY OF THE GANGES, *end of April*

Before going down the passage that leads to the quay on the Ganges, you take your sandals off as at the entrance of a temple.

A bell tinkles incessantly. There are illuminated niches in the wall, and beneath them, the shops of the garland-sellers.

The passage descends steeply and turns a corner. You meet village women in red gipsy dresses striped with yellow zigzags, coming up from the river with empty sacrificial bowls. Their ankles are imprisoned in heavy silver bangles, and rings moulded in the shapes of flowers or shells bite into their toes.

Here at last is the sacred river at the beginning of its journey through the plain. It is narrower here than the Seine in Paris, and not very deep, but it rushes like a torrent.

The porticos and the steps that plunge into the river are crowded with worshippers. The houses facing the water crowd together, old, rickety and daubed with different colours. Humble, whitewashed cupolas squat on their flat roofs. Beyond the river, meadows spread and starry-leaved trees rise and, further off still, the distant outlines of the mountains overlap each other. And the countryside is green with all the greenery that surrounds Krishna-Gopal in the pictures where he stands with his flute between his fingers, leaning against the cow that is licking his heel.

The gladiola-coloured robes of the monks glow on the red sandstone quay. The young Ganges in his green vigour scours its steps. Green and yellow china fish are lying in tight rows, in line with the current, some as big as two hands, others as long as a leg, equals in divinity with the river and living profiteers of that divinity, waiting for sacrificial offerings. As soon as a wooden or copper or silver dish is emptied, they whirl upwards, leap on to the stones, gobble up the flour and rice, leave the fleeing petals to be swept away by the water.

*

He is crouching on the first step, his back to the river, his heels and his buttocks in the water, and before him, on the quay, lies a tray piled up with flowers and pebbles. From a spoon which holds only a drop, he pours water, taken from a vase, on to the pebbles. At the same time, with one finger, he follows in a book the proceedings of the ceremony and the prayers to be recited, lest by uttering one untimely syllable, he turn these against him. From time to time he shakes a bell over the mixture.

*

Your face is hidden, man of God, for you have thrown your coat over your head and for the world you remain as sightless as a haystack. But from the depths of your darkness, your eyes can see the lines in the book placed before your knees. Beside the book is a begging-bowl into which I willingly throw a pice[1] so as to acquire merit in the sight of the divinities you serve who would languish and die if you deprived them for one moment of the nourishment of your reading.

*

Behold, like rows of tree-trunks in a burnt forest, the sages with flowing beards and hair, their eyes rooted on the spot between their eyebrows. Motionless in the sun and the flies, some have built little huts round their heads, or perhaps worshippers have built them round their immobility, or perhaps time and the all-powerful stillness of wisdom have made them grow.

*   *

A chain of murmuring rises at the approach of the passer-by as soon as he sets foot on the bridge. A double hedge of twisted limbs, dry and pitted with scabs, or oozing pus, springs up from the paving. These are the beggars, a single tree when they are lying down, with a single common voice.

This voice is like a mill grating and grinding, or turning emptily, but turning incessantly and tirelessly; it quickens or slows down its output according to the number and the attire of the passers-by.

When a pious person wants to give charity, his best way of going about it is to put the pennies for alms, or the pancakes or nuts or sugar, into a bag or a fold in his robe, then having gathered speed, to rush across the bridge scattering them while taking the utmost care not to be caught or tripped up.

Oh pitiful beggars! I wonder why you do not become saints like the others: you would have food, shelter and leisure and perhaps praise as well, just like the holy men, many of whom are merely dishonest beggars.

*

Women seated in a circle are singing and clapping their hands or slapping their thighs to beat time. Others, further off, are smacking

their wet linen on the stones, for the river is as useful as it is
sacred: Ma Ganga, Our Mother the Ganges.

Hawkers are selling rosaries and things to eat.

*

The barber puts his little iron suitcase on the ground and opens it.
It contains scissors, razors and soap-pastes. He operates on those
who squat and pay. They get their money's worth, for not only
does he shave and shear them, he also massages them, cuts their
fingernails and toenails and removes every hair of their bodies
except a wisp on the back of the head. The current carries off the
clippings, which the fish treat with as much contempt as if they
were flowers.

The small, old man is naked and smooth like a pebble from the
river. His arteries twist like worms round his skull. He is 'taking
the name of God', that is to say, he is repeating 'Ram, Ram, Ram'
without giving himself time to swallow his saliva. Day and night,
his jaw, already a plaything of death, grinds nothing else, for it is
his whole function, his happiness, his reason for living. And when
his exhausted voice becomes soundless, his nose continues to
quiver like a rabbit's with the word inside him which will not be
silenced until he has breathed his last.

*

There are four of them under the banyan-tree, naked except for a
rope round their loins and a string of rag between their legs. They
are smeared with ash from head to toe; it makes their skin dark
purple and puts it into mourning.

The tow of their hair, powdered or dyed red like that of ageing
actresses or bawds, hangs like the bushy roots of the tree whose
self-appointed priests and guardians they are. The first is tending
the sacred fire, the second is doing needlework, the third is smoking his hookah, his eyes dazed and bloodshot. And the fourth is
doing nothing. He yawns, and the pink oven of his mouth gapes in
his heavily coated face. His hair is drawn up into a bun and
wreathed with flowers.

4

At Hardwar, I went to Gurukul. I was to have presented myself to
the head of this school with a letter of introduction, but had lost it.
So I introduced myself to him empty-handed and was welcomed
with open arms and treated with honours of all kinds.

Children enter the school at the age of six and stay there until
the age of twenty-five without any holidays or contact with their
parents or contamination by the thoughts of the world. It seems
that it would require force to make them leave school for a single
day.

They have all taken vows of chastity and service for the period of
their education. I asked some of them what their dreams and am-
bitions were for the future. 'We shall have no money,' they
answered, 'and shall probably never marry. We shall serve.'

They venerate Gandhi and follow his precepts. The food is the
same as at Wardha. In the dormitories, they sleep on the floor.
Their board and education cost about three annas a day.[2] They
study Sanskrit, Veda and Vedanta, English, mathematics and
science.

They can all spin, and weaving is done in school.

Teachers and pupils form something like family groups and the
teacher remains with his pupil throughout the latter's schooling.

These teachers have inherited the prestige of the gurus, the
spiritual masters who were God incarnate for their disciples. The
affectionate trust and profound respect they win from their pupils
make severity needless.

Beautiful young people, clothed in white, frank, their black eyes
full of light, their teeth shining and devoid of any ferocity. I felt as
if I were surrounded by a herd of does and fawns.

I was asked to talk to them. Nothing bores me more than lectures
and speeches, especially when it is I who am speaking, but this
request from my hosts obliged me.

I spoke to them of our guru Gandhi, and of several thoughts
which so fill me that they spoke for themselves. Thus I was not
really talking to an audience, but to someone whose eyes I could
look into.

5

RISHIKESH, *April*

Rishikesh is higher up on the Ganges, just where it comes out of
the gorges of the Himalayas whose first slopes shut off both sides
of the horizon. It is the city of men who have left the world. Three-
quarters of its population wear the red robes of anchorites. Their
greeting is the syllable *Aum.*

There are hardly any houses in this town. The walls hide courtyards surrounded by arcades into which rows of doors open with
darkness behind them; these are the shelters of the wandering
hermits.

You can see them everywhere, lighting fires for meditation, for
sacrifice or for cooking, coming and going with their bamboo
sticks and pitchers.

At sunset, everybody squats in the town square to listen to a
text chanted from the book and the master's commentary on it,
and to take part in common prayer.

The cupolas of the temple are hung, day in, day out, with
yellow oriflammes.

I am the guest of the Mahan, the High Priest of the Temple and
the religious leader of the district. More than one man of God has
come to visit me, approaching me with the reverence thought due
to one who has come from afar in quest of truth. So much homage
weighs on me.

They ask me what progress I have made. The geography of the
spiritual continent is familiar to all here. From the fatigue of the
first physical exercises, the dizziness engendered by the first controlled breathing, to ultimate, perpetual ecstasy, all the tracks are
well beaten, their crossings and detours have names, the stages are
marked. They comment on my answers, exchanging nods like
doctors consulting each other. They ask me to bare my breast, for
it is there that spiritual fire leaves marks visible to those who have
eyes to see with. I open my scarf and stand before them like a leaf
whose veins can be seen against the light.

*

There are log huts at the bend in the river where bathing is truly meritorious and purifying and sacrifice valid. Crowds of people, jostling one another as in a fairground, undress and dress there pell-mell, buy and sell, haggle, bawl, sing and give thanks.

Hermits live in the holms and in the neighbouring forest. One of them, in a hut on the bank, has had himself walled in and stays there without eating or moving or letting his breath out. You can watch him through a hole in the wall. When his vow comes to an end, men with pick-axes will come and free him from his tomb, alive. Another stays for twelve hours a day immersed in the water which is icy even in summer, and when summer comes, he goes up to the everlasting snow and lies down in it uncovered and motionless. Another stretches out on a plank bristling with nails. Another spends his days standing on his head. Another has been holding his arm up for ten years and it has withered like a stick. Another, they say, is sitting in the air a little above the water with no other support than empty space, and the crowd rushes to see the sight.

*   *

The jungle begins on the other side of the Ganges and covers a patch of mountain which breaks off in a sheer cliff. This precipice drops to deep green water. Sometimes a chain of monkeys hangs from a branch over the cliff face.

There are bands of them on all the roof-tops, which resound with their thumps as they spring and caper.

Sometimes a herd of wild elephants comes and tramples down some quarter of the town and it is not always easy to persuade them to retreat.

Fortunately, the tigers avoid inhabited places of their own accord, for nobody here would take it into his head to use force against a creature of God.

6

I have got myself a staff, a fine male bamboo stick from the Himalayas, which I have decorated with copper nails. It feels good in my hand and reaches my chest. I have also a calabash that gives the water in it a taste of plants. The heavy roll of my blankets is slung across my shoulder and I have tied my sandals to my waist so as to walk more easily on my way to the mountains.

The path rises steeply through the jungle. It is the month of

May, the season when leaves turn yellow and fall and when the
light pink and tender green of young leaves burst from the bud.
Here and there a tree stands bare while others spread in full leaf.
From time to time, one of them flames with bloom. Thus each tree
here respects its own season as each man in the dense multitude
respects the religion of his birth.

The ant-heaps look like rotten stumps. Bushes suddenly tear
themselves from the ground and flee: they were the antlers of a
herd of red deer.

The far off Doon³ is now only a slab of marble and the Ganges
a vein in it.

*   *

Now the flat country is lost from sight for a long time. The path
passes below the first crest of the mountains, a ridge of black rock
torn like a storm.

On the tall, candelabra-shaped cacti, there are tiny, red, flesh-
like buds. A religious fig-tree has looped its tentacles into the
highest rock. The trunk has ringed the rock with its flow of lava
and the stone and the wood are so intermingled that they have
become indistinguishable, while the great head majestically crowns
the mountain.

7

On the first night, I was the guest of three princes of the reigning
house of Nepal exiled to these slopes through palace intrigue.

There are two reigning houses in Nepal, I have been told. The
first is that of a king reduced to purely ritual and decorative functions, the second that of the mayors of the palace whose divan and
dictatorial responsibilities have become hereditary, as have their
sovereign titles and honours. The father of my three princes was
to have been the legitimate usurper if their uncle, a general, had
not usurped his place.

They lived in a big villa, a cross between a Gothic church and a
Swiss chalet, with a French garden, amid ornamental marble
bowls and very white statues in pure *fin de siècle* style. On the flood
of Victorian furniture there drifted some flotsam of rare beauty,
such as a painted silk from Tibet or a gold dish engraved by some
humble Nepalese craftsman.

The three young people had slit eyes, faintly yellow ivory skins, wore loud sports suits and reclined on silk cushions.

The only court dress I was wearing was a cloth round my loins, and my feet left the mark of dusty toes on the carpet.

The first asked me whether I 'objected to cakes', and as I did not, they served me some with tea in the English manner.

They asked me if they might smoke. As I begged them to, three turbanned servants came in with three hookahs, and as soon as each prince had put his pipe into his mouth, the vases began to bubble.

The first asked me whether God existed, and if so, why did suffering and injustice exist. I answered the unanswerable question as well as I could. The second told me with a complacent smile that he was bringing his last years of worldly enjoyment to a close, after which he would adopt an anchorite's way of life. The third, whom I liked best, kept quiet, but when we found ourselves alone, said, 'I am ashamed of our clothes! Oh, you have come and made us feel ashamed!'

They opened a house for me at the bottom of the garden. It contained a great number of rooms for nothing, populated with all kinds of furniture with legs serving no purpose, including a bed with sheets.

* *

While I was standing in the flower-garden, at a certain moment a gong sounded. About fifteen women, all young, all pretty and graceful and wearing silk veils shot with gold thread, appeared on the far walks, came through the flower-garden without speaking a word and without looking my way, and disappeared.

In the evening, my three hosts came down to visit me in the garden. 'We must get him to pay her a visit. She must meet him and get to know him,' they were saying to each other. And turning towards me:

'At Dhanolti, which is on your way, a little higher up, our sister is staying, or, rather, hiding, during the hot season. She wants to spend some time alone with her children without seeing anybody. She has taken the smallest, most inconvenient, most inaccessible house you can imagine, but of course one must not expect a woman to account for her whims.'

'If she doesn't want to see anybody,' I objected, 'a visit from me might put her out.'

'You're not the sort of person to disturb one's solitude,' was the answer. 'She would never forgive us for neglecting to invite you on her behalf . . .'

*   *

Next day, at dawn, the one who was ashamed of his clothes came and knocked at my door. He was wearing suede gloves and carried a riding-whip with which he was hitting his boots. He had come to see how I was getting on and to apologise on behalf of his brothers for anything of which I might have had occasion to complain in their house. He gave me a letter for his sister.

Then he accompanied me to the place where the path disappeared into the forest. I thanked him. 'I should like to go with you always,' he said.

8

The second evening I was the guest of the mountain.

Twilight was coming down but the path was still going up. I had been told that I would meet black bears in this part of the country. I met nothing but the more frightening than anything else in the world loneliness of unknown, inhuman country.

I used a hole in the rock as my bed. The air of the abyss whistled all night at this mouth.

The rousing chill of morning, the rousing brightness of morning, the rousing beauty of the new world in the young air, made me get up.

At the first bend, the wall of ice appeared. The valley, then ten, then twenty valleys, separated me from the everlasting snow.

There were neither peaks nor sharp ridges, but, on three-quarters of the horizon, foam rolling like the crest of a wave.

A rhododendron tree had broken into scarlet flower on the brink of the cliff.

I walked on and on. The even hours glided over the shining tops of the trees.

And further up, I entered spring, spring as it is in the sweet, far off country of my birth. I came once more into the refreshing shade where thousands upon thousands of little suns dance: I found firs again, and a night of moss studded with white stars, and violets, sweet violets trembling in the tender shade; and far off, from the depths of the forest and the years, the ridiculous call of the cuckoo pierced my heart. But the marvel of marvels was waiting for me on the other side of the woods, for when I came out, there lay a meadow and an orchard of apple-trees, which so thoroughly completed my sudden transplantation in place and time that I was astonished when, from a branch within my sight, a big, ash-coloured monkey swung down.

I was nearing Dhanolti.

9

As I was trying to get in, a voice shouted, 'Oh, there's another of those fakirs coming to ask for money. Run, Govinda! Throw him out and don't listen to him!' But I had already pushed the gate open and over the servant's head I called, 'I am not a fakir and I don't want money. I want to see Princess Bhubana.'

The servant turned back sheepishly, carrying the letter from the princes, which I had put into his hand. There was some talking in the house, followed by a great silence.

Then I saw coming towards me the person who had shouted in the first place. It was a young man, of small but good build, wearing flannel trousers and a silk shirt. He had wide cheek-bones, almond-shaped eyes and slender hands. He greeted me ceremoniously and made me take a seat in the garden.

Shortly afterwards, the princess herself came down, slight and supremely graceful in her veils. She bade me welcome. 'For the first time, I am sorry this house is so primitive,' she said. 'I am not going to be able to give you proper hospitality.'

She clapped her hands. At the signal, the whole household came running out and lined up in order of dignity. 'Now I am going to introduce them all to you,' she said, and, pointing to the one who had shown me in, 'First, this rascal who was almost rude to you— my son.'

'Mr Saint,' said the young man, 'you will forgive me, for I regret it bitterly.' (He did not look in the least contrite.)

'. . . and next, Bhagavad Gītā, my daughter.' She pointed to a little girl of twelve on her left, peach-skinned, with beautiful, black, lustrous eyes, who was wearing thick mountaineering trousers and over them a shirt with the tails hanging loose.

'And then,' she went on, turning towards the uneven row of servants, diversely but all equally badly dressed, 'these are our brothers and sisters.'

She said this because here, as elsewhere, the servants belonged to the same caste as their masters, in this case the Kshattri.

'But you too, sir, judging by your name—you are also a Kshattri, so you are our brother.'

'And your servant, madam.'

10

'It is so pleasant,' she said, 'to be able to eat together and touch each other without fearing pollution.'

As far as eating was concerned, we were served on the spot. Like everywhere else, we each had a round copper tray placed in front of us, and on it, rice, vegetables and a peppery sauce which we licked with our fingers.

As for the second point, the privilege remained on an abstract plane, for it was never given me even to touch her hand.

11

One would think the Princess twenty-five or thirty years old at the most if one did not see beside her this sturdy fellow who came out of her and who is twenty-two.

It is customary to say that Indian women, who reach puberty earlier than women in the West, also fade earlier. Like most things one hears said in one country about another, sometimes even when both are within Europe, this is not only not exact, but is exactly the contrary of the truth.

Nothing is more striking than the look of childhood that the Indians keep all their lives, and the youthfulness they retain into their last years. This would be more apparent if the age of the Indians were known, but often it has to be guessed by putting two and two together, since they generally do not know it themselves.

They can therefore just as easily forget the number of the years which have left so little trace on their hair and teeth, the freshness of their skins, the slimness of their waists and the suppleness of their movements. When one sees a woman from the back walking some distance ahead, one is hard put to say whether she is nineteen or fifty. The old men gradually dry up but hold themselves straight to the end. As for the old ladies, one sees them in the course of their household tasks sitting down on the backs of their legs as easily as little girls making sand-pies. The reason for their prolonged youthfulness, in spite of their being much weaker, bodily, than we, no doubt lies in the life they lead, a life free from anger, haste, ambition, envy, worry and erotic excess; also, toxic, heating and fermented substances are excluded from their food by the law.

Not a wrinkle is to be seen, even close up, on the face that is smiling with lowered eyelashes. There is a round spot of saffron between the two eyebrows. A touch of kohl heightens the brilliance of the eyes. One of the nostrils is studded with a tiny rose of rubies.

The Princess's husband is heir to an estate situated not far from Lucknow.

Her round-headed, cat-eyed son has taken upon himself all the bodily characteristics of the yellow race. But her brown daughter with the big, round eyes is wholly Indian, apart from something rough and boyish in her movements which belongs to neither race.

12

I accompany the Princess on her walks. We go along the forest path to the edge of the terrifying cliff and look across the vast abyss, slashed by a thousand crests, to where the half-circle of everlasting snow shines, and we wander through fields lit with flowers. She wears linen gloves and in the sun opens a small, ivory-handled parasol; just as our grandmothers did when they were young.

The pleasure of walking beside her is rare and fine, like seeing a doe leap, or the leaves of a plant coming to life in the breeze. It is the pleasure, after so much austere thought and harsh solitude, of hearing her chatter and seeing her live.

There are women whose touching fragility and delicacy caress in us some obscure, vital pride and make us aware of our greatness of stature and the vigour of our limbs. The feeling that with a

backhand blow we could snap them like a stalk makes us want to
keep them safe from all harm and serve them reverently.

Furthermore, I have not always enjoyed such freedom in the
presence of a pretty woman, whoever she may have been. I am
harvesting the fruit of a long effort to control my inclinations and
my dreams.

And I am enjoying the double pleasure of seeing that she is
desirable and of feeling free of all desire towards her.

13

'You can mortify yourself for all you are worth,' she said to me one
day, 'fast two days out of three and pickle yourself in piety, you
red-haired, full-blooded giants, you're still Rakshasas[4] for all that.'

'I haven't got red hair,' I protested, rubbing the glossy ball that
serves me as a head. 'It is light brown, and in any case I haven't got
any hair at all now that I shave my head.'

'Shave it as much as you like, you are a Rakshasas all the same.'

'Your son calls me "Mr Saint", which makes me feel like
laughing, and you say that I am a demon. Perhaps the truth, as
always, lies somewhere between the two.'

'Be one or the other. Be both if you can. Don't be somewhere
between the two. Shantidas, I beg of you, let your truth not be
somewhere between the two.'

14

The young Prince had only one subject, but he ruled him thoroughly. This was his servant, a little boy perpetually flustered and
on the run.

The Prince kept him busy all day and busied himself with him:
he was teaching him to read and also teaching him manners and
religion, and constantly found occasion to whip him.

He made him polish his boots, darn his socks and iron his shirts.

And when the master went into the woods to ease himself, his
subject followed him step by step and with dignity, carrying the
little copper jug needed for the ceremony of ablution.

15

Bhagavad Gītā has a follower too: a strong girl of fourteen, pleasant to see and almost a grown woman.

They accompanied us on our walks and ran ahead of us.

They both wore mountaineering trousers of thick, brown wool with pouchy, hanging seats which gave them comical behinds.

'That slovenly little thing is the daughter of a soldier we have taken in,' the Princess explained.

Occasionally, the young lady and goddess[5] would be found hanging on the other girl's hair and slapping her face for all she was worth.

But the soldier's daughter would be taking an eye for an eye and giving slap for slap.

16

'I admire you, Shantidas, for everything you have left, and I dream of it.'

'And what have I left?' I asked.

'As a child I used to dream, and still dream,' she went on as if talking to herself, 'of all the splendour of the West that I have never seen.'

I burst out laughing.

So the royal children of Nepal, draped in silk and loaded with chased jewels, dream under the solid gold roofs of their palaces, of our tinsel glories.

17

On another occasion, she said to me, 'I admire you for your indifference. I envy you for having found the strength to leave everything and go. There are days when we, too, feel disgusted with everything we have, everything we do, everything we are, everybody around us and like us, all those who force us to be what we are. Those are the moments when we gauge the power and price of what we haven't got—indifference. For indifference is more powerful than power and more precious than wealth.'

'I feel you admire me mistakenly,' I said. 'Nothing is more foreign to me than disgust, and nothing seems more undesirable to me than indifference. I have not severed my ties with the world. I have only come away to stretch them, so that they sound and sing like tightened strings. I had rather suffer a thousand deaths and all the suffering of others added to my own than win the sort of wisdom you mean and which would make everything indifferent to me.'

18

I keep putting off my departure. Every time I mention it, they insist on my staying. Besides, since I have been here, my legs, for some reason or other, have lost all desire to go.

19

I have got into the habit of slipping out of the house a little before dawn. Wrapped in my blanket, and seated with my chin on my knees, I rise step by step with the morning.

A mighty tree-trunk stands shattered on the edge of the precipice. A few tufts of young leaves sprout from this charred bone. My sight climbs over its boughs and drops on the other side to where the valley, furrowed by the plough, splits in two.

The first mountain has the sturdy back of a shaggy beast. The second has the consistency of leaves. The third is of water. The fourth is the shadow of a wave upon another wave. The fifth is of air. The sixth has the shape and colour of nothing.

The seventh and last is white like a thought of the Absolute.

20

Sometimes, while we are talking, little Gītā throws herself into her mother's arms.

She falls into them like a may-bug into a wild rose.

Then the Princess's sweet face hardens and she stops in the middle of a sentence to push her away.

'I wonder where my daughter picked up her country-bumpkin ways.'

When the child had gone off, I said to her:

'What makes her clumsy is above all her overwhelming need of love which she does not know how to express. Be careful not to disappoint her or to drive her unwittingly to despair. A child's heart seems light and clear to us. We don't know how shy and vulnerable it is. We all know somebody who has been marked for the rest of his or her life by some unfortunate gesture or remark made by a mother who at the moment was perhaps a little pre-occupied or absent-minded.'

'I didn't push her away unwittingly, but on purpose, to teach her to restrain her impulses. Is there anything more disgusting than not containing oneself? Do you know of anything, Shantidas, as low as attachment? Mother, daughter, son, wife, husband—we have all met here in a shelter for travellers. At dawn, we shall each go our separate ways. That is what one must learn from childhood. I shall have gained only one thing from life, learning that. I am attached to nothing, neither to my dear children, loving as they are, nor to my husband, an excellent man, God keep him; you may be sure *I* shall not hang weeping on their necks on the day of farewell.'

'Yes,' I agreed, 'attachment is a dirty sin, because it is miserly love. It is an obstacle to love, and consequently a sin. There is attachment without love, and it should be torn out by the roots mercilessly. But there is no human love without some attachment, just as there is no living body that has no waste matter. Attachment attaches itself to human love just as the shadow attaches itself to a living body, not that the shadow is the body or that the body's dejections are life; they are their contraries, but life leaves trails of waste in its wake. Whoever knows how to love without attach-ment, and whose love is pure enough to cast no shade, deserves the name of saint. We must all achieve such love, similar to fire whose body casts only light. But how many of us can? Some of us cannot love without attachment, so it is better that we should attach ourselves to something and love, rather than un-love, every-thing; for the un-love of everything is the death of the soul.'

'It is rare,' she said, 'to hear love spoken of as you speak, for neither lovers say these things, nor wise men. Who are you, then? Oh, Shantidas! Why didn't I know you before? Perhaps I shouldn't have lost my life then.'

21

In the evening, we meet to talk on the verandah by starlight or, when it is too cold outside, in the drawing-room, by lamplight. The arm-chairs are fortunately big enough for us to be able to sit on them as if we were on the floor. The princess is the first to drop her tiny slippers and draw her naked feet under her in a flash. I do the same, for I now feel dispossessed somehow when I am sitting on a chair with my feet dragging down below. We leave the young man to play the Englishman all by himself with his fine golfing shoes.

She smokes a narghile which has been stuffed with tobacco and sugar. As I turn the pages of the family album, she comments on it page by page.

Here is the Maharajah with his fine turban surmounted by a spray of plumes. Here is the uncle, the usurping General, with his sweeping moustache, his round belly and his curved sabre. And here are the garden-parties long past, the outings on elephants and the returns from big-game shooting and the heaps of antelopes and tigers on the ground. But wait! Here is something that prevents me from turning the page.

It is a tiny photograph, gilded with spots like an old mirror. There, on a heavily carved throne, sits the royal child in its robes of stiff silk embroidered with gold, a gold crown blazing on its forehead, dragons and serpents of gold twisting in its bracelets, its chains and pendants. There she sits encased in gold, the little girl who has suffered a sea change.

But more than any gem, the beauty of the face glows out, set in its perfect oval.

My eyes linger on the proud, shy mouth, the lips like the calyx of a hyacinth or lotus-petals, and come to rest on the impenetrable onyx of the eyes.

'Do you recognise me?' asks the Princess. 'It's me in my wedding dress.'

'I recognise you,' I say, looking into her eyes. And in the secret of my heart, her words rise like a sigh: 'Oh, Shantidas; why didn't I know you before?'

22

The following evening, when darkness had fallen, we found ourselves together in the drawing-room again. The draught was making
the brazier in the middle of the room crackle, and from it, the
fourteen-year-old maid, the soldier's daughter, boldly picked out
glowing embers one by one which, without a grimace or a cry, she
placed in her mistress's narghile.

That done, she straightened herself abruptly, and her breasts
punched the coarse linen of her blouse like fists. I glimpsed the
ardent coals of her eyes and her smile flashed like a knife. She
disappeared.

'You will do well,' I said to the Princess, 'to marry off that girl as
soon as possible if you don't want her to run away with somebody.'

'Oh!' she exclaimed, 'how do you know that? It's true that she's
a hussy, and I worry about her every day, but how do you know?
Is a look enough for you to see through people, and a word enough
for you to say what they are?'

Then, after a moment, with a hint of uneasiness in her eyes and a
touch of defiance in her tone, 'And what about me, Shantidas—
what am I?'

But here the young man entered into the game excitedly.

'Tell her, tell her that she is a dreadful coquette and that she
tries to seduce every man she meets!'

He shouted this in a jocular tone and accompanied it with a
laugh which failed to disguise a little growl of tigerish jealousy.

'On the contrary, I think she attracts every man without trying
to, but nothing gives her less satisfaction than attracting just anybody. She has had only one great love in her life—a disappointed
love, a disappointed love of the Absolute. Having little inclination
for piety or study, she has placed the Absolute where there is no
place for it, in honours and in love. You received as your lot,
madam, noble birth and rare beauty, enough to make any other
woman's cup run over. Love of the Absolute has made you conceive a distaste for these privileges. It is a very great humiliation for
you to be a princess when the empire would scarcely have been
enough to satisfy your little heart the day that, adorned for your
wedding, you forced your frail neck to bear the weight of the

diadem. You have had children. Every mother finds hers perfect
and marvellous because they are her own; you can only see defects
in yours because they are yours; it is difficult to love the Absolute
and somebody else as well. Your parents gave you in marriage to an
honourable man. He has only one fault where you are concerned,
but it is an irremediable one—that of not being Rama himself . . .'

'Oh, do go on!' she begged, grown humble. 'I see that nothing
is hidden from you. Go on!'

But it was she who went on. Forgetting her son's presence and
perhaps even mine, she revealed herself completely. She only
needed the support of my unflagging attention and a word or two
to supply her with some links and footholds. From time to time I
made her draw breath by recalling some point that she had not
made clear.

'I was right in thinking you can guess everything!' she exclaimed
when she had said everything. 'Now I feel stripped bare, but
delivered too. I feel naked in your sight.'

23

In the morning, I found her pale, and there were shadows under
her eyes.

'Are you ill, madam?' I asked.

'I had distressing dreams last night. I can't tell you all of them
because they were mixed up. In any case, I don't want to. Especially to you. But I shall tell you the last one so that you can explain
what it means. I dreamt that I was Sita, and that, like her, I had
been captured by the Rakshasas and like her snatched back from
them again. And then I was back again in my house in the plain.
It was not Rama who had saved me as in the poem, but someone
else who was no other than my real husband; and you were beside
him, but a you diminished, foolish, overflowing with sickening
goodwill. And both of you kept congratulating yourselves on your
victory and lavishing encouragement on me. And my husband was
saying, "Here you are, back again at last! Pull yourself together
again! Open your eyes and see our beautiful house, our beautiful
furniture, our beautiful children, so loving towards us; and see
your dear faithful husband. Look at me! And look at our friend
Shantidas who is going to teach you to overflow with love for me!"

And I could have slapped both your faces. I could have killed you both. For I *loved, loved, loved* the king of the Rakshasas with the red hair, but like cowards you had smothered him under the drawing-room cushions. I woke up weeping and am still weeping. Is it absurd?'

I had understood. No need to be a wizard to understand that. While she was still speaking, a demon had started up in my heart, a red-haired, full-blooded demon brandishing his weapon and exulting in the dear face harrowed with grief, and its guileless tears, exulting over the nakedness of the dream she had shown.

Measuring my words, I said, 'Compose yourself, madam. Don't attach so much importance to mere images. Drive them out, don't try to understand them, there is no good to be got out of them. Madam, I have come to take leave of you. I must set out this forenoon.'

She caught her breath. 'It had to happen sooner or later,' she said. 'I wept so much in my dream that I have no sadness left for a friend's departure. Go, Shantidas, since you are free. God bless and keep you.'

*

The whole family accompanied me to the first bend in the road, and the servants, our brothers and sisters in nobility, came too.

As soon as I was out of sight, I broke into a run.

24

This time, the paths are not deserted as when I first set out. I have caught up with the procession of pilgrims who have taken the road during my stay.

I have seen them all before and know them all—these God-the-Fathers, these Moseses, these Jobs and Melchizedeks, St John-the-Baptist, the Apostles St Peter and St Paul and all the Saints, those that Duccio painted, and Giotto, those Michelangelo sculpted, those that only God could imagine; clad in white, draped in red or faded pink, or bare and bony, and shaven or black-furred with tousled hair and beard, or hoary like clouds. And when they catch sight of you, they bow their venerable heads to greet you, for great is the politeness in Paradise. And you can also see them crouching over their pots and pans, for (you would never have believed it) they eat.

The women advance in separate files. They are from every caste and every country: from Travancore and Coromandel, black, with scarlet veils and gold ornaments; from Lahore and Bihar; from Gujurat and Orissa; the Marats who pull their violet-coloured saris up between their legs and make trousers of them and those who wear saffron and are no longer of this world; almost all poor and old, labouring along on their staffs with bundles on their heads, dragging sandalled feet that can do no more, murmuring, 'Rama, Rama, Rama, Sita Rama', in complaint, in self-consola-tion or in greeting to some other poor wretch on the road, eyes lowered and almost closed throughout the successive marvels of the sky and earth.

They will wake up tonight in the smoky dharmsala. The coolies have already arrived; they have unloaded the baggage, almost en-tirely composed of pots and pans of all shapes. Then the women begin blowing on the fires, sprinkling water on the ground, smack-ing between their flat palms the bread to be baked on the cinders, diligently mixing the peppers and spices for the sauces. But woe is me! The pepper mortar is missing. Ah, Lord! what a sacrifice!

*

Neither inwardness nor unction reign in these pious gatherings. In spite of the loud, hoarse voices of those who are hailing each other or laughing, the noisy prayers of the others proceed without interruption.

*   *

We lie on the ground, side by side in tight rows in the big room that is open on all sides to the night wind, men and women, young and old, families and monks as well as children who have been brought in the luggage-baskets.

Sometimes a man coughs until morning because he did not know what a cold night is, and all the bed and blankets he has is a rag of coloured cotton.

Or else somebody wakes up suddenly and begins beating a drum in the dark or blowing a trumpet or else singing off-key at the top of his voice. All the others keep their heads rolled up in one end of their blankets; those who want to sleep show the greatest respect for the din set up by those who want to stay awake. There is no such thing here as quarrelling or disturbances of the peace.

They leave the place in silence, before dawn.

*

Sometimes the palankeen of some wealthy person breaks up the column of walkers. Four men are harnessed by one shoulder to the poles. They pant as they go uphill but trot over the loose stones on the downward slopes, almost always barefoot. The bearers who are going to relay them cluster round them. Sometimes they chatter light-heartedly as they go.

The luggage-carriers take short cuts and climb alone with their great wicker baskets on their backs. They are nearly always men from the mountains, short and thickset, with broad, yellow faces. They climb, leaning over thick staves with perpendicular handles on which they rest the bottom of their baskets when they stop to get their breath back. Their legs and feet are bare, but they wear long, woollen jackets slit at the sides. The braces by which the basket is attached to their shoulders only serve to keep the load balanced. Its entire weight is borne by a strap round the top of their foreheads.

The basket is stuffed with cooking utensils and rolled bedding, but occasionally, instead of baggage it contains some tiny old woman drowsing or 'taking the name of God'; and sometimes there is a rich, fat man in it.

The man who sweats and toils under the halter gets the money. The man sitting in the basket reaps the merit of the pilgrimage. That is in the order of things.

25

At the cross-roads there is a small sanctuary, a humble roof upheld by two short columns and a wall at the back. In his niche, riding his rat and waving his trunk and arms, Ganesh awaits the homage of the passers-by.

A woman with a look of studied piety brings him her sacrifice, makes a multitude of hurried signs of respect, and goes. I suspect that she is murmuring something like this prayer:

'Hail, Ganesh, the seated, who only movest
to the beat of the drums; I love thy great round belly
Full of love for the people, and thy divine
Elephant's nose, so useful and so fine
Which fits my smooth palm; I shall anoint it
With red saffron. Quickly take these flowers
and hold them tight lest the wind carry them off.
I may not linger long before your door
For I belong to Krishna, the great Seducer.
Forgive me, merciful one! For here he comes.
Great is this god, but also a jealous master.
The flute in his fingers sings and perfect beauty
Shines on the lashes of his eyes. With us
Poor women, he is a rascal. The more he cheats us
The more he watches and keeps guard over us.
Oh, if he knew that I have touched thy trunk! . . .'

26

This abrupt descent leads into the gorges of the river. It has
narrowed to half its width since Rishikesh, but makes up for it by
roaring twice as loudly. It has turned a muddy colour because of
the snow thawing in the hills, this being the hottest time of the
year. The steep banks that enclose it rustle with cacti and insects.
Butterflies as big as your hand and birds of different colours respond to the heat of the sun. All around, slopes rise carrying rocks
and trees: it will be a long time before we see the snowy summits
again.

*

The thunderstorm which had been weighing on us all day broke
loose in the evening and fell.

27

A last dip in the Ganges before turning away towards the Jamna.
Between burning rocks the water of the Ganges remains so icy
chill that it makes one's teeth chatter.

Although mud-coloured, it is purer to drink than even the

clearest mountain springs. Even when kept in open phials for decades, it does not turn foul: its flesh is immortal. A few drops of it are poured into the throats of the dying to help their souls to break free.

I am leaving you, Mother Ganges, but only to meet you again higher up. I am going where the most faithful go, where you spring up to the light between the crevasses of ice and meadows full of flowers.

28

It was raining next day on the high path. I had entered the country of streams.

Opposite, the fields cut out in uneven scales made the hillside look like the bark of firs, and from a distance, like old pottery decorated with clumsy geometrical lines.

Then I entered the country of pines, pines with rosy trunks and hair of long needles, as high as steeples, swaying like masts in the rumour of the wet breeze, with a sound of travel.

The rain woke the red of the dead pine-needles, the smells of resin and of earth. The purling of brooks filtered through rain-drenched foliage. And these scents and sounds took me far away, for the smell of wet grass is the same the world over. I let the rain run down from my new beard on to the skin of my chest tanned by the sun and wind: it didn't matter, for I had entered the country of the marvels of memory, and there I wandered till the day's decline.

*   *

From very high up, between the tall, downy grasses and the lofty pines, I looked down on the blue Jamna eating its way through huge chunks of yellow marble.

And then I entered the country of torrents.

Deafened by the roar of water, you cross trembling bridges. The surrounding air, so roughly scrubbed by so much water, suddenly turns chilly. Sometimes, the bridge is made of faggots laid across two parallel tree-trunks, sometimes it is only a trunk on which a few flat stones have been balanced. Sometimes the torrent rushes across the road so that you have to jump over it or cross on stepping stones, or wade.

Further on, from up above, I saw the torrents hanging and floating like horses' tails, with their bordering streams of plants.

And then I entered the country of bearded forests.

Brown moss clothed the trunks and branches up to the ears and from every twig there hung grey hair. The leaves gleamed like tarnished steel.

And at last, my sight reached the country of everlasting snow.

Beyond a tree hung with traveller's joy in full bloom, I first saw the great splendour of the country I was bound for.

29

And now, the first patches of dirty snow. Around me, the forest is still tropical, entwined with liana and agitated by troops of monkeys. It is midday; my shadow falls on my feet. A blue lizard half an arm long throbs on a hot stone.

A few more hours of walking, and the path abuts on a wall of rock, our journey's end. On the top of this rocky wall sits the wall of ice that mounts to the sky.

From inaccessible heights, the sacred Jamna gushes out, springs three times into space and falls into a crust of ice before taking her roaring leap between the rocks.

Clawed by the white peaks of the mountains, the sky advances, foaming.

Not far from the tumult of the river, over rocks coated with greasy, sulphureous rust, flow the hot springs. Through the steam, you catch sight of two lopsided little temples. In these holy places they are seldom bigger than huts. The temple is the mountain, God is the river and the altar, its source.

30

The paving gapes with four-sided mouths like the tombs in our pictures of the resurrection of the dead.

In each of these tombs, the water bubbles and boils. Priests and the faithful sit on the edges and officiate, shake out the saffron and the flowers, raise their hands, put marks on their foreheads and utter the appropriate words. Silver coins chink on the stone and in the dish.

The yatris bathe naked, and the women wholly wrapped in their veils, in the sulphureous, steaming pool. It is square and steps lead down into it on all sides. You have to stop up your nose, close your eyes and plunge under the boiling[6] surface. Your sins sink to the bottom and stay there.

I, too, went down into this purgatory. The cuts the road had made in my feet and the scratches made by thorns and all my other sores cooked in the sulphur-seasoned soup. I rushed to rinse myself in the river that flows from the ice and slid into a clear pool between the two big, round stones to which I clung so as not to be sucked under by the swirling current.

*   *

Night is cutting cold in the shelter made of loose planks stuck like a swallow's nest under the roof of the world.

*

When you have spent the night hugging the slight warmth that is your life, the best thing to do at daybreak is to throw it overboard and plunge into the coldest of all waters. Then you will recover your life whole.

*   *

The Jamna is so chill this morning that my heart shrinks and hurts and dizziness blackens out my sight. Shall I be strong enough to bear you, clearness of the diamond, purity of the heights, milk of the summits?

Jamna, can you be the same river as I saw sluggish in Agra the day the heat was so intense that I longed to bathe, and your water was so dirty that I wandered helplessly on the bank? (That was when I came across some people stooping in a circle over a sleeping child. They were shaking it, perhaps to wake it up. They lifted it up, cradled it, and the child flew up. A garland was tied to its waist, and a stone. In the eddy, the mouths of the tortoises that eat corpses came to the surface.) And it was the same river that I bathed in at Delhi, diving from the wharf among the miserable multitude. The current was pulling and I swallowed water, swallowed the suds and the slops and the sins of the penitent, swallowed the dead. The same river.

G

And I, standing in the dawn, naked in the water from the melting snow, the same man as used to take his mistress dancing in the
night-clubs, the same man come back to the Source.

31

Now I must get to where the Ganges is a ravine a little before
Uttarkashi. I am wandering vaguely in that direction. So long as
the provision of brown sugar and seeds in my handkerchief lasts,
I shall enjoy lingering by these lakes, a frontier of blue between the
jungle of the monkeys and the glaciers of the eagles.

32

On a plateau patched with ragged fields, the village comes into
sight. It is a square of outsize crazy paving on which houses are
placed like the sacrificial pebbles on to which the holy water drips
to the tinkling of a bell.

The houses are linked by a heavy black chain, and from this
chain hangs the bronze bell that marks the entrance to the village.
The walls of the houses are frames made of thick beams filled in
with layers of grey stone. Their roofs are paved as if with tomb-
stones.

On the side of the village opposite the cliff, there stands a square
tower. It has no windows, only a door halfway up, at the top of a
steep staircase. This door is studded and tightly shut and has
richly carved side-posts.

Beside or opposite each house is another building of equal size,
made of wood. At first one takes these for sanctuaries, so much
storeyed carving is there on their fronts. Each of these façades takes
the shape of a triangular pediment placed on three carved columns
and framing a panel which looks like the door of a tabernacle. I
think they are just granaries. They are surrounded by colonnades
in which baskets and ropes are hung up, and as soon as the
snow has withdrawn to the upper slopes, the villagers sleep
there.

The temple closes the ring of houses at the point furthest from
the bell. It does not dominate the other buildings, and indeed
looks even squatter because of the heaviness of its decoration.

This is a cluster of symbols and figures with horns and claws and numerous arms brandishing weapons, all entwining.

From the eaves, the peak of which you can touch, hangs a mobile fringe of wooden beads.

And all the dark madrepore of the triple porch glints with metal studs shaped like shells.

I recognise the two fabulous birds that support the architrave. I have seen them in the crypt of Canterbury Cathedral and on a capital in the church of the Crusaders at Vezelay. I have seen them in an Arabo-Roman cloister at Palermo and on a farmhouse chest in the Abruzzi Hills. I have seen them on an ebony paddle worked by the Negroes of Benin, those two birds that have never flown anywhere else than in the head of the craftsman carefully biting into some good chunk of wood or stone with his chisel. They belong to the style which people who are knowledgeable about art call *Romanesque* and which I call *human*.

33

The weavers in the square are pulling the weft across the teeth of the combs. Everybody here, men and women alike, is dressed in the same way. They wear big jackets of brown or fawn-coloured wool tied at the waist, slit at the sides and hanging to the knees; and trousers with baggy seats, tight from knee to ankle. The holes in the cloth show that they do not wear shirts.

They press round me and, in chorus, all start begging. Even from a half-naked pilgrim, they beg.

They seem poorer still, if possible, than the peasants elsewhere in India, perhaps because they are the subjects of a petty tyrant himself held on the end of a lead, a rajah who pays tribute to England. There are thus two of them gnawing this bit of earth which is all rock.

These villagers, today as in the past, remain talliable and liable to unpaid labour at will. When the Rajah of Tehri Garhwal, an extremely pious man, goes to the Holy Places, he raises a thousand men to carry his baggage and lead his mules, but he does not pay them, and scarcely feeds them. At the moment, the Rajah of Tehri Garhwal has gone to London to see the coronation of a King of England. What a lot of milk from the old woman's only cow, what a lot of the peoples' sweat and blood the crown of a King of England costs!

34

The women wear necklaces of hammered silver and bracelets decorated with dragons' jaws. Big rings go through their left nostrils and cover one half of their faces. These rings are so heavy that they have to be supported by a thread that passes over the head and is attached to another thread stretching from ear to ear. The tops of the women's ears (not the lobes) are burdened with so many pendants that they bend over like the stems of fruit-laden banana-trees.

It is the law here that a woman should marry several husbands; and the custom that she does all the heavy work while her husbands, sitting at home, spin and embroider.

One woman, out of family feeling, has married seven brothers. Whether she deceives them with the eighth-comer, history does not tell and I have not had leisure to observe.

35

The eagle. His flight slashes the air with a sound that makes you shiver. At the ends of his wings he has five feathers spread like a hand. He swooped almost across my face as I was standing on the edge of the cliff.

Gliding beyond, he tied the weight of the abyss round my neck and made me stagger.

36

She is young and her skin is fresh and though she is wrapped from throat to ankle in rough, hill-spun cloth, three big folds in it show that her long arms and legs are finely shaped and her waist is slender.

On her back she is carrying a great bundle of fodder for the cattle: branches and leaves stick out all round her. At every step the flesh of the leaves yields, trembles, reveals its mother-of-pearl underside, loses a drop of recent rain, gives out its bruised green smell.

37

The sky is overtaking me with thunderous strides. The fleecy belly of the cloud rubs on the furry back of the mountain opposite, then covers it, and is torn to shreds on its thorny rocks.

The wind comes out of the mouth of the chasm and is in front of me like a thing. It is at the foot of a solitary tree whose foliage it is ruffling, then turns and seizes me by the shoulders and knocks me over backwards between the slippery rock and the lightning-stricken tree.

The flashes swim round and below me. A shock darts through my limbs and bursts in my fingers and toes into stars of pain. I grind earth with my teeth.

38

Uttarkashi is the last holy city on the Ganges before its source, the pendant of Benares, a Benares of the north.[7]

Walled in by four mountains and sheltered from all contact with the outer world, this city is a meadow inhabited by a tall tree.

Round the tree and in the meadow, the two temples and a score of sanctuaries are scattered. There are also thirteen houses and two shops.

39

A little further up I had to stop.

I was lucky enough to find a small field on the cliff at the foot of which the river thunders past; a little field fringed with agaves and in it a black rock bristling with fleshy-leaved plants. The black slopes of the jungle cut off the view all round. I dropped my bundle of blankets on the grass and said to myself, 'Here we are!'

For I did indeed believe that I was going to end my days there. I was short of breath, my lips were parched, my legs swollen to half their size again by poisonous fly-bites.

At first I had attributed the fever and suppuration to some contagious disease I had caught in a shelter. But I observed that only the uncovered parts of my body were affected. I remembered the tiny, almost transparent gnats that had harassed me on my way to the Jamna. The sulphur and the heat of the baths had transformed the bites into pimples. But whatever sort of poison my body was full of, I had less to fear from my sores than from total abandonment, for I was now in rags, penniless and deprived of my own strength in a region haunted by all the beasts of the jungle, hundreds of miles from the plain and all likelihood of help.

I unrolled my blanket and lay down on it, facing the sky.

And like every simpleton who thinks he is about to die, I saw my early childhood again, the white house with its arches and terraces opening on to the vines, the sunny heath and the sea. My mother, young again, standing on the tiled floor of the big room, her laughter echoing clear from the high ceiling and now from the vaults of remembrance. My mother again, frail and ancient, in my arms when we said our last farewell on the jetty-head amid the cries of the sea-gulls. The days of my life following one another without order. My boat had not left much foam in its wake. Lying there, I saw it all from a great distance, and the faces and landscapes I loved. But I looked back on it with sadness in which there was no trace of bitterness or regret.

Not that I did not feel displeasure at having to leave. For I have always been filled to overflowing with joy here below. Joy that has been steadfast throughout contentment or grief. Besides, I love the broad light of day and shall never tire of it.

But no doubt it would be discourteous to insist, for such paltry reasons, on staying all the time.

So I made the sign of the cross over it all and shortly afterwards fell asleep.

40

Half waking, I became aware of the presence of an object at my right ear.

It was a bowl full of warm rice. I emptied the bowl and turning over on my other side, fell asleep again.

Next day, I saw a child coming along the river bank below, taking great care to balance a big copper mug on a tray.

When he had reached the spot where I was holding state, he stopped and laid the tray down on the grass. Then he folded his arms and waited. I saw that the mug contained tea with milk in it and understood that it was intended for me. I drank, and thanked the wind, for the child did not understand me and carried off the empty mug without speaking a word.

He came back in the evening again and every day after that, sometimes carrying cakes, sometimes fruit, but I never found out who sent him.

41

When night came, I kept looking at the stars, immortal eyes which would watch and wake instead of mine. I clung to them a while before sinking back into the sweet darkness I call 'me'.

42

At dawn, my eyelids open on the spread wing of a vulture. There are ten of them, and ten more, and ten higher up, going the rounds of the castles of morning.

A sunbeam strikes the metal of the one in the zenith.

How noble you look, far off and flying, you eaters of the dead! I contemplate you and you wait for me: every living thing that lies down on the earth belongs to you.

But so long as the soul inhabits the body, you will be careful not to come near. Surely our last breath peals out in the bell of the sky, for you recognise it without fail. Then you will perch in clusters on the surrounding trees, your too big wings flapping in the stiff, glossy leaves. From there you will drop on to the grass and hop round in circles, you crooked, hunch-backed, bald-necked, hideous birds. It is true indeed that we come to resemble what we desire.

Then the feast and the fight will begin. And some of you will fall and stay where you lie. For death, on which you live, is a bigger bird than you.

43

One day, a gentleman wearing a sun-helmet and city trousers came to pay me a visit while I was cradling my foot in my arms.

I was astonished to see him fall full length on his face. He was kneeling now, and touching the ground with his forehead. This indicated to me that he took me for a sage. And, as a matter of fact, he touched my foot with the tips of his outstretched hands.

Finally, he sat down opposite me with his legs crossed and began chatting gaily, for nothing is more common among the Hindus than mingling gestures of the most profound veneration with those of the friendliest familiarity.

When he had finished his chatter, he did more kneeling and went off. But I called him back because I had noticed that he had dropped something.

'It is impossible for me,' he protested with his voice, his head and shoulders, 'to take back something I have given.'

I looked for a long time at the big, silver coin. A beautiful thing indeed, precious, and useless, as a sacrifice should be.

44

Since I have been lying here, I have been hearing the cawing of the crows again. It is the first sound to strike the traveller's ear when he lands in India, like a loud reminder of his loneliness, his fragility and his being far away from home.

And step by step, from dawn till dusk, from south to north, throughout this compact land with its natural barriers of still water, black rock and glossy vegetation, their cawing will pursue him until at last he becomes unaware of it.

In my present immobility, I can hear my heart beating and feel the life in me drifting up in slow bubbles. The voices of the crows darken the funereal blue of the sky.

45

An old woman coming along the path with a faggot on her head stopped to ask me some questions. Seeing that I was having difficulty in understanding her, she started shouting, opening her toothless mouth wide without, however, overcoming my mental deafness.

Finally, she heaved a sigh, and crouching in front of me, remained silent. She remained thus for half an hour, an hour, two hours, without tiring of staring into my eyes, while I, just as untiringly, thought of other things.

Once, she stretched her hand towards my foot and one by one touched my wounds as one washes the stains from a precious vase. Her fingertips were very smooth.

Almost in a whisper, she asked me a question I understood: did I, in my country far away, still have a mother? I nodded. She then ran her fingertip down her cheek to suggest tears.

Other little, old women joined her and came and looked at me for a few hours every day. They brought me hot bread, and peppered rice in a wooden bowl.

46

One day, just beside the rock that was overgrown with thick-leaved plants, there rose a bare, bald head with the widespreading ears. The mouth in the head said '*Aum*'.

Then the trunk and the rest of the body, no less bare than the head, grew from ground-level, coming up by the cliff face.

And before me stood an elderly man who, in irreproachable English, made me more or less this speech:

'Honourable sir, you have been here for five days—I was informed of your arrival. My eyes fixed on the holy water of the river, looking neither right nor left, I was made aware of your arrival by a kind of beneficial influence on my meditation, a privilege which I attribute to your welcome presence and from which I conclude that good neighbourly relations have already been established between us. That is why I should feel very happy to be able, in my turn, to render you some service. If you need a roof, or a bed, attention or medicine, or special food, if you need or would simply like something, I beg of you, honourable sir, to let me know. For fifteen years I have been living here, and all around me are my friends. I, therefore, consider myself personally responsible for the manner in which this country treats you. Under this rock there is a hole; now you know where I live. I shall welcome as an honour and a favour any request you may care to make to me.

'Moreover, I beg you to consider me, sir, in everything and for ever, as your own self.'

Having concluded this speech, he turned his back, gallantly hung with a string in guise of breeches.

47

The police have been. They had no difficulty in arresting me, since I cannot move. They told me what I already knew: that I am in forbidden territory. Tibet is closed to people of our race except if they are on a special mission. The source of the Ganges lies beyond the frontier. It is even forbidden to approach it within some scores of miles.

They had been looking for me for a week; they had let me pass by mistake, failing to recognise the European in this bearded, blackened man wearing a torn loin-cloth. They had taken me for an Afghan fakir.

They made me sign a paper promising to go down into the plain as soon as I am fit. They were willing to come to my aid. 'I have everything I need, thank you,' I answered.

For a vagabond to accept anything from such as they would be to betray the dignity of his condition.

48

So that's that. I shall not reach the source of the Ganges, the place where the holy river springs forth alive from Shiv's brow and leaps out of the sheer ice to spread roaring among the flowers. In any case, I have always preferred the journey to the journey's end.

And a journey from which one returns is a fine thing. I gave my calabash to the child who brings me the milk and signed to him to go and fill it from the river.

And now I drink the icy water in long draughts, the 'white water' of the Ganges. However many corpses they throw into it, it remains pure, and purifies. Its body is incorruptible. It will wash me of my ill.

49

Although the young man was still a long way off, as soon as he caught sight of me he put his hands together before his lips and shouted '*Aum*'. He approached and asked me if I was going to the source of the Ganges. I replied that as soon as I could get on my feet again I should, on the contrary, go down towards Tehri. 'And what about you?' I asked.

'I was on my way to the source of the Ganges,' he said, 'but since you are going down to Tehri, I shall go down to Tehri with you. I shall follow you everywhere and serve you in all things.'

It was not an easy thing to make him understand that it was all I could do to cope with the disciple I was myself, and that I was not in a fit state to take on another.

He withdrew, grieved.

His cheeks and head were shaven and his robe was saffron-coloured. He wore the cordon of the Brahmins. From time to time his left eye languished and sought the shelter of the eyelid as a bird puts its head under its wing before going to sleep.

The spurned one remained at some distance from me and spent half a day looking at me from afar. At long last, without another word, he pursued his way to the mountain.

50

Things had turned out badly, and so had the weather. The poison was working on my entrails. Thunder swelled the devouring roar of the river down below. I was beginning to feel restless under my goat-hair blanket which was now fluttering in the wind that precedes a storm.

Then, in the agaves, a face appeared, darkened by its own beard as much as by cloud and the twilight. Beard and hair, entwined like branches and liana in the jungle, hung down to his belly.

He beckoned to me. But while I was limping towards him, he came towards me, passed me, bent over my blanket and rolled it up, took it under his arm and carried it off. I followed him, with the help of my staff, to his house.

This house was nothing other than the temple of Kali which the clump of agaves had hidden from me and of which he was the priest.

51

So I slept in the temple of Kali, on a soft carpet and in clouds of
incense while thunder rolled on the mountains and rain battered
and furrowed the ground.

Those were days of heavy storm outside, and atrocious pain in
my entrails, but days illuminated by doctrinal talk and entirely
filled with the joys of friendship.

In his dark fleece, my friend had teeth of laughter and splendour; eyes shaped like half moons, a brow polished like the
morning sky.

He bore the name of Krishna Chandra and had honoured himself with the title of Brahmachari, which means 'seeker on the
roads of Brahma' or 'the novice', and, in a word, 'the chaste'. He
carried the double burden of chastity and silence with virile and
youthful courage. One of the first things he did after taking me in
was to write on a piece of paper, 'I know English and I would
speak it, but four years ago I took a vow of silence. You can speak
to me—I shall answer with signs or in writing.'

The liveliness of his face, his boyish impatience—he would
shake his head or tap with his foot when I took him up wrongly or
was slow in understanding—were proof enough of the violence he
had had to do himself never to let his heart cry out. I quickly became accustomed to this way of communicating which leaves the
tongue time to turn before speaking and gives the written answer—
sometimes reduced by haste to an enigmatic snippet—the solem-
nity of revelation.

The chaste one wrote to me: 'I like your words but they are
going to trouble me in my meditation, especially what you say of
your mother countries in Europe. Your words will remain between me and myself, between silence and me.'

'How many hours a day do you give to meditation?'

'Few: five or six a day at the most.'

'And have you achieved the absence of all thought, the obscure
night which, in the common experience of our saints and yours,
opens the way to the divine descent?'

'Once or twice in a flash, and it left the whole of life illuminated.
But for some years sterility has afflicted me again. For—more than

evil or desire—it is difficult to overcome the waywardness of a day-dreaming mind, especially for us Bengalese who are song-loving people and inclined to easy life.'

*

Krishna Chandra's eyes kept coming back to the cross on my breast. At last he asked me what it meant.

He only knew Christ by name.

So I talked to him of my Lord and my God and soon I surprised myself preaching. Meanwhile, beyond the grille, the wooden goddess reared up black, her red tongue hanging down to her breast, her many arms brandishing trident, knife, club and bowl of blood; her neck hung with skulls and her feet trampling the prostrate body of the white god.

When I had finished my sermon, the priest of Kali raised his finger towards the goddess and then wrote on a sheet of paper: 'But Power is one.'

52

My friend has left me in order to prepare the meal. I see him at the bottom of the garden, under a roof, crouching amid fires and clouds of smoke. He pours out, cuts up, crushes and tastes things with priestly care and cleanliness.

Then he hurries to the foot of the altar and presents the steaming bowls before serving them to me.

Seated before me on the ground, he picks up the morsels that he has so carefully cooked for me and places them on the leaf that serves as a dish, his eyes asking me if they are to my taste.

When the meal is over, he pours water on my hands, removes the leavings and throws them away, then goes off and sits on his heels, facing the wall, and there, in great haste and secrecy, eats for himself.

53

At twilight, the Brahmachari shuts behind him the door of the temple and then the grille of the inner sanctuary. Alone there with his goddess, he officiates.

A short cloth is fastened tightly round his loins; he wears no other coat than his hair. Standing amid the dim lamps and the smoking incense-burners, he has become solemn to the point of being almost frightening.

Now he prostrates himself, his forehead on the ground, then stands up again, raising in his right hand a burning oil lamp while his left, with sustained energy, shakes a bell. With the flame, he draws large circles round the effigy of the goddess then, slowly turning, repeats the circles towards the four horizons so as to unite himself with all the shining bodies, and the circulation of the planets, and the perennity of the fixed stars, and the rising and the setting of the sun, and the cycle of the seasons, and the crown of invisible light, chief of all marvels, that invisible light which belongs only to the few awakened ones who are embraced in the circle of the One.

After which, underlining the act with the same vehement ringing, he begins to form similar circles with an ember of incense in order to evoke fire; fire which gives man power, makes demons terrible and the gods light of heart; fire that kindles health in every living creature or burns the flesh with fever; fire that spreads the ravaging dance and rage of God; fire that fosters the meditation of saints and like a tongue and a mouth consumes the sacrifice offered up by pure hands; fire that forged this world and will devour it.

Then he describes the same circles with a conch full of water, to call forth the waters that come down by all the steps of heaven, by all the rocks of the Himalayas, by all the rivers of the earth: the raining and the singing waters, the leaping and the still; the waters frozen like diamonds and the low ones that carry death; the waters that play in the leaves and in the green of every plant; those that fill the heart with forgetfulness and the eyes with sleep; those that steam in smells and those that wait, hanging in the clouds, for the cycle of life to begin again.

Now that he has scattered the water, he puts the conch to his mouth and sends through it a bellow as wide as space, like an answer to all the voices in the world, to the secrets of the soul, to words of power, to charms and spells, to the strength of the prayers that swell the breast and make plants grow as well as the immense tree of creation, whose roots are in the air and whose branches are on earth.

And now, making a fan of white feathers into a wheel, he addresses himself to the four winds, to the winds that uphold the vaults of heaven, to the winds that quicken flesh, to the winds that are the very body of the spirit, to those inevitable encounters between laws and destiny which in our ignorance we call 'chance', to the course of events, to the breathing of the worlds in their adventure, to the play of the universal illusion which, reflecting what we believe to be *us* in what we believe to be *other*, hides from us the unique Self that we are and which alone is.

By the cessation of all invocation and by prostrating himself motionless before the goddess whom he calls 'Our Holy Mother' (who at her pleasure creates and destroys, terrorises demons and consoles the humble), he offers up each element cut off from its roots and gathered like a flower.

Meanwhile, on the other side of the grille, I admire the enacted poetry that a rite is: the bridge that it is, built of all the things a man throws between himself and power, power which is one, as the chaste priest of Kali had affirmed, his finger raised. The thought came to me that little boys play with wooden swords and will be soldiers when they grow up, and little girls play with dolls and will be mothers tomorrow. And we humans cherish certain images and with them play at religion, but when we have grown, what shall we have become?

54

When the time came to part, the chaste one took me tightly in his arms, an unusual farewell even between intimate friends in a country where greetings are made at a distance and every man is untouchable to every other. He looked into my eyes to make me understand the words that, even if he had spoken, he could not have said.

Round my waist, instead of the old loin-cloth, he had tied a long, white, immaculate robe and round my shoulders he hung a scarf as clean as an altar-cloth.

55

The Philosopher from the hole in the rock was waiting for me on the road. He had come to inquire after my health several times during my stay at the temple and he now insisted on accompanying me for a few miles.

My eyes were drawn to a certain pair of rope sandals with square soles, the only piece of clothing the old sage was wearing.

As soon as he noticed this, he took them off and slipped them on to my feet, and behind his polite remarks his pressure was so vehement that I had no choice but to accept them. And, indeed, illness had made my feet sensitive again, and I also knew what to expect of the sharp, stony tracks of Uttarkhand.

Giving in, I thanked him. 'Why do you thank me?' he asked. 'Why do you smile to me? Why do you look at me like that, from the outside? Am I not your own self?

'Why do you force yourself not to accept the things that you need for travelling and which are offered to you? I hope that on the road back, at least, you are going to learn to beg, sir.

'You are on the right path, and you have made good headway on it, but I am telling you, so long as you cannot beg you will not attain true philosophy.

'It is a duty for every head of a household, every father, every labouring man and every worker for gain to supply your wants. It is a law. The Code of Manu says, "Whoever prepares a meal for himself alone, eats sin."

'So take what is due to you. They owe you so much! They owe you everything: are you not the Creator of heaven and earth? The everlasting, limitless, all-powerful Self?

'My friend, since it pleases the everlasting, limitless, all-powerful Self to go wandering in the heart of a man, it follows logically, as you clearly see, that you must go begging. . . .'

For a number of years, of which he had lost count, his own hands had not touched the metal of a coin. He had left his already grown-up sons, and his wife weighed down by age, had left his business and its worries, his house and his garden. Later, he had given up his blanket, then his book, and, later, the last rag that covered him.

'If there is some shame attached to the naked body, that is the body's business, not mine. It is not mine; I am not that. I am the everlasting, limitless, all-powerful Self.

'I have laid down all hate, all fear, all hope, all love. Things come and go, men pass and die; they undergo the fate they have woven with their own hands. What does it matter to me? It is not mine, I am not that, I am the everlasting, limitless, all-powerful Self.'

The naked one spoke to me of the body as well. He told me about the five elements of which it is composed and the quintuplication of each which results in the structure of the organs and the knot of their living: each element halved complicates itself with four-eighths of the four other elements and health or illness depend on the balance of things. 'Air, water, fire, earth, ether—what is it?' he said. 'By whom is it? Can I call mine any of their encounters? That is not mine, I am not that. I am the everlasting, limitless, all-powerful Self.'

He taught me some moral precepts as well. 'If you want to lead a holy life,' he said to me, 'do not pray. What can you ask of God that you do not already possess? And who is God if not yourself?'

We reached the bend in the road and the time to go our separate ways. We each put palm to palm before our lips in farewell, but at that moment I saw an appearance that caused me some surprise.

It seemed to me that a little of the water which partly composes our body-which-is-not-ours was gathering in drops on the Philosopher's eyelashes. And his voice also moved the surrounding air, and I heard it sounding like this:

'It is strange, my friend. Here is my heart full of emotion as if we were really separating. And yet I know for certain that separation is the favourite game of Maya-Illusion, a game of reflections, a game . . . a game . . .'

And quickly turning his back on me, the old man hastened home to the rocks and thorns of solitude.

56

The monsoon caught me by surprise on the way back. The Philosopher's sandals became tufts of hemp, then clods, and returned to the elements.

For three days, I rolled down screes, got stuck in mud and had to jump newly-sprung torrents. The wind leapt out of ravines and threw me on to my face while the rain battered my legs and ribs.

As night was falling, I arrived at Narendranagar in the outermost spurs of the Himalayas. I was starving, for so far I had eaten nothing; water was streaming off me and I was utterly exhausted.

Then I remembered the teaching of true philosophy.

Picking out a house of good appearance, I went up to the door with what resolution I had left and dropped my soaking bundle on the threshold. I then asked for the master of the house.

He soon appeared. He was fat, surly and surrounded by a great many other persons. 'I don't know who you are,' I said, 'but I know that in every man I meet a friend is hidden.'

And the persons with him looked at each other and smiled.

Only the master of the house continued to be surly. He asked me who I was, where I came from, what I wanted. I told him briefly, on which he turned his back and disappeared into the house, followed by all the others.

I was just about to pick up my bundle when a servant came running and snatched it from me, begging me to follow him.

I found a room ready, and a bath, and a bed. Shortly afterwards, dinner was served me.

'By the way,' I said, 'whose house is this?'

It belonged to the Divan of the Kingdom of Tehri Garhwal, a man hated by some, feared by all and accustomed to being constantly surrounded with flattering smiles or looks of terror.

I have been here for eight days and feel I could stay here all my life, for in this man, indeed, a friend was hidden.

1. Worth about a halfpenny.
2. At that time worth fourpence.
3. Name of the valley.
4. Demons who play a great part in the Ramayana. They carried off Sita, and Rama her husband won her back again by killing them all.
5. 'Koomari-Devi'.
6. At this altitude, the temperature of boiling water becomes bearable.
7. Uttar—north   Kashi—Benares.

VI

THE BANK OF THE GANGES

OR THE NOVICE

'So now,' says the disciple in the red saffron robe, 'stay with us, work on yourself perseveringly and become a true yogi like our Lord Jesus Christ.'

The small monastery stands with its back to the jungle and monkeys come and play there. Closed to the road, it opens on to the Ganges, whose impetuous torrent has widened into calm, like a plain moving at the foot of the slopes.

Day and night, storms rack the sky and split the mountains. The river is yellow. The rain is a ceaseless exchange between the equally murky sky and earth. Cloying and mouldy smells hang in the air. Vapour rises from the soil with swarms of insects. Glossy leaves are thrust down by the smack of the rain and throw their heads up vigorously when the downpour stops. The rutting elephant trumpets in the distance and peacocks dance in the clearings.

It's done. I am a novice. If truth lies in yoga, one can only go in and see so as not to have been born in vain.

If my body is what prevents me from seeing truth, I must learn to pierce it through, raise it like a veil and put it aside.

2

Swami Ananda has a good reputation in the region. There are about ten disciples in his monastery. So I have presented him with my modest offering of milk and fruit and the little heap of pride and ignorance I call 'I', begging him to teach me.

'Is your health good?' he asked me.

'It can stand anything,' I replied.

'That is an indispensable condition for entering religion,' he declared.

'How do you feed yourself?'

'Like a poor Brahmin.'

'That's good: pure food is necessary to anyone who wants to approach the things of the spirit. How do you sleep?'

'Like a stone.'

'And you don't dream?'

'No, I don't.'

'That's a good sign: you may become one of the truly awakened. Is your manhood healthy and strong?'

'A horse difficult to master.'

'All the better; chastity must have strength in it.'

'Have you a good voice? Can you sing?'

'Yes.'

'Sing.'

I have a strong, deep voice and sing in tune. I make great use of it, especially when travelling in the plains, so as to rhythm my step. So I made a tune up, as I am accustomed to do on the road.

The Swami turned a joyful face towards me:

'It's good to have a fine voice to keep silence with and to offer up in sacrifice. All the yogis have powerful lungs and beautiful voices. You have in you what is needed to make a yogi, provided you have enough will-power, ardour, devoutness and fearlessness. I am sorry for my own sake that you cannot become my disciple. You are Mahatma Gandhi's disciple: a man cannot have two masters, and you would lose too much by the exchange. But at least be my guest for as long as you like. I shall endeavour to put you on the way and teach you the little I know.'

I thanked him and told him that I was a demanding guest. 'A guest who wants to be done the honour of being treated with terrible severity. If you think there is a spark hidden in the stone that I am, strike me hard to get it out of me. I am ready to bear anything. You will get nothing out of me by gentleness.'

Throughout this conversation, the Swami's eyes kept coming back to the cross hanging on a chain round my neck.

'Have you anything against my wearing it here, as elsewhere?'

'On the contrary,' he replied, 'I want you to make the cross the constant theme of your meditation. I shall give you my teaching in the symbolical language familiar to us. It is up to you to translate it into your own inner language, into Christian language. What we want to reach remains beyond names, forms and distinctions, does it not?'

3

My cell is whitewashed and paved with bricks. It is furnished with a jar filled with water from the Ganges and a board that serves as a bed. I have put my stick in a corner and unrolled my striped blanket and laid it on the board. I have brought a smooth, round stone from the river, marble with black and yellow veins, and made a pillow of it.

I am grateful to the Swami for his welcome, and at the same time deeply disappointed by the ease of it all. Ordeals and terrible maceration should mark entrance into mysteries. But I do not know where I am. They simply said to me, 'Come in'. So my entry is just a word.

At three o'clock in the morning, a long *Aum* resounds in the dark. It is the signal for getting up and the call to prayer. I run and plunge into the black river before joining my companions in the portico.

The prayer begins, sustained by drumming; then hymns are sung to Shiv, Ram, Krishna, Sita, Gowri and many other names of the only One. Half an hour later, we proceed to meditation, for which we take up the position of the lotus—a sweet-sounding word. As for the attitude, easy and natural for all Indians, it is torture for us, at least, to start with. It consists in sitting on the ground and taking one's legs and twisting them one on top of the other into a sailor's knot, so that the two feet lie soles upward in the groins.

We should then be able, by crossing our arms behind our backs, to seize the big toe of the right foot with the left hand, and the big toe of the left with the right hand. Thus, strongly based and painfully tied to ourselves, we must make our heads, necks and bodies into straight, unshakable tree-trunks and stay thus for several hours without weakening, moving a muscle, or blinking; neither stiffening ourselves up nor drooping. Breathing becomes peaceful and deeper; facial wrinkles disappear, the knots in the body are loosened.

Another *Aum* announces that the sun has risen and restores us to everyday life. I go on sitting for a while in the midst of my ruins, fingering my legs to make sure that they still belong to me. (Long, long after, they still recall themselves to me by the groans of their forced joints, and cramp, and tingling.) Then the stone of the floor seizes them with its chill. I get up and drag them together. Legs, oh my legs—the best I have had for many lives, do not betray me, for I need you—without you how could I have got here? I shall always need you, legs, to follow Wisdom. For I clearly see that it is I who shall always have to go to Wisdom and that I shall never be able to wait, motionless as the Absolute, for her to come to me.

It will take more than gymnastics—which my companions are already doing—to limber up my stiffness. These are gymnastics of attitude rather than of movement—the contrary of ours. Ours exercise muscles and constantly throw the body out of itself in all directions: theirs exercise breathing, the nervous centres and the internal glands, and tend towards stability.

Yoga moulds the body in a series of poses forming closed circuits. The body becomes boneless, stretches and glides over itself as it passes from one attitude to another. Each attitude lasts for as long as one can hold in one's breath. But sometimes, one breathes in just before diving and one goes through ten or twelve attitudes before letting one's breath out again. I do my utmost to imitate the others but lose my breath, and start to suffocate. So I gather myself up in a corner and watch them. The coarse angle that elbows and knees make has been smoothed out in them. They turn into liana, snakes, flowers; then from being snails, embryos or corpses they rise and marvellously become themselves. Sustained effort has left their breathing even, and their faces are even too, like smooth pebbles in the clear, furious water of a torrent.

The same ritual takes place every evening. All day we are free to exercise ourselves alone, to meditate, to pray, to read and to walk. When the sky clears, I marvel at the clouds standing on the glory of the trees. Just as in Sicily, a carpet of clover lies under the orange-trees, so a veil of feathery-leaved plants mingled with maidenhair covers the earth in this forest. I climb the slopes of the jungle by the slippery paths of the brooks, crawling under the dense, glossy leaves of the bushes up to a tunnel of light at the foot of a ring of cliffs where white waterfalls, black branches and grey liana twist and rise and fall at the bottom of a lake of motionless greenery.

4

Even if I only leave my cell for a few minutes, when I come back I find it sprinkled with water, swept and sometimes perfumed with incense; and lying folded on the plank is the linen I had left hanging on the rope.

My companions are all, like the Swami, Indians from the south, that is to say, particularly black, particularly clean, gentle, courteous and discreet.

And the abyss dwells in the night of their lustrous eyes.

5

I am beginning to be broken in to corporal exercise. I have forced myself so much that I can now bear the position of the lotus with an even mind. I can stand for a long time on my head and elbows, which has the effect of irrigating my brain with blood and fighting off the drowsiness that becomes disastrous when one must remain motionless in the same attitude for a long time.

The Swami shows that he is pleased with me and lavishes praise on me in the presence of my companions. But instead of encouragement, it is severity I need.

*   *   *

I tried to fast properly, but after three days the Swami came down to my cell. He did indeed speak to me with severity—but in order to make me break the fast. 'Yoga is not for the man who eats too much, nor for the man who fasts too much,' he quoted, 'nor for the man who works too much, nor for the man who does nothing.'

To which I replied, 'I know that verse of the Gītā by heart, thank you, but it does not apply to me, since I am not a yogi. I have so many desires, so much vanity, attachment and inattention

216 to expiate that I should be an impostor even to call myself a novice.'

'Instead of inflicting penance on yourself,' he answered, 'train yourself patiently. Too much severity would eventually dry up the very germ of your acts.'

'Swami, I shall obey you without discussion, since it is my duty to do so, but I know myself well enough to tell you that you will get nothing out of me by gentleness.'

6

The Swami carries high his fine golden-bronze head and has a certain stout and jovial majesty. There is gravity in the shaven forehead and the masterful clear-cut features, lightning in his look, and in his smile, artlessness.

7

Our monastery possesses a small library. It contains the Vedas in Sanskrit and in English, so I have resumed the study I began at Wardha.

Easy study, in which one only has to receive. The hours pass and are lost in it. For what grips me is not the desire for sanctification or the love of ultimate truth, but rather the impure, boisterous curiosity of the intellect.

Sometimes a monkey clutches the bars of the window, pokes his head between them and peers into the darkness of my room with a busy, questioning look.

8

I know that the whole secret of yoga lies in two practices concerning which I have been unable to obtain any guidance from anybody else or make any progress myself; control of breathing and meditation.

Of all the functions of the body, breathing is the only involuntary one that can be performed at will. The object is to make it voluntary and take possession of it. Through control of breathing, step by step, one can gain control of the other functions. And to will is to know. If you want to know your body from within, this is the rope that goes down into the well.

Now, our body is the summing up of the whole of creation, the only object that we can know from inside at the same time as from outside. Knowing the body, we know everything else. So control of breathing is the philosopher's stone and the principle of transformation. By control of breathing, the yogis manage to suffuse their flesh with so much vital air that it rises of its own accord and floats like a cloud; they can also intensify the heat of their bodies until they burn like glowing coals in the ice of the Himalayas; or reduce themselves to the state of stone, be buried and come to life again at a chosen date.

All *we* have been taught to do is to breathe in through the right nostril and out through the left, stopping our nostrils up alternately with the thumb and the ring finger. There is nothing difficult or interesting about that.

As for the other practice—I mean meditation—we are told, 'Fix yourselves and stop thinking', which does not seem difficult to me but just impossible.

Until now, meditating meant, to us, reflecting on a given subject, going into it thoroughly and conducting our inner talk to a logical end. Until now, knowledge was the result of well-guided intelligence. From childhood, our minds had been trained to seize upon the brilliant threads of relations, to hoard up the riches of memory, to force up the springs of inventiveness. So it is vexing to learn one day that in order to attain truth it behoves us to give up altogether the childish habit of thinking.

And yet, if you are not content to reflect, but also reflect on 'reflection', you cannot escape the obvious fact that you must *divide in order to think*. The subject of your thought must be distinct, that is to say, exterior and multiple. The function of thought is to unify the multiple. Faced with the *one*, it has nothing to do. It can only try to break it up. But the purpose of meditation is knowledge of the one, of the inner one, of the self. Thought cannot therefore force its way in there. The very nature of thought, and not a failing of thought, prevents it from penetrating the mystery. Thought must renounce itself in order to conceive the one. That is why Christ has said, 'If thine eye be simple, thy whole body will be lighted.' But I am far from being simple. I am double-eyed and troubled within myself. I am just trying to achieve this difficult simplification.

*

Meditating is entering truth without discovering[1] it, without seeing it from outside, without opening it into words.

9

As I was endeavouring, with my face to the wall, to keep my inner tumult in check, I thought I heard something behind me like the whirr of an insect's wing or a slight draught.

I turned just in time to see a bare heel going out of the door. The man who was fleeing like a thief had just swept and tidied my room.

So I ran after him and caught him still holding the broom. It was the Swami's favourite disciple.

'Why,' I shouted at him, 'why do you do that?'

'To serve you, sir.'

'You must not serve me or call me "sir" either. Don't you know I'm called Shantidas?'

'I shall try to obey you then, to please you, Shantidas-Jee.'

10

There are what look like broad patches of yellow leaves on the ground. When you approach them, they turn into clouds which break up into butterflies. For the rainy season is the season of love for butterflies, as for nearly all the beasts of the jungle.

Sometimes a monkey, unhurried and lightfooted, saunters carelessly up to the golden pool, springs and lands in the midst of the whirling cloud. His two fists are full.

He sits down to munch them at his ease.

11

'Well, you see, it's because we admire you so much.'

'You do indeed surprise me,' I exclaimed, 'and whatever for?'

'For your great simplicity.'

'Admire yourselves then, since we live the same life.'

'But we have no merit, since we have been brought up to it since childhood.'

12

Sometimes I am told that I have visitors. Now, I know what good manners are, and what I must do.

I must sit on my plank with my legs drawn up. The person who has come to see me touches my feet and then settles himself on the ground in the same position.

He looks at me his fill, for half an hour or an hour. When he has seen enough of me, he gets up, touches my feet again and goes. He always leaves me a gift of fruit, cakes and milk which I hasten to give to the Swami in the same way as they have been given to me.

Sometimes it is a whole family that comes to see me. They come in with their baskets and umbrellas and seat themselves in a row along the wall, down to the small five-year-old who, like a good boy, ties his soft legs into the knot of the lotus and gazes up at me, his beautiful eyes wide with innocence and such as mine should be.

These people have such a thirst for saintliness that they see it and do homage to it even where it is lacking. So much the worse for me, but as far as they are concerned, it does not matter; the very sight of me will sanctify them, even if I am only a poor man and less than they, as the following story proves. Rama Krishna tells it.

'Tapobana, the Master, had a disciple who served him with irreproachable diligence. It was solely because of this diligence and the services he rendered that Tapobana kept him, for he found the disciple rather stupid.

'One day, the rumour spread throughout the whole region that Tapobana's disciple had walked on water; that he had been seen crossing the river as one crosses the street.

'Tapobana called his disciple and questioned him.

' "Is what people are saying about you possible? Is it really true that you crossed the river walking on the water?"

' "What could be more natural?" answered his follower. "It is

thanks to you, Blessed One, that I walked on water. At every step
I repeated your saintly name and that is what upheld me."

'And Tapobana thought to himself, "If the disciple can walk on
water, what can the Master not do? If it is in my name that the
miracle takes place, I must possess power I did not suspect and
holiness of which I have not been sufficiently aware. After all,
I have never tried to cross the river as if I were crossing the
street."

'And without more ado, he ran to the river bank. Without
hesitation, he set his foot on the water, and with unshakable faith
repeated, "Me, me, me . . ." And sank.'

13

Morning and evening, while my companions invoke Shiv, Rama
and the others, I say my own prayer apart, 'God of truth, grant me
purity of heart, strength of will, mastery of my breath, control of
my mind, blessedness of soul.'

When I was a child, to make fun of me, they used to say, 'It's
not difficult to catch a little bird—all you have to do is put some
salt on its tail.' And like a silly boy I would run after the blue-tits
in the garden with my pinch of salt at the ready.

The method I am being taught here to achieve absolute truth is
likewise childishly easy. 'All you have to do is to know yourself
and seize your own thought.'

When I think of my own thought, the thought I think is not the
thought that thinks. I only have to seize it for it to be of no more
use. I am like a man trying to get rid of his shadow by jumping
over it. I reflect, I turn upon myself, the thought I am trying to
seize is always behind me and I turn round and round like a dog
trying to bite its own tail.

When I try to think of nothing, I think of nothings. When these
nothings flit away, I fall into nothingness and fall asleep.

I struggle with myself and it is as if my right hand were fighting
my left. There is no danger of being wounded. There are neither
losses nor victims in this battle, nor defeat nor victory. It is the
indifference of despair that wins.

I force my breathing, I adopt what is called 'the smallest
measure' here, that is to say, twelve seconds for breathing in,

forty-eight of holding one's breath, twenty-four for breathing out. I sweat and tremble and my eyes stick out of my head. The Swami becomes alarmed and urges me to be patient, which, when all is said and done, amounts to giving up the effort completely.

The Swami's extreme prudence is due to his having had serious trouble with one of his disciples—the one who last occupied my cell. This man rushed into dangerous practices so rashly that he went off his head.

The Swami is wrong to worry about me—I am bursting with common sense—the commonest sort of sense there is. For no sooner am I left to my own devices that I start arguing, theorising and reasoning with utterly boring accuracy.

14

'Oh mind of man, you drivel like a fly
Hungry for shit and thirsty for the sun,
Hither and thither flitting, nothing done,
A speck of waking dust with restless eye.'

15

I thought there might be someone among my companions who could help me to study the sacred books, but they all speak Tamil or Telugu, and none of them can read Sanskrit—not even the Swami.

Sometimes at the hour of meditation I can only day-dream. Occasionally I push hypocrisy to the point of taking advantage of my free time, to write verse. I also walk a lot, which will no doubt *not* lead me to my goal.

16

The monkeys that haunt our austere monastery are shameless, bare-arsed red-heads; vulgar and ugly show-offs and cowards; cynical and deceitful, familiar and cantankerous, idle and perpetually restless, self-indulgent thieves—quick as the devil to profit by the slightest lack of attention on the part of unfortunate human beings, diligent in doing mischief and altogether insufferably like us. To the stupefaction of the people around me, I love them.

The ugliest are transfigured by movement, take on the grace of birds, the strangeness of fish, and blossom like flowers.

I have seen mothers lavishing attention on their hideous little nurslings, coaxing them with coquettish pride and pouting tenderly.

It is a marvel how the string-like babies tie themselves round their mothers' flanks and hang from their bellies when, at the slightest alarm, the mothers leave the ground to seek refuge in the forks of the branches. I have observed prolonged mourning when one of them, in consternation, turns and shakes and questions the poor corpse of the little creature that a few minutes earlier was coming and going as lightly as a downy seed. She raises her eyes to the sky, her arms fall to her sides and then she hugs the little body to warm it, cradles it as if it were sleeping, despairs and lets it fall and finally, making herself blind to what should not be, takes it into her arms again, stroking and caring for it till it falls apart in putrefaction.

*

The big male has been watching me since the beginning of the meal. As I get up I throw him the pancake I have not eaten.

He picks it up with both hands, sits down and raises it to his mouth, but at that moment, stops, darts an indignant look at me and suddenly jerks his head in my direction and shows his teeth. 'Well, what is it then, what else do you want? I've got the pancake. Get away!' But I don't get away; confronted with such artless ingratitude, my heart melts. I want to kiss him.

When we lived in the world and somebody turned the same face towards us after receiving some good from us, why did our hearts not overflow with the same tenderness for him?

17

The pure scientist ignores God. 'He does not need that hypothesis.' Likewise, the pure yogi does not need what men call God. But the man who is not journeying towards God has made some false semblance of God his goal.

The scientist knows only the external God he calls Matter, an unknowable principle whose existence can only be affirmed by an act of faith, but this faith is so strong and so unreflecting that it takes itself for an affirmation of something obvious. Discipline, patience, self-forgetfulness, scrupulous obedience and ascetic self-sacrifice earn the scientist the marvellous empire he holds over things. But, on the other hand, he lets his inner life lie fallow, or wrongly tries to subject it to the laws he had deduced from external things.

The yogi's purpose is to know only the inner God called Self. It seems obvious to him that this unknowable principle exists and that it is one and the same in himself and in all other beings. This is the axiom from which the method, experimentation and knowledge spring which lead the yogi to supernatural power over himself and other people. On the other hand, he lets the outer world drift or else inaptly applies to it a rule he has taken from within.

But who places God in God, that is to say, above? Inside, outside and above, all at the same time?

*

The Catholic faith shows God at the end of three roads that part in different directions to meet again in the Infinite.

This faith always goes further than those who follow only one road.

It shows God beyond the outside, beyond matter, in being: the Father.

It shows God in a me more myself than I, in the Son of Man, in Christ the heart of hearts.

It shows God in a rainbow higher than the seven heavens, the absolute relation beyond relations—the Holy Ghost.

18

Precisely because yoga is not attached to any particular religion, I can practise it without apostasy.

Yoga is not a religion, but a philosophy in the proper and first meaning of the word: wisdom of love.

Yog means 'yoke' and also 'joint'. Moreover, *yog*, 'yoke' and 'joint' are the same word. Yoga is therefore the yoke we have to submit to in order to reach the 'joint', that is to say, inner unification and union with the One.

It is thus the rational method of reaching the supreme plane. It is the joint between the mysteries of absolute truth, the problems and dialectical contradictions of thought, and the actions of this limited body.

Yoga with its four branches,[2] yoga of knowledge, Royal Yoga, yoga of action, yoga of maceration, is not a philosophy, it *is* Philosophy.

Philosophy is practically non-existent in the modern West. The occidentals who talk about it and teach it do not know what it is about.

The religion revealed to the West is no doubt divine in its essence and the richest in truth that there is, but because philosophy is lacking in the West, the truth of Christianity remains separate, as it were, from those who should adhere to it. Faith, devotion, knowledge, charity, justice, courage and goodwill are as frequent in the West as elsewhere; what is completely lacking is a direction. The joint is missing between what they believe, what they think, what they know, what they feel, what they want and what they do.

Since the joint is missing, everything is missing, for they themselves are missing from themselves. Consequently, the outcome of all their undertakings can only meet with absurd failure.

'Truth does not need you, my friends,' Buddha used to tell his followers. 'Truth is perfect, complete, blissful, unchangeable and radiant even if no one knows her. It is you, my friends, it is you who need her. So it is you who must set about seeking her.'

19

The leper is lying naked at the cross-roads. His nakedness is not immediately noticeable, so obscene is the rest. His very form gapes and its nudity is the rawness of the flesh of suffering. His hand is a mouth that slavers and spits out bits of bone. Flies form a quivering scab on his wounds. They even cling to his lidless eyes. I can't help the grimace that twists my face, so strong are

the pity and disgust that grip my heart, whereas he smiles to me
from the depths of his stink as I pour hot vegetable stew into his
bowl. He doesn't seem to be suffering. The deepest evils are
beyond pain. Corruption is one of them.

*

Since nobody will go within ten yards of him, I offer to carry him
wherever he wants to go. But he wants to stay there.

Not far from here is a leper-house where he would be given
shelter, but he refuses to go into it.

An onlooker explains, 'This is a busy road. Religious persons
throw alms to him. He makes a lot of money.'

'I don't understand. What does he do with it?'

A stupid question. For what do the other misers, whose leprosy
is invisible, do with *their* money?

20

Just as, in calm weather, one pushes one's boat up to the cliff
hollowed and sculpted by the sea, and with the oar noses it between the reefs, behind the pillars, under the arches of rock,
right into the cave whose mouth is blackened and worn by rough
weather, but whose interior is richly green, so do I navigate my
approach to the banyan in the jungle.

They call this tree the 'religious fig-tree', and the name suits
it.

To begin with, every tree is religious, since the trunk forms a link
between earth and heaven, constantly aspiring to the light, and the
foliage is a globe of green from which blossom springs and from
which fruit falls, and round which the seasons turn according to
the stars.

But this tree, thrust into the blue in the full power of its metallic
leaves, remembers the cool freshness of its first deep sources,
regrets its greatness and longs to return.

And from its outer branches it drops a lead-line. The rope
swings in the air with a tuft of red roots at its end and as soon as it
has touched bottom takes hold, becomes a beam, a flying buttress,
a bridge, or the roof of a mountain cave. And the life of the
pontifical tree passes over.

H

With raised arms it gropes on the walls of future heaven, its multiple steps stride across time. Its traces follow it, the acts it has accomplished are still standing and surround it. Its immortality is there to see like a tangible truth.

And the tree is a family, a tribe, a people, a temple. Ancestors, fathers, children, husbands and wives stand hand in hand and serried side by side, bequeathing one another the burden of glory. The love they bear each other makes an arch full of sap, crowned with the life of leaves, flowers, berries, nests, the song and flight of birds, and all overgrown with a profusion of starry liana.

And the banyan is the inverted reflection in the lake of illusion, of the supreme Brahma, whose roots plunge into the heavens, while our world and all the others nest in its eternal branches.

21

I had to leave Munikereti and Swami Ananda—discipline there remained too lenient in spite of my insistence, and although I wanted to remain ardent, I was becoming lukewarm. Moreover, my companions went on serving me in spite of my protests and I was eating twice a day and very nearly putting on fat.

I had met Sadhak Bhairab Sharma three times. Three times he invited me to follow him, and the third time, I did.

The first time was at Rishikesh. He was one of the group of holy men who came to visit me as I was passing through on my way to the Source. He took me aside and said, 'For several years now I have been following the Way I was led to by a good teacher. If I have found anything there, you are the one I should like to entrust it to—not as a teacher to his disciple but as friend to friend. There are powers in you of which you are not aware. It only requires an accident to reveal the science that is in you without your knowing it. I should gladly be that accident. I feel correspondence between you and me.'

I looked at him. Moon-faced and big-eyed, with a lion's mane; discreetly polite, almost shy. Small in stature, with puny arms and legs, and crooked nails on his fingers and toes; livid and smiling, he looked as if he had just come out of the ground. 'Perhaps,' I thought, 'it is the correspondence of the dissimilar.' I thanked him and said, 'I'm sorry, I'm leaving tomorrow and I don't know where the roads will take me.' 'I shall see you soon then,' he said, 'for they will bring you back and I shall be waiting for you.' Whereupon we parted.

The second time we met was during the last stage of the pilgrimage between Tehri and Narendranagar on the third day of the monsoon. I was taking a short cut downhill in thrashing rain. I was astonished to come face to face with someone at a bend in the path—indeed, I had nearly knocked him over. I was even more astonished to recognise the person I had bumped into. It was he, his mane dripping, looking like a root risen from under the earth. He was smiling. 'I was sure I should meet you,' he said, 'for I dreamt of you last night. Nevertheless, our friendship is not for today. I am going up to the hills to keep a vow. In a month's time I shall meet you at the temple at Rishikesh.'

He did not seem to doubt for a moment that I would keep this appointment tossed to me, in passing, in a downpour of rain.

He had reckoned rightly. Discouraged at having had to grope my way without firm guidance, I now deserted my cell and went for more and more walks. That day, my steps took me to Rishikesh, which is half an hour's walk up the river. To my surprise, I saw him coming along the road towards me. His eyes were brimming over with pleasure. 'Brahma-Chari-Jee-Shantidas,' he called out to me, 'I was expecting you. It shall not be said that a European doesn't keep his word or that he forgets the appointed hour.'

Now we had not fixed the hour, but the month.

'Your hut is ready,' he went on. 'It is beside mine, on the bank facing the Holy Waters.'

*

And indeed, on the high bank, not far from the temple, the two huts stood side by side.

A hardy hedge enclosed the grassy space round them so that we could do our exercises without being seen, while nevertheless having a view down on to the pebbly beach, the river, and the cliff and jungle beyond.

The huts were made of clay and wattling composed of branches and bamboo. They were thickly thatched. Mine was a little lower. A big pumpkin was ripening on its roof.

And there I lived till the end of the rainy season.

22

First of all, it was given me to have a surfeit of fasting. This was so much to the taste of my new guide as a preliminary that he offered to accompany me on the trip. Day after day we dried up in front of each other. He shrunk rapidly, and his head started shaking. I admired the inflexible willpower, the vigilance, the cheerfulness and the unfailing courtesy of the frail little man. The ordeal he was enduring in my honour obliged me to him.

On his advice, I also took up silence for the duration of our fast. I am not inclined to be talkative by nature, so giving up speech cost me nothing. I was very surprised at the benefit I immediately gained from it. It enabled me to gauge how much we unwittingly lose by dispersing ourselves, how much of our substance a futile word carries away. The silence of the mouth gains thought and the heart. Inner life takes a peaceful turn and gravitates more freely. Things and people are seen as through a glass. We draw back; go up a flight; the hollow we have created resounds.

When we had not eaten for two days, he said to me, 'Don't let yourself be oppressed by fasting—don't let yourself be humiliated by it. Raise your heart and head. Purification by water and control of breathing will help you to do so. There lies all the difference between the person who is suffering hunger through misery and the one who is fasting for his deliverance.'

Indeed, my shoulders were beginning to drag on the sinews of my neck, my throat was tight, my heart would sometimes miss a beat and sometimes accelerate; my breathing was feeble and in the full heat of the sun I would break into a cold sweat.

But my venerable friend's words, and the sight of him, uplifted me. I noticed that the emptiness of my belly left the field free for breathing exercises, that I was holding my breath much better than usual and that I could widen and deepen the intake provided my attention to it never failed.

Every quarter of an hour I drank the life-giving water of the Ganges. I was animated by a happy fever. At night, I slept no more than two or three hours and during the day I no longer pined. I had ceased to waste away. This is how, by persistent watering, one can make plants grow in ground glass and thrive on water, air and light, without any contact with earthy manure. This burning of water only is life in its pure state. When images no longer seethed in my mind, I thought myself purified.

We returned to a normal diet, taking rice at midday and in the evening a bowl of milk and a mango.

When Brahmin Bhairab Sharma had finished preparing the meal, he would turn towards the south and scatter a handful of rice for the spirits of the dead and throw another towards the north for the spirits of light. And the Gods and the dead would come down in the shape of crows to taste his offering and commend it with loud cries.

23

As for meditation, my venerable friend described to me how vain the attempt was to think of nothing. It is an undertaking well beyond the strength of a novice.

Even the divine Rama Krishna, who at the age of six was visited by mystic visions, succeeded in thinking of nothing only later in life, after meeting Tota-Puri, the ascetic.

Till then, Rama Krishna had lived with the goddess Kali like a son with his mother and rather like a lovelorn suitor, calling to her on the terraces of the temple, singing and raving for her.

But Tota-Puri, the old ascetic, made fun of his visions and called them childish, much as a hardened old sinner might have done.

And one day, when his disciple had been raving at length, he picked up a shard, pushed it in between the young saint's two eyes till it hurt and shouted at him, 'Meditate on that!'

And Rama Krishna at last entered bliss in its plenitude without any image whatever.

'So, far from pushing every image aside,' concluded the Sadhak, 'try to set one up and to leave it full scope within you. Take such an image as you can fix yourself in entirely.'

'The cross.'

'Yes, take the cross.'

Thenceforward, I advanced rapidly along the path traced since my childhood and worn by the feet of my forbears and along which I might hope the Saviour would come to meet me.

For meditation, I surrounded myself with incense, in whose perfume nothing persists that has any bearing on taste or desire.

24

> 'The aching spine is the upright post,
> The bone of the shoulder the arm of the cross
> That thought has put together with its timber.
> The nail of the scroll pierces my brow,
> A last cry relieves my darkness,
> My bleeding heart is the body of the Lord.'

*

Now he feels the cross growing in him and in the hollow of his hand the nail sprouting like a bud.

25

I think I am now approaching the fields of heaven; I feel myself surrounded with sweet perfumes and music never heard before. I walk on stones as if they were clouds.

'Don't believe in it,' says the Sadhak, 'don't believe in it. These are only illusions of the senses, but let us rejoice, for it is a sign that something is on the way.'

I now fill the 'smallest measure' without suffocating.

I asked my friend to observe the fact this morning. He rejoiced and praised me for it—'You are not a novice any more, you are a sadhak now. The measure is small but it is already a yogi's.'

He gives me the order not to try to push myself beyond it, but to stick to it for several months. 'If you force yourself too much, an accident is to be feared.'

26

Consequently, I took care not to force myself, but the accident happened all the same.

It was an image so fleeting as to be scarcely perceptible, but it came back again. I brushed it away as one brushes away a fly but it came back again and stung me to the blood.

Then I had something like an epileptic fit. The dam that act by act and refusal by refusal I had built up over the years suddenly broke and I was overwhelmed.

Every girl I had known more and otherwise than I should have done came back to me. They came back one by one, or, rather, several together, mingled brazenly.

Those I had once cherished in every detail were restored to me, not in dreams, but to my waking eyes, in the fullness of their flesh and more than naked.

Through fasting and nights of waking given up to devotion I had acquired the power to make images more concrete than stone and more lively than a snake. Looking at them brightened them as when a beam of sunlight breaking through a storm-cloud strikes the grass on the crest with such dazzling light that it hurts the eyes.

My sight clung to the form from the front and from the back, below, inside and through and through.

And there were no longer, as in the days when my pleasure was my only law, there were no longer the natural limits to my frenzy that fatigue or diversion or disgust impose. There was no longer the limit of satisfaction. There was no longer the limit of decency, or care about demeanour or horror of the coarse gestures that spoil pleasure. There were no longer the delays that a refined lover can contrive to prolong the anticipation of pure pleasure. There was no longer the veil that a tender impulse, a genuine desire of good for the object of desire can cast over sin, there was no longer freedom in my lewdness or the old unconstraint. There was only the boundless tumult of a tempestuous sea or a tower ablaze with raging fire.

On this background there appeared the tear-stained face of Princess Bhubana. I cried out to her, 'Don't weep any more! It's I, the real one, who loves you. The other one, the idiotic sage who left you, was only a mask and a disguise.'

I supposed that she must now have returned to her house in the plain which was not far away, and said to myself, 'Since what she loved in me was the full-blooded *demon* . . .'

And I mulled many another vulgar thought.

*

I could no longer meditate. Instead of the cross, some other image would arise and bind me to it with hellish attachment.

*   *

At night, I no longer dared to lie down, even on the ground with the stone from the Ganges under my head—the inside of the hut was feverish with sleeplessness and mosquitoes.

I went and leant against a jamb of the ever-open doorway and breathed the warm wind. A moon of blood hung heavily over the black jungle. A cloud slobbered in the disastrous sky. Beyond the livid beach the everlasting growl of the river filled the night. I went down to it. It is icy in all seasons. I plunged in, up to my throat in the strong, nocturnal current. The terror and the power of God seized all my flesh with the chill of the mighty waters and their superhuman roar. I went back into my hole, my teeth chattering, and fell into fitful sleep till the vacant hour of dawn.

27

At this point, my venerable friend took to eating grass. 'It is holy grass,' he explained to me as he browsed. 'It is very rich in magnetic power.'

I thought the moment could not be better chosen for myself to eat grass like a cow. Perhaps this food, as unheating as I could wish for, would give me cooler blood and the desirable serenity of cowhood.

But I was mistaken, for I ate grass like a bull. It is quite mistaken to think that poor, tasteless, indigestible food will calm irritation of the senses.

As for the magnetic power of the holy fodder, I had enough and to spare, for my skin thrilled all over with electric current and crackled with sparks like the fur of a cat in heat.

28

I tried long walks. I set off in the small hours with nuts and brown sugar in my handkerchief. Since the flesh was willing but the spirit weak, I tried to use up my over-abundance of bodily strength on the stony tracks.

But the swarm of gadflies follows the galloping horse and buzzes persistently in his eyes and ears.

I returned to the tunnel of light in the jungle, above Muni-kereti, where I had not long since been in the habit of going to look at the waterfalls and the green and the shade.

But the jungle was full of beasts at rut and smells of musk and tuberose. There was women's laughter in the streams, four women in the white cascade, others in the liana, others tumbled with their legs up in the fig-trees and another one lying on the top of the cliff in a beautiful flesh-coloured cloud.

29

I tried the graver. Every time my thought deviated, I stuck it into my thigh up to the handle. The flesh bore the stabs without flinching. I even believe the bitch enjoyed it in the end; it was one way of relieving herself for lack of another.

30

Without any doubt I should have finished up in madness, as so many other seekers after saintliness had done before me through knocking at the wrong door, had I not, by a grace for which I thank God, discovered the real remedy just in time.

The real remedy was to want to be cured of my lack of will.

How the will manages to make up for its own lack is a mystery that it is better to enter into in practice than throw light on by talking. I believe that the will only has to become aware of its own weakness in order to heal itself. And the Hindus very rightly say that every sin springs from ignorance.

I perceived that during these troubled days and nights I had not wanted to put my house in order. I had simply desired to do so and entertained that desire along with many other conflicting desires. But a longing for order cannot bring about peace, it can only clash with longings for disorder, and by the very clash, add to disorder.

The limits nature imposes make swift work of establishing order even where there is no desire for it. For that reason, a mere brute sins less than a man torn between his good and evil desires.

In vain had my longing for order dictated resolutions and bullied my body in order to appear important, it had not become the will for all that.

The will belongs to the race of rightful princes who have only to flicker an eyelid to be obeyed. To conquer, all it has to do is be born.

It has no battle to fight, for no desire can compete with the will in its own field. As soon as the will appears, desires vanish like bad dreams at waking.

One morning, pale and drawn like a convalescent, I took up the lotus posture under the mango-tree. And the tree sang glory to the delivered soul.

31

The great danger of yoga is that it makes a man grow.

Now a tall man can fall just as easily as a small one but he falls from a greater height. When a tree grows and spreads green in the sky, that is the time that the root is spreading black under the earth.

The righteous man keeps his evil behind his back and under his feet.

The righteous man keeps everything in its place. Low things serve him as a foundation and a resource.

But the submission of low things does not wipe out their existence. Inhibition irritates them, on the contrary, and repression gives them explosive force. The orgies of the Sybarites were never troubled by the demons and the swine that tormented St. Antony in the desert.

The saint shouts more loudly than sinners 'great is my sin' not out of humility, but out of terror of the danger he knows only too well.

For every enlightened thought that illuminates the righteous there is a demon lurking underground.

The depth of a man is the measure of his place in hell, dug to size and ever ready to receive him. At every step he takes he may stumble and fall headlong into it.

The man who is sublime without depth is not a saint, or a sage or even a man. He has no roots and no substance. Oh! Oh! What a wise image and a pious lie!

The emasculated can hope for nothing from yoga, no more than can the dissolute. The roots of the former have been cut, those of the latter have rotted. Whole and unblemished must be the sacrificial horse. So, likewise, must be the virility of the penitent, and as intact, constant and active as his chastity, since it is their impact on each other that generates magic powers and the saintly elevation of the soul.[3]

32

Full of courage and joy, then, I harnessed myself to yoga again. But another accident was lying in wait for me.

I was coming up from the river at dusk when, unexpectedly, I thought of my mother and wept.

I was like a child whose soul is suddenly cracked and flawed by the discovery that death exists, obvious as the moon, hard and real as the stone at his feet. And he weeps for the old gentleman he saw once, two years ago, and who died last year, they said. And that girl who was laughing, she is dead too, and he can still hear the sound of her laughter like the water in a brook, but a brook that comes from nowhere and falls for ever into nothingness.

Likewise, for no reason at all, I remembered that my mother would die and that I should never see her again.

And what good has come to her from me for all the good she wished me? How have I rewarded the hopes of the mother who reared me with such delicate care?

Would today's nakedness and poverty please her more, if she knew of them, than the rebellion and scandal of other days? And Bhartriheri's verse came back to me:

'We have not enjoyed our pleasures:
Our pleasures have enjoyed us.
We have not done penance
But our sorrows have punished us.
Time has not passed: our lives have passed.
Ambition has not grown old
In us grown old.
We have been the axe that felled the tree of our mother's youth.'

I thought of my brothers, of our beds side by side in the nursery, and our long, heart-to-heart talks in the privacy of the dark, and then the shared wonder and delight when we discovered an idea or a book. I remembered the friends we had in common and the poets and heroes we admired with the same love; the dreams we cherished for the future, dreams that were a bond between us, and, later, of our love affairs, linked but always pure of jealousy. There were three of us, sufficiently different and alike for our agreement to be perfect. And now we are scattered over three continents, but how much more apart in our inner ways!

Drawing in my breath, I let out the high modulated call which was our rallying cry and it rang out just as it used to behind the house, in the garden or the vineyard or the familiar wood or in the crowd in the streets or on station platforms or up to a window, at night, when we returned unexpectedly from our travels. And my cry tore the solitude, fell back on me and pierced me.

I thought of my friends, those who spoke the same tongue as myself, and to whom I confided my secrets, my heart-ache and my hopes. In what language could it be understood now, and by whom, my soul now utterly alone, hardened with dry silence, lonely unto death?

I remembered the girl I loved for so many years for nothing. I remembered the look she used to have, her eyes lost their outward looking when they met mine; I remembered her hand that used to melt into mine, her intact body and the heart she used to have, and the dress and the ribbon that lasted one day, the girl I hadn't seen for twelve years; gone another way, married far away, mingled with others, become someone else. I must have been remembering her as we think of the dead with the faces they had when alive, with their warmth and the voices they have no more, for we should shudder with horror if the earth that hides them gave them up to us as they now are.

I thought of the country where we lived when we were small. It fitted our smallness. A country of pale sunlight, grey men and poorish plants, whose summer stars were clumps of wild violets: a fitful, shifty climate, the sky intimate and inclined to pity; the houses of good stone built to defy sea-wind and rain and lined with carpets and furniture—where the mean ugliness of towns and their pointless busy-ness, their meaningless habits and comforting vanities are contrived to shelter our souls from the unbearable greatness of the world and the fire of truth.

A demon had taken possession of me, but unlike the one from which I had just freed myself, was not honest enough to show his demon face or to speak to me improperly. This was a maudlin, wheedling demon. He drooled out his confidential banalities in a mournful tone. If I had gone to the trouble of writing to his dictation no doubt admirable poetry would have come out of it and I could have passed it off as my own.

The fact was that during meditation I could no longer keep my eyes fixed and dry nor my heart pure of all memories and all melancholy.

Besides, the rain kept pouring. The washing no longer dried, the air was stagnant and heavy with depressed smells. My friend had also grown tired of looking at the cloud from underneath. But when we went up the mountain, the summit was muffled in mist. The mountain shelter smelled of mould and scorpions and insects filled it with sly, scraping sounds.

So we climbed down again, step by step through the glaucous, steaming gulf of the forest. Behind us, the hollow, broken roar of the tiger. The song of the birds and the screaming of the monkeys ceased and the silence fell heavy as before thunder. The tiger followed us for some time; perhaps the golden fern of its body would spring up between two clumps of bamboo.

A curtain of rain fell, then rose. The birds and monkeys took up their chattering again.

I took advantage of the great, green calm between the showers to tell my friend about my homesick heart-ache and my confused longings. The holy man looked surprised. He was sorry to be so stupid but he was unable to understand what I meant.

It was very aptly said, with a suitable air of stupefaction. No affectionate consolation could have comforted me at that point. I was grateful to my friend for doing me the honour of completely failing to understand the state I was in. I felt the only thing left for me to do was to put order into my inner life so that it would not belie my outward appearance and that I had to achieve another sort of sincerity than oh-so-easy confessions of weakness.

I came back to my hut in gladness of heart.

<h2 style="text-align:center">33</h2>

But I had scarcely settled when a third demon called on me. This was a soft one.

He took advantage of my lying down for the night on my mouldy mat with the stone pillow, to glide into me.

And the memory came to me of the sheets at home—the sheets that years of wear and laundering and lying on the shelves of fragrant presses had worn delicate as young leaves or petals. And I thought to myself that I should like to stretch out once again— even if only once—in linen sheets.

And one after the other, I remembered the things that suddenly I felt it would be good to enjoy again, even if only once. And a hundred times in succession I longed for each of them, for just once. In consequence of which I lost the sleep which would have made my mat a place of bliss.

But towards morning, I pulled myself together and said, 'Oh comfortable God seated on the generality of people while from your arse oozes the satisfaction with which our world stinks; Prince of Capitulations, Father of Compromise, Mirror of Ugliness, Source of Inexhaustible Pettiness, is it all in vain that I have hated you so valiantly, and have I brought my body to the bank of this holy river only to render you the homage of my thoughts?'

34

I was washing my linen in the river when, raising my head, I saw a low cloud brushing the wide, stony beach and a group of monks running. The wind was lifting their saffron robes and baring their black legs.

The first was blowing into a sea conch; some others, in a group, were carrying a big bundle which they tugged this way and that as they ran; the others, talking and shouting, straggled after them over the shingle.

They hurried to a flat-bottomed boat which had just unloaded stones. When I went closer they had already heaved the bundle on to the boat. It was wrapped in a blanket and tied with ropes. A man's head stuck out of it.

Two monks were holding by the ears this head that kept wanting to rest on its knees. The two knees emerged naked from the heap formed by the bent body, the knees on the shoulders, the heels on the behind. From a hole in the blanket some sand and gravel were trickling.

The head thus upheld kept its eyes shut and its mouth open, revealing hideous teeth, and the grimace of death split the layer of ash with which Sadhus smear their faces when they are alive.

The escort pushed off from the bank. Sudden rain spread a white sheet over the face of the river when the boat, caught in the current, began to revolve at the bottom of the cliff opposite, under the hanging jungle.

Then a clamour arose and the bundle disappeared.

The boat came back to the bank downstream; sunlight wove its rays through the threads of the rain and the monks, standing, blazed like tall flames.

The corpses of ordinary people are burnt on the other side of the town. Only their ashes are thrown into the Ganges. So the man whose funeral had just taken place must have been a man of exceptional merit. He was a Great Delivered One.

35

Now the monks are bathing, for service of the dead always ends in purifying ablutions. They shower themselves, rinse their mouths, gargle, and spurt the water out at a distance. They talk loudly and laugh.

Oh the holy laughter! The dignified funeral! Oh, the perfect celebration of detachment!

The soft demon that had weighed on me during the night fell into the Ganges with the remains of the Great Delivered One.

36

Having escaped from the slough of temptation, I entered a desert of sand and rocks.

In losing the thread of my desires, I had also lost all reason for living. I had displaced my inner centre and no longer knew where I was.

I was not even very sure who I was, for I was not a man, but a shadow, a vacant form, a wandering ghost.

'Know thyself . . .', or, rather, 'He that loseth his life for my sake shall find it.'

Yet I kept working patiently, gnawing the daily exercises like some insect preparing for the end of a winter of which he will not live to see the first days.

And in the middle of this desert, I met what I had never in my life sought, what I had never done anything to deserve, what I was furthest from expecting to meet: happiness.

37

Yoga is learning to live and die as one learns to play an instrument.

It requires the same part of patience, technical skill, convention and artifice, and the same part of inspiration.

The musical instrument is the living body, the inner body, unknowable by those who look at it from the outside or those who kill it to open and dissect its visible remains.

The strings are the conducts of vital breath and magnetic fluid.

The fingers that strike out the notes are the reflective attention brought to bear on it.

Freedom comes from mastery and belongs to it.

The melody is the joy of the player and of those who have ears to hear.

Whoever can play that music not only has joy, but becomes joy.

*

The blending of the tones, the consistency of the outlines, the harmony of the whole, the unity in the contrasts, the symbolical value of the shape make the beauty of an object.

The beauty of an object makes the joy of the eye.

The play of appearances makes and unmakes beauty; the spirit receives from it a reflected joy.

Whoever wants this joy for himself must himself make the beauty of the object. He must blend the tones, trace the outlines, bring the different parts into harmony, conceive the work and bring it to fulfilment. By expressing himself in the work, he himself enters beauty and the beauty of the form becomes a joy within him.

But as soon as the work has come out of him, he comes out of it, and whether he admires or forgets it, he returns to his own darkness.

If he wants all the joy to enter him, if he wants to enter wholly into joy, he must do the work inwardly, out of his own substance. Let him contain himself and draw his own outlines, bring the different parts of himself into harmony, unite his contradictions, blend his tones, know that he himself is a living symbol of the One; let him be the beauty of his own work.

One only knows what one has made; let him know himself by making himself.

And let him enjoy the joy he is.

*   *

None can take my joy away—it belongs to me as the red to the ruby.

Light of the jewel playing in the light.

The pleasure of this body is a froth on the surface. It soon loses its savour, a trifle spoils it, its very excess turns into sickness, its duration into weariness.

The suffering of the body is deep unto death.

The suffering of the soul lies on the surface; the body suffers in its stead.

The soul in its depths unto infinity is joy.

38

Was I born of myself? Did I bring myself up? Is there anything in my mind I could enjoy if I had received nothing from anyone? Did I invent writing? Did I bring the various arts out of myself? Could I even think if I had not learnt to speak among men? Could I pray to the Father in secret if there were no human family anywhere?

If I shut myself up for ever in my secret joy, shall I be paying my debt to others?

Now is the time when, alone, free, poor, naked, comforted with wisdom and pleased with my self, I must take care not to have left like a thief.

*   *

I had heard the song of the Sirens from afar. But I had had myself tied to the mast beforehand. I had stopped up the ears of my oarsmen with wax. My deaf boat held to its course and passed. And so I escaped the danger of infinite happiness. My whole life long I shall regret that I did not let myself drown in its waters. The reason for my journey won. The reason for my journey was the return.

For I had not left my country in order to seek adventure, but rather to be set free from adventure and to find a way out of our disorder.

The customs and mental habits of Europe, which inevitably and logically result in deserved upheavals and suffering and ugliness of all kinds, constitute a system which some uphold deliberately and from conviction, others by acquiescing to it. I felt an urgent need to escape from it.

The problems that we have—mechanisation, enslavement to convenience, lucre, violence and irreligion—were solved at one

stroke by Gandhi. It seemed to me that it was my duty as a man
to go to him. I intended, when I had finished my apprenticeship,
to shut myself up in some Indian village and serve a general
human cause there till the end of my days.

I had undertaken my journey to the Source in order to steep
myself in the traditions of the country I wanted to settle in and had
undergone the ordeals of my noviciate in order to strengthen
myself and prepare myself for the task.

But now a new thought was dawning in me: that by virtue of the
very principle of Swadeshi, the place of a Western disciple of
Gandhi was in the West and his task to sow the seed on the most
thankless of all ground—at home. For nowhere was the need for
his teaching greater.

I knew that to give this truth life it was vain to expose it in
books, or scatter it abroad in lectures or public speeches; vain to
theorise and polemise, vain to appeal to those who read out of
curiosity or to the crowds that howl and forget. For it is the kind
of truth one can learn only by living it and teach only by helping
someone else to live it. It was therefore necessary to found a
brotherhood of men, bound by solemn vows for the purpose of
learning to live together according to the rule of Ahimsā and
Swadeshi; and to make this community thrive in poverty and hard
bodily labour and grow in independence, while nevertheless subject to civil law, so that in time and with the help of God, without
preaching revolt or forcing destiny, it would transform the life of
the peoples from within, eliminating bloodshed and revolution and
the endless chain of wars.

With deep emotion, I wrote to Bapu-Jee about my project; the
letter was clear and well written. That done, it seemed to me that
the peace of the world had been achieved.

By return of post, the answer came, 'You will do what your
inner voice bids you. But if it is at all possible, come and look us
up before you leave the Indian shore.'

39

My venerable friend has come to the Punjab to visit his Master and
since he wanted to introduce me to him, I am here too.

We left Rishikesh, where everything was rotting in the rain, for

this sky of molten metal and this cracked, baked earth. It is flat
country where rain never falls and it owes its fertility to the canals
that cross it.

                                    *

The camel drags a plough. The peacock pushes its ship of feathers
through the maize.

                                    *

At the foot of a tree we find the man to whom we have come to pay
homage. He is seated under a canopy hanging from the branches
and two turbaned men fan him. We touch his feet.

He is an old man with heavy, powerful limbs, naked but clothed
in his beard. Blind in one eye, he has the face of a bird of prey and
a crest of tow-like hair. Crackled with age and self-denial and
exposure to all weathers, profusely hairy and visibly full of sap,
he looks like the tree itself.

This spreads around with its hundred pillars, like a city. And, as
a matter of fact, the inhabitants of ten villages have deserted their
houses and fields to spend their days and nights in its shelter and
under the protection of the saint.

They live together in families and in clans, light fires, come and
go under the arches of the tree and along its galleries as if it were a
fair-ground.

In almost uninterrupted succession, baskets filled with fruit or
fried food and jars of milk arrive at the Master's feet. He takes
from them all and gives to those around him and tastes for himself.
The givers carry away the rest and hand it out to the people till
there is none left. Not one person in this revelling crowd raises
anything to his lips that has not been carried on this ebb and tide,
and every one of these good things from just anywhere has gone,
blessed by the Sage, to just anybody.

The Sage welcomed my companion. Concerning me, he spoke
loudly, staring at me with his one and only eye. What he said to us,
or about us, I do not know, not understanding Punjabi. His words,
no doubt too benevolent by far, unexpectedly shifted the adora-
tion of the ten villages on to us.

We were immediately wreathed in garlands, crowned, enthroned
on trestles and placed on a level with the gods.

I had begun by protesting, but my friend begged me to submit with grace, 'otherwise you will dismay these people and they will think themselves cursed'.

Seated and motionless, we therefore bore with equanimity the sacrificial offerings, our praises and the heat.

'This undeserved homage will be profitable to us,' said my venerable friend, 'if it forces us to consider the humility of our condition with severity.'

But instead of humility the constraint inclined me to sarcastic and rather vulgar reflections. As nobody could understand us, I communicated them to my friend who looked up at me with bewilderment. 'I am joking,' I said, 'just joking.' One must never joke with an Indian without warning him, otherwise one risks becoming inextricably entangled in explanations. But if he has been warned, he gets ready to laugh, and at the end of the sentence laughs very politely. Joking seemed to me to be the only way of getting out of our predicament and passing time.

Going back to a conversation we had started on the road, I said to him, 'You fear reincarnation more than death. But I love this world—I shouldn't mind at all coming back after death. I even think nothing could be more desirable than what you most fear— coming back in the body of an animal. A frog, for example. Yes, a frog at the bottom of a cool pond, its tongue made for tasting the coolness of the pond and uttering the laughter of leaves and water, green with life, its mouth full of bubbles and a song full of bubbles and jubilation and golden bubbles for eyes. Yes! I shouldn't like to miss being a frog at least once . . .'

My venerable friend smiled feebly.

'No doubt you are joking now.'

I declared I had never spoken more seriously. He sweated, opened his mouth to speak but could not reply. My words went beyond all the limits of sense and verged on blasphemy.

'In any case,' I added, 'there is one thing I never want to do, and that is be reborn in Punjab in the shape of a god.'

40

A mere mortal again, I sang and capered on the way back. It was
a pleasure to feel myself wedged on to a third-class bench in a
crowded train.

We did not return to Rishikesh. My friend had to go home to
Dehra Doon for the annual family festival of the Renewal of the
Cordon. Only now did I learn that he had a family and a house and
even a wife.

To tell the truth he and his wife had been living like brother and
sister, or rather like master and disciple, since they had agreed to
enter religious life.

She was a small thin woman with pale, tight lips and downcast
eyes, and she walked with mincing steps. She wished me welcome
and gave me a garland without raising her eyes.

They bade me sit on a rug and served me with a mug of milk.
A shower of flowers without stalks rained down on my head.
I looked round just in time to see my friend's aged mother
hurrying out of the room, casting all kinds of blessings in my
direction.

Then the elder brother, girded with his becoming corpulency,
his beard spread like a peacock's tail and his turban the colour of
glory, advanced. Rolling his big eyes, he made me a speech in a
tone of finality and at the end of it presented me with the rose he
was holding in his fist.

Finally, the little niece approached, draped from head to foot
in an amaranth veil from which emerged only the yellow wisps of
her hands and her triangular face with its cat-like eyes. She might
have been twelve. The awkward grace of this budding fine lady's
movements as she turned and stooped in the solemn drapery of the
ancient costume enchanted me. No doubt she took a fancy to me
too for she laughed and held out her lump of sugar to me. Her
younger brother Krishna stood back and looked at me with
thoughtful eyes.

Naturally, I made up games, and tumbled and pulled funny
faces to amuse the children. The family massed on the steps,
watched me, wondering whether they ought to smile at the sight
or let their consternation get the better of them.

My behaviour was a disappointment to them, for they had intended to venerate me with almost religious awe.

41

Hindu families grow bigger and bigger without breaking up, sons living with their wives under the roof and rule of their father. When the father dies, the eldest son inherits his possessions, his authority over the other brothers, nephews and cousins, and his priestly functions.

For the family's purpose in life, its basis and justification, is sacrifice and the need to perpetuate the five Oblations: to the Saints, the Gods, Spirits, Men and the Souls of the Dead.[4] Here the sacrificial fire is the life of the home as it was for the Romans. Thus families grow in tribes, sometimes numerous, in strict hierarchy and possessing everything in common. There is no law standing in the way of brothers separating if they want to be independent, but, actually, families consisting of one couple and their children are not frequent.

Generally, a Brahmin has only one wife, although he is not restricted to one by law. Men with big farms have two, for the sake of convenience. Only Rajahs keep harems. One wife is what best satisfies the loving heart of the Hindu, with his disciplined and— judging from what I have been told—undemanding and un-inquiring senses.

A virtuous woman must perpetually revere her husband like a god. This is what the Law of Manu[5] demands of her in explicit terms. Even if he misbehaves, even if he loves other women, even if he has no good in him, he nevertheless remains the form in which god has become man especially for her. The husband's defects are the various moves through which it pleases the Lord to test the faith of the wife. Of what worth is faith that lets itself be blinded by appearances? She must overcome appearance and keep intact her vision of the perfect husband. This mystical precept is beyond all doubt the most effective method with which one can arm a woman against the real failings of her husband.

Whatever her rank or wealth, she prepares his food for him and serves him at his meals. She assists him when he offers up a sacrifice. She keeps the fire burning when he is absent. She renders

him service by advising him. The man commands, but the woman
rules by her advice. She shines with the brilliance of her jewellery,
for the woman's jewellery signs the dignity of the family. She must
also adorn herself lest joy be extinguished in the heart of her
husband and their union remain sterile. Motherhood fulfils her
longings. Worship occupies her leisure. The verses of Ramayana,
the glory of Rama, Sita and Krishna haunt her memory and
magnify her dreams.

> 'Fathers, brothers, husbands, brothers of husbands,
> Lavish homage and gifts on women
> So that prosperity may smile to you.
> But to worship the gods without honouring woman
> Is to undo every pious act' (Manu III, 55, 6).

Never have husband and wife chosen each other in an honourable family. Taking a wife, whether by seducing her or running
away with her or asking for her, is what Manu calls 'marriage in
the Rakshasas way'.

The choice belongs to the parents. There is therefore no need
to have grown up in order to marry. One may find oneself married
at the age of five.[6]

Western people, whose sensitive hearts and sensible minds raise
a clamour of criticism when the customs and institutions of other
peoples are in cause, feel the deepest indignation at these child
marriages without love beforehand but nevertheless indissoluble.

But since we pride ourselves on founding our opinions on
experience, we ought to notice the fact that the marriage tie of the
Hindus remains unbroken throughout all kinds of strain—even
the death of one of the partners—and brings them—if not happiness, at least the opportunity and the training for achieving it if
they are capable of doing so. Founded on ritual, not illusion or
greed of gain; on ancestral memory, not on fleshly desire or
covetousness of riches; on ancient tradition, not the whim of the
moment; their union is not exposed to disappointment or doubt;
and quarrels, drama and scandal are excluded from it.

*

The Sharmas live outside the town in a modest house set in a
garden planted with banana-trees whose great leaves flash and

gleam like deep, tranquil water, and slender papaw-trees carrying high their double fruit under their plumes as a young mother carries high her breasts; and jacks whose fruit hangs green and black like shellfish and whose flesh is fish and meat; and bushes with starry leaves, and clumps of flowers in profusion; and jambus.

I have never been shown over the house although I have lived in it for several months. There is only one storey, and it is divided up into non-communicating apartments in which the widowed mother and the two brothers live. On the façade there is a verandah where I have taken up residence.

Through the openings, you can glimpse the votive lamps lit around the images. There is a ceaseless murmur of mantras or poems and the crackling of ghee poured on to the fire, and even during the night, you can hear the conch being blown and the sacrificial bell tinkling.

42

'When the guests first, then the kinsmen,
Then the servants have eaten their fill,
Let the master of the house and his wife
Eat the remains of the meal.

When the gods and the saints, men and the dead
And the household gods
Have received their share, let the master
Eat the remains of the sacrifice.

Whoever cooketh his meal for himself alone
Eateth sin' (Manu III, 116).

'A man exact in reading holy scripture,
Exact in offering sacrifice
Upholds this world and every motionless
And animated thing this world contains.

Ghee poured on the fire in accordance with the law
Rises to the sun; from the sun comes rain,
From the rain the plant and from the plant all creatures.

Everything that has the breath of life
Owes it to the air;
Likewise, every creature breathes
With the help of the master of the household' (Manu III, 75).

'To earn his bread, lest he neglect his task,
Let the father of a family have little to do with the world
And avoid busy-ness' (Manu IV, 11).

'One man in his granaries has a three-year hoard of grain.
Another has stored some jarfuls.
Another only has enough for three days,
And one has kept none for tomorrow.
Of these four householders and Brahmins,
The last is better than the others,
Worthy, by his righteousness and his virtue,
Of conquering the Kingdoms'[7] (Manu IV, 7).

'Some profound men, well exercised in the rite,
Imbued with understanding of the Five Great Offerings,[8]
For perpetual sacrifice offer up instead
The five organs of sense.
Some sacrifice their breath to the Word,
Some sacrifice their words to Breath
And find in the Word and in Breath,
The eternal benefits of sacrifice'[9] (Manu IV, 22).

43

On the day following my arrival, I attended the ceremony of the cordon. It lasts all day.

The white cordon, made of three intertwining threads and worn next to the skin by all Hindus of honourable caste, is the symbol of their dignity in the eyes of men and the gods. They are never without it, even when they bathe, in which case they loop it up over one ear while they anoint and rinse themselves, then wash it in the bath without removing it from their necks.

They renew it once a year and with it their religious and family bonds.

In the morning, I went with the men of the house to the bath of purification in the water-pool of the quarter, behind the temple.

To the usual dinner-meal were added some round fritters and puffed rice sprinkled with sugar and eaten dry.

Like the others, I had been marked on the forehead with a spot of red saffron and, like them, I had a tuft of coloured string attached to my wrist.

My venerable friend officiated on the threshold, poured the water and recited the mantra, gave to the fire ghee for the gods and cakes for the dead.

Finally, to bring the ceremony to a close, the bearded elder brother, the head of the family, raised this prayer to the shades of the dead:

'May our house grow in generous men
And zeal grow in our descendants
And never may faith abandon this house of ours.
May we have much to give, and always' (Manu III, 258).

44

My plan to return to Europe has hardened. I shall not go light-heartedly, but go I must. Besides, the opportunity has arisen sooner than I wished. By some unexplained accident, I have not lost my return ticket from Colombo to Port Said. It is valid for a month yet. Now, I have taken up the study of Sanskrit again with the help of my venerable friend. I should like to go on with it a little longer. Besides, I want to go back on foot through Afghani-stan and Persia. The journey will be interesting in itself and also present the advantage of being slow. Indeed, I know that I am not yet ready for the great enterprise I want to undertake in Europe. The trials of travelling on foot would prepare me for it. I shall go to Jerusalem and visit the Holy Places, which will comfort me even more.

Things will decide for me. I have sent the ticket to the company asking them to take it back and reimburse me (which would pro-vide for the journey over land) or if they will not accept this, to prolong it till next spring. Or if that is not possible either, to book me a passage on the first boat leaving for Egypt. But if things make it necessary for me to board the first boat, I must get to Ceylon in time to do so. That is a long way off and I cannot afford to travel quickly. Moreover, I must visit my Master before leaving India, and want to. I shall therefore travel towards the south and shall wait at Wardha for the company's reply.

*   *

The suitcase with which I disembarked has been sent here. I had left it at Madurai with Gandhi's disciples, those who keep the Khaddar shop. It had been thoughtfully packed by a far-seeing friend and contained a whole outfit of 'elegant, rational and practical' clothing—tussore silk jackets, light trousers, cork-soled shoes, linen socks, a toilet case, a thermos flask, filters and a panama hat folded in four like a letter.

I begged my venerable friend to set about distributing them. Seeing that Indians drape themselves in anything whatever, that they unhook a curtain, or take a tablecloth or a towel or a sack and clothe themselves in it or else walk around in shirts and under-pants without anyone making the slightest remark, I had no doubt that several in the neighbourhood would be pleased or amused to have this brand-new finery of such a queer cut. As for the dressing-case and other shiny objects, they seemed to be made for the little nephews to play with. For myself I kept the coarse linen shirts and blue jute trousers that had already done good service on many roads. I didn't want to over-stuff my rolled-up blanket but, on the other hand, I did not care to disembark at Genoa or Marseilles in a cotton robe.

*

The dress coat was still swinging from a branch, upright, closed, complete as if the man were in it, with the waste-pipes of the sleeves and legs, the false metal of its razor-edge folds correspond-ing to the false armour of the shirt-front, the false geometry of its outlines, the calculated meanness of the seams, the false utility of its pockets, its buttons without buttonholes, buttonholes without buttons, braces, buckles, hidden hooks, elastic, all the strings that pull its scenery and support its machinery, the lapels flat and shiny like bugs or wood-lice, the indecent fly, the sinister and skittish tails.

I contemplated this splash of oil, this smear of coal on the tapestry of the sunlit banana-trees. I thought of the people who decorate themselves with it when they want to look their most stately, their smartest or most solemn.

It was a visible summing up of the funereal futility of their philosophy.

As well as evening dress I had taken with me some letters of introduction to different maharajahs. I had forgotten them for another king with whom one does not dine in tails.

Gopal the servant, padding through the garden, stops to contemplate the dress too. Marvelling admiration shines in his eyes. 'Do you want it?' I ask him. He doesn't understand. 'It's yours,' I tell him. He does not move. He does not yet understand that he already possesses the exotic, mysterious object before the desire to possess it has even dared to take shape in his heart. I unhook it and put it on his arm then place the patent-leather shoes and the silk socks in his hands. He goes off without a word, dazzled and weeping with happiness.

Gopal will never put the dress jacket on. In the first place, it would take two Gopals to fill its vertical space. The idea of possession and the sight of the object of his desire are enough to overwhelm him with joy. Sometimes he will leave his chores and run to his tiny room just to lay his long flat hand on the silk lapel. But he does wear the patent-leather shoes and makes great use of them. He uses them to sleep in. He puts them on at night when he goes to bed. Then in his dreams he takes sparkling steps and walks among the gods. In the morning, become himself again, he runs about his duties barefoot as usual.

45

I have set about acquiring some money for my journey. A rich person who lives near here, a friend of the Sharmas, greatly admired a goblet I had engraved during the halts in my journey to the Source. He wanted to buy it and offered me a very high price for it. However, I intended to keep it, so I proposed to engrave a ring for him. He supplied me with the gold and a fine, deep sapphire.

I decided that the ring would represent Vishnu in his incarna-

tion as a fish and the sapphire would stand for primeval water or
the night sky, that is to say Krishna.[10]

I started work at daybreak, after my morning meditation. It was
a Friday, a day uninterrupted by a meal.

At the point of the graver my mind went entirely into the gold.
Hardened light, seed of the sun, matter that reflects the essence
of all things, drop of the blood of things, solar species of our blood,
bond between the stars and souls—gold, inalterable as truth,
shining inexhaustibly, like grace, measure of every earthly value
and mirror of the royalty of the Heavens.

In its turn, this luminous point entered my mind. It became its
one point, the point the meditating ascetic seeks to sharpen. And
extreme joy rose and burned me.

But a moment came when I sighed, 'I'm growing old: my sight
is failing. I can't see at all.' I raised my head: it was night. Day had
blazed without my moving from my place or noticing the time.

Nevertheless, my hands had not ceased working according to
the order and the impulse received and the ring was finished.
Vishnu had entered the gold and was living in the fish, the night
sky and primeval water in the sapphire.

46

SEGAON, *September 1937*

The Wardha countryside, yellow with stubble and winnowed by
the great March sun when I left it, is now slimy with mud and
green to the horizon, refreshed with breezes and showers, interrupted by stretches of white-plumed grass that look like fallen
cloud from close up and from afar, like lakes.

This time I am not staying at the Maganvadi School. Gandhi-
Jee insisted on giving me a mark of his fatherly benevolence and I
am now living at Segaon in his household.

A whole month has gone by like a necklace of thirty pearls whose
evenness adds to their value.

The day begins two hours before the light. At prayer we sit in
two rows facing each other—men on one side, women on the other,
in the meadow if the stars are shining, under the roof if it is
raining. At the end of the space between the two rows, closing one

side of the rectangle, Bapu-Jee sits on his small mat. At the other end, the musician, fingers poised on the strings of his vina, waits for the signal. After the ordinary prayers comes the psalmody of the Ramayana of Tulsidas. The tune still sings in my ears:

This covers two lines. After that you begin again and again until time and self are completely forgotten, lulled into nothingness by the tune.

One never quotes a line of the Ramayana in conversation without immediately humming the familiar music. The metre of the Ramayana is decasyllabic with hiatuses after the fourth and sixth syllables; it is the metre of the Chanson de Roland and the Divine Comedy. From the moment that poetry is no longer sung, there is no longer any reason for metrical form, till eventually there is no longer any reason for poetry itself. When one has sung a hundred, a thousand or ten thousand lines of the Ramayana, one begins again, for the Ramayana, and all other Hindu poems, like the sound of the sea, is meant never to finish.

But in Gandhi's company moderation in all things is the rule. Half an hour later, at a sign from him, we go our ways. Each of us sets to work. The spinning-wheels hum, and when day steps on to the great scree of cloud, she finds us all at work. It is up to us to keep on the note now and make our waking hours sing in tune.

When night has come and the prayer[11] been said we can lie down where we like, outdoors or in, the girls here and there among us. There are always four or five of them in the company that lives with Gandhi-Jee. He likes to see them near him. They serve him with veneration tempered with tender concern and cheerfulness.

The Mahatma who took the vow of chastity at the age of thirty-six when he entered public life and who constantly urges his own people to live in chastity and bind themselves to it by vows, has always particularly esteemed and delighted in women 'the better half of humanity'. He has attracted great numbers of them in his work of setting free and rehabilitating the Indian people. They have responded to his appeal and fulfilled his expectations. In all kinds of hardship, in imprisonment and in bereavement, they have set an admirable example of courage, devotion and constancy.

Nowhere in India do men and women associate with each other as freely as they do here. Not even a semblance of an amatory relationship can arise between us, brothers and sisters.

One can tell a saint by this fact, that every profane thought is wiped out in his presence. As for sin, it inspires us with no longing, but it does not arouse loathing or indignation in us either. It makes us laugh like something quite absurd. The saintliness of man is an impenetrable thing; we cannot understand it in him because he is greater than us, but something of it enters into us from him and we can then see and touch it within ourselves.

47

You who have been so good at slipping round the law and smiling your way out of subjection or laughing off the advice and tyranny of other people—have you scoured land and sea only to find a master? Does freedom weigh on you already?

'I searched for a master so that he would teach me to set myself free.'

'Free from what, from whom, from what laws?'

'From the laws of weakness and my whims.'

Not without some pleasure, a man thinks, concerning other

people—'I am worth more than all these.' And if he is mistaken he does not like to be told. Or else he says, 'All men are bad', to make it clear that at least none are better than he.

Now I have often been accused of pride and it is indeed a wretched and very common failing. So why is it that I feel so much joy to think, 'This man is better than all of us', and that I am so exalted when I cry, 'I am not worthy to wipe the dust from his feet'?

*   *

On clear nights when we sleep on the ground in the yard, my bed is only two steps from his. And when the moon has risen I sometimes raise myself up to see him sleeping the sleep that is still action, since he keeps the thought of God throughout it in his heart.[12]

He is wrapped from head to foot in soft wool that glimmers like a lotus in the moonlight. His slight body is effaced by a fold in this whiteness. I hear his light, even breathing, the scarcely perceptible thread that binds him to the earth. He can break this thread at any moment: his task is done. Like Manu's just man 'he has freed himself from this evil by fire' and can 'reach the heights of light' carried up in the hub of his celestial body.

48

The ministerial elections have taken place. Out of the eleven ministers elected, six belonged to Congress. The day following the election, the six ministers arrived at Segaon to ask what they had to do.

They discussed the reform of primary education or, rather, they noted without discussion the method Gandhi advises.

The question was how to rid official teaching of its fundamental vice, which is that of all our culture, namely the divorce between practice, theory and morality.

Practice, says Gandhi, is the root and stem of the plant, science its foliage, virtue its flower and fruit. Separating disciplines is cutting up the plant.

The child should first be taught a craft, and from that stem the branches of his culture will grow.

I

The child's body should be busied, exercised and fortified at the same time as his intellect and heart.

No knowledge, no principle should be revealed to him without their point of application, their use, their connection with reality being made tangible to him.

Now, everything is connected with everything else. It is up to the educator to discover the joints. If he starts from spinning and weaving, for example, it is not difficult to spin and weave a whole history of the civilisations from that subject. The study of cotton leads on to botany, agriculture, political economy and so on.

The child should be taught the dignity of working with his hands, and from that, the dignity of working on himself and mastering his senses, which leads on to all duties and all the virtues.

From the outset the child should be made to understand the price of knowledge and he should earn it himself in the sweat of his brow. A school must be productive and self-supporting through the work of its pupils.

Boredom must be banished from school. Boredom is useless mortification by bodily idleness; it is dead science, dead principles forcibly inflicted on children. Children are the most lively creatures there are, the most open, the most inquiring on all subjects. Imposing silence, immobility, dead science and dead principles on them is not bringing them up. 'Dead' means 'cut off at the root'.

*   *

Next morning all the newspapers described 'the Segaon method'; a week later it became law.

*

Gandhi is not the head of State; he holds no government post; he is not a party leader; he broke officially with Congress; nobody has elected him, he imposes himself on nobody by force; he does not seek for support from an army or police or secret agents; he does nothing to win popularity; he has no fields, nor even a penny of his own, and lives on a plot of land lent to him; he has neither a telephone nor a secretary, nor a car, nor a typewriter, nor a servant; you can come from the plain and walk right into his room without meeting a door. At every hour of his life, he is exposed to the eyes of one and all. No one can surprise his secret, which is that he has given himself to truth; no one can snatch away his power, which is to offer advice that immediately convinces everybody at first sight of its obviousness.

He is indeed the mediator and the judge in this world, he who is not of this world; who has nothing to lose, 'who desireth not death; who desireth not life; who awaiteth the time appointed for him, as the servitor awaiteth his hire'.[13]

49

One morning I entered his room while he was shaving. Seated on the ground, his eyes fixed on space, he drew the blade down his cheek and now and then touched his skin with his fingertips to find out whether the beard had gone.

'Bapu-Jee,' I asked, 'why don't you use a mirror?'

'Because I haven't got one,' he said, continuing his performance. 'Someone broke it. That was two or three years ago. A good thing too; it taught me that I could do without it. And even *should* do without it—since there are people who cannot even afford shaving-soap.'

50

Every other day, Gandhi-Jee grants me an hour. This gives me time to talk to him about the questions that haunt me and to reflect during the two following days and nights on his answers and the new questions they raise.

When I spoke to him in great detail of my plan to go and implant his doctrine in the West, he simply said to me: 'Are you called? Or is it you who are calling yourself? Or are you forcing yourself to believe yourself called?

'Is it you who consider the thing opportune, necessary and urgent? You are right, it is. But is it you who consider it so?

'Is it because you are eager to undertake the thing, to fulfil yourself, to sacrifice yourself? It is highly praiseworthy. But is it you who are eager?

'Are you counting on your own intelligence, on the resources of your nature, on your various gifts, on your courage? If so, understand that all these will be of no use to you whatever.

'Ask yourself, "Is it God's Will or mine?". That is the only important question.'

It was enough to throw me into confusion. How can I know for sure? How can I know? God knows I believe it. But how can I know whether I am right to believe it?

Torn between conflicting thoughts, harrowed by doubt, suddenly struck by lightning flashes of certainty, at other times utterly depressed or cast into a void, I tramped the black and green countryside.

And still I walked, relieved to be thrashed by the rain, plunging belly-deep into bogs and thorns. Men and the waters had exchanged their paths; the streams were being used as roads since the roads had turned into rivers.

My thoughts went round and round and kept coming back to the cardinal points. For four days and four nights it rained. The earth brought up its waters and split into pools. Then dawn rose like silk and like newly washed linen.

*   *

The monsoon is drawing to a close. An answer has come from the shipping company, which fixes my departure for the 15th of March. Thank God, I still have a little time left.

What transpires most clearly from all this is that I must wait. The hour has not yet come; far from it. I must prepare myself painstakingly and be ready for the call. The time has not yet come for our countries either. The war that cannot delay much longer will have to pass over them; they have done so much to deserve it that it is inevitable. After that the horizon will perhaps clear. Perhaps the time will even come when those who want to found peace on the principles of justice and charity will cease to be considered as rebels against all civil law and enemies of the human race.

51

DEHRA DOON, *October/November 1937*

Here I am, at my venerable friend's again. The rainy season is over. It has left the earth soft with silt and green with thick vegetation. The shadows are hollow to the eye and dazzling light falls harshly on the fields of violet-stemmed sugar-cane, and the limp blades of the banana-trees by the canal, and the rice-field coming up yellow.

Dew makes the night and the morning fragrant. A flamingo pulls the stalks of his legs from the mud, spreads his wings, folds back his neck and takes flight. A long-tailed bird shoots like an arrow into the open heart of a tree and vanishes in the starry thicket of its leaves.

A marsh half a league long is covered with lotus-flowers—moonlight blue like the body of Krishna. A jet-black buffalo lies down in the water, then gets up and walks, pushing through the greenery a wave that rolls all the way to the bank. Finally, he snorts and comes out with flowery wreaths dripping from his horns.

At the other end of the plain, a dead tree thrusts its silver corpse into the blue sky.

The light of day would be enough and more to make me happy, but I am not allowed to content myself with it. The days go by crowded and too short with their close succession of exercises, prayer, meditation and study.

With the aid of my venerable friend, I have entered the un-fathomable Upanishads, the never-ending Ramayana and the in-extricable knot of the Yog-Sutra.

In this we are conforming to the 'Segaon method' since from our apprenticeship to Yoga we are proceeding towards knowledge of the holy books.

*

I am not good and patient enough, and I hate Too Much too much to love the Ramayana[14] as the Hindus love it.

The good in it are too good and the wicked too childishly wicked, and the strong too comically strong. The accumulation of these marvellous or formidable adventures reduces me to tears of boredom. I confess it to my shame: I am not good enough for such poetry.

But as there is no excess the Indians will not gladly go to, as soon as they start being brief, they abound in brevity. This is the case regarding the *Sutra* or Precepts.

It is said that an author of a Sutra will celebrate the economy of one half letter with more joy than the birth of his first-born. Consequently, the line of poetry turns into a riddle or puzzle

Be that as it may, the Yog-Sutra of Patanjali or the account of the doctrine and practice of yoga in a hundred and ninety-five lines is of highly ascetic aspect and hard and dense within.

As for the Upanishads, I shall never forget the booming and flashing of the maxims when my venerable friend recited them in his rather hollow voice. For the first time, perhaps, human thought pits itself against the abyss and comes out of the struggle intact and victorious.

Like the Pyramid, like the Sphinx, this monument to truth keeps as many secrets as it tells.

Oh puny latecomers that we are! Lord, have pity on us! And if we should ever feel pleased with ourselves, if we should ever believe we know, Oh Lord, cover us then with your mercy and hide us under your pity!

1. Etymologically, to discover is to take off the cover.

2. The yoga of knowledge (Gyana-Nyana Yoga) consists in *realising* the discernment of what is true from what is false. Because evil, and the very existence of separate beings, results from ignorance, salvation comes through this discernment. Royal Yoga (Raj-Yoga) consists on mastering the passions and the restlessness of the mind. The yoga of action (Karma-Yoga) consists in acting rightly with complete surrender of self-will and with no regard for the fruits of action. The yoga of maceration (Hatha-Yoga) consists in overcoming the body and through it the whole of nature. There is a fifth yoga (Bhakti-Yoga), the yoga of devotion, which is entirely religious and consists in perpetual worship with its ecstasies, its visions and graces. The system is complete. All the roads are well trodden and landmarked. Every ascetic chooses one or other of these methods according to his temperament and inspiration. Most of them combine the practices of the five methods.

3. For the same reasons, the Catholic Church insists on the continence of her priests and refuses to ordain a eunuch.

4. Law of Manu IV, 21.

5. Ib. V, 154.

6. As I have already said, their children are not more precious than ours. A

second ceremony, this time strictly private, completes the marriage when the wife reaches puberty.

7. The 'three kindoms' of the Universe.

8. The five family sacrifices to the saints, the gods, spirits, the shades of the dead, and men.

9. That is to say, some breathe only to pray, others remain silent in order to exercise their breathing.

10. Krishna—etymologically the Blue-Black. He is constantly associated with the moon, Chandra, so he is indeed the night sky. On the other hand, Krishna is the Avatar of Vishnu, the sun-god, for whom gold is proper. So much for the symbolic content of the jewel.

11. 'Prayer is the key of morning and the bolt of evening.' Gandhi (*Young India*, 23, 1, 1930).

12. Gandhi, Letter XII to Ashram.

13. Law of Manu VI, 45.

14. I am speaking here of the Ramayana of Valmiki.

VII

FROM ALMORA TO CEYLON

OR THE ROADS BACK

ALMORA, *December 1937*

Here, I am between Tibet and Nepal, on the hill as they say. The hill is over six thousand feet high, but since it carries meadows, trees, houses and people, it is the hill. For mountains are inhabited only by rocks and ice. Indeed, 'Himalaya' means 'House of the Snows'.

A wall of that house rises opposite.

*   *

From this little town, the view plunges on all sides into deep valleys. It is partly populated by the tribe of the Sharmas which has also settled in the villages of the district. My venerable friend has come to visit relatives and to look after the affairs of his elder brother who has two houses here and another higher up.

The house, which is lived in and kept by some poor relative, has given us a cold welcome. It is centuries old, unfurnished and open to four valleys. The wind whistles through it.

Last night I shared my blanket with a pariah who would have been made to sleep on the balcony for fear of his presence contaminating the room. He would have died before morning, for the stones are splitting with frost. All night he scratched himself, belched, farted, sang and shouted in his sleep and all day he has sat silent, his palms on his knees, looking at the world with ship-wrecked eyes.

*

The morning air carries us the din of a caravan of Tibetans coming down the road from Mount Keilash. They are wearing cone-shaped hats or leather bonnets with horns over the buttered thongs of their hair, and carry bronze lances to each of which is tied a bunch of bells. Their broad, hairless faces look like rising moons and it is not always easy to distinguish them from their wives who are also as massive as boulders or buffaloes. Their steps shake the great red robes that fall from their shoulders to their feet. Their boots are plated with copper trinkets and amulets studded with uncut gems; their necklaces are metal collars that clink and the silver bangles on their ankles add to the jingling.

The horses, short and shaggy like sheep, the goats trailing their cloaks of hair on the ground, all carry bunches of bells and tinkling amulets. These ornaments are weapons. The metallic sounds with which the Tibetans surround themselves frighten off demons and wild beasts during their travels through the jungle at night.

2

A month ago I sharpened a reed and began to write. Not much, of course, and for myself alone. The book is called *Principles and Precepts of the Return to the Obvious*.

It is a little handbook for ascetic tramps. As I have only one disciple who is myself, its teaching is addressed to myself. God grant that my only disciple be faithful to me. Every word in the small book is a pact I seal with myself. God grant that the other one shall not betray me.

I have collected in it the finest honey of my travels. I began the book on the road in Italy after setting out from Rome on foot for Jerusalem. I had to stop halfway. Now I have taken it up again and want to end it, before the year ends, between jungle and glacier on the edge of the roof of the world. And I shall also be taking the road to Jerusalem again soon.

*   *

This week we went into the Koomaon district. The village notables came to visit me. The visit consisted in sitting on the floor in tight rows and keeping quiet out of respect. Or else they asked questions about me and answered them among themselves, while I continued to write the *Precepts* by candlelight.

The houses are built of big stones and are roofed with slabs of

stone. The windows are framed with thick, carved timber, and
there are no window-panes. Sometimes an icy cloud crawls up the
slope, comes in through the window and goes out by the door.
At night one can pull the heavy carved shutter close; during the
day one can also pull it close and make night. One can light a fire
in the middle of the room and oneself act as the chimney for the
smoke. What one cannot do is warm one's feet at the flame, for the
Law of Manu does not allow such an insult to Fire.

The monks who live naked in the snow between the Great
Lake and Mount Keilash often make a fire but only to keep ten
paces away from it and fix their eyes on it in meditation. My venerable friend teaches me that twisting one's legs together correctly,
breathing suitably and thinking of God, suffices to keep one warm.

Seated on the paving in my loin-cloth I therefore concentrate on
finding that it is warm.

The people here are more like the country people of Europe than
are the other Indians, for they wear sewn clothes made of wool,
eat meat, quarrel with each other and do not wash at all in winter.

Consequently, my morning bath was the occasion for an
assembly in the yard where it took place. A few willing hands passed
the buckets of water as if a fire were raging, and my back did in
fact steam as they slapped the water on it. Other spectators,
muffled up to the eyes in scarves, commented on the scene, explaining that this was the fashion among the mahatmas of Europe.

3

My friend has taken on as a servant—unpaid—a young Brahmin.
In exchange for his services (which, by the way, are rather vague)
he intends to make a man out of him.

I call him 'Chotaylal', 'the kid'.

He has vague legs, his mouth and eyes turn upwards and are
also vague. His father married him at the age of fifteen to a girl in
his village who is twice as big and fat as he, and for this he loves
her.

But life, which is a vague thing, having taken him away from her,
he thinks of her constantly, day and, above all, night, and stains his
linen despondently.

'Run to the river,' his master then orders him, 'and as the law commands, go into it with all your clothes on and put your head in it, too, and recite with compunction, "May my seed come back to me". The law is kind: it is a bath in fire you need to wash yourself of such a dirty sin.'

But Chotaylal did not find the law kind, especially in winter. He contented himself with going and reciting 'May my seed come back to me' while he vaguely watched the river flow. As a result, it only came back to him in order to flow once more.

I give him English lessons while my friend does his best to make him understand the beauty of celibacy.

Sometimes, for no reason at all, he goes to bed and the fever takes him. 'Don't you think of your wife!' he is told.

One morning, Chotaylal announced to us, 'I didn't think of my wife. I thought of another big, fat girl in my village.' And he smiled upwards.

But the effect on his linen was the same.

'I fear you don't quite understand my teaching,' said my venerable friend severely.

4

I went out of the house to go up to the summit. But there I discovered a higher one, and climbed to it, and after that I saw another.

It began to rain. Hugging my knees, I made a little heap of myself under a pine-tree and waited for the shower to pass.

Then I came down again, at the place where I expected to see the village roofs. I saw only a torrent and branches.

I started to walk. It is a big country, Koomaon. I discovered valleys, slopes cut into terraces, meadows, torrents and jungles, peaks, clouds, and peaks above the clouds.

Several times, I met women carrying great heaps of grass on their heads but I did not know the language, which differs from one village to another and, in any case, it would have been difficult to ask the way to a village of which I had forgotten the name.

At last some houses came in sight and I went that way. The country people at their doors greeted me as if they knew me. They showed me the way as if they knew where I wanted to go. I obeyed this sign of God.

Following the steep path, I reached the top. A fire was burning under the tall trees and sacred banners were streaming.

There, too, everybody was expecting me, it seemed. They spread a blanket on the ground, settled me on it and regaled me with a glass of hot milk.

A little old man sat on his heels in front of me and gave me the local news. It was thus that I learned that a famous mahatma from Europe had arrived the previous day at Palyon and that many people were going there to see him. I asked him excitedly how to get to Palyon, for I too wanted to go and do homage to this famous mahatma.

He told me, adding, 'Take what I've said with a pinch of salt, because I am a lunatic number five. I haven't been out of the asylum very long. But this road will take you to Palyon all the same provided you walk perseveringly enough and always forward.'

So I stood up. But they begged me to stay because they were presently going to sacrifice a male buffalo and two black he-goats to the goddess Kali. They worship her in these highlands and the ash of the fire that burns everlastingly stands man-high.

At night, to the beating of drums, the men of the mountain, convulsed with dizziness, leap about and utter prophecies. But I insisted on leaving.

A ragged, wretched group barred the way into the path, looking at me silently. The lunatic spoke for them and said, 'These people are anxious to help you with some money.' I refused, and likewise refused a meal that the women had begun to cook for me, so eager was I to meet the famous mahatma from Europe before nightfall.

5

KOTWALGAON, *Christmas*

On Christmas Eve, having climbed by steep tracks, we reached the house where my friend was born, a low, massive, ancient house with heavily carved architraves and beams and doors.

Since there were about ten men talking and shouting in the room, and the last pages of my book were already in my head, I asked for privacy.

The only empty place was a stable which had just been white-washed. Rice straw was spread on the ground because of the intense cold, and a fire had been lit against the wall. The open door and window competed for what smoke I was not swallowing. A wick burnt in a goblet of oil. The great silence of Christmas Eve reigned on these star-frosted heights. And there, holding my temples, my eyes streaming because of the thickness of the air, I finished *Principles and Precepts of the Return to the Obvious*.

When I had finished, the fire died down. A great crescent of moon rose between the branches. I opened my missal and read out the night office.

Then I fell asleep in the straw, full of the joy of the nativity.

6

Christmas is a feast-day in India as elsewhere. It is called Bara-Deen, the Great Day. The cowherds gild the horns of their cows; in town, fireworks are let off as if for one of Rama's triumphs and railway engines are decorated with leafy branches and garlands of flowers.

My friend announced that the heads of the village wanted to give a feast and that there would be dancing, in my honour and also because it was Christmas.

But it was Bara-Deen rather than Christmas. A strange Christmas indeed and a gloomy feast.

We gathered then, when dark had fallen, in a little field high on the hill, in front of a small sanctuary dedicated to Shiv, where ten tree-trunks or so laid criss-cross were already burning, while from every path men were arriving with more. When the fire was a mountain on the mountain and sparks and smoke were covering the stars, the orchestra struck up. It consisted of only one drum and four kettle-drums.

The man who had charge of the drum was standing, tall as a black god in the flickering light of the flames, his head halved by a pink turban, the bottom of his deep drum hanging about a foot above the ground, the blades of his moustache sticking out from the sides of his mouth. He brandished his whirling drumsticks then fell upon the drum with redoubled rhythm while the four squatting kettle-drummers, playing now with their palms, now with their fingertips, prolonged his thunder like an echo in some watery cave or dispersed it in a flight of bats and owls.

At regular intervals, the man with the turban would raise his drumsticks, open his mouth like a cavern, and shout an imperious and monotonous summons to the Powers Above and the Powers Below, then release the thunder of all his drums and once again shout the unvarying summons.

Around me the Brahmins were grouped; further off, on each side of the fire, the pariahs, wearing brown woollen stuff or grey cotton, were massed in a dense crowd. Above our heads, between the bushes and trees that the ever-widening arena of firelight illuminated, a glimpse of a blue veil, a trail of ash-coloured cloth, a stifled whisper, a movement as if does were fleeing through the forest, revealed the presence of women.

The rolling of the drums, interrupted by invocations, went on for an hour or two longer while the fire roasted our faces, the damp penetrated our shoulders and the ground froze beneath our feet. Fatigue was overcoming me.

But suddenly a scream twisted my stomach and I saw, above the squatting pariahs, two knees fly up and clap together. I thought it was an accident. But it was the feast beginning.

The man who had screamed seemed to have been sent flying over the heads of his neighbours and he rolled up to our feet, his knees bent, his arms stuck to his sides, palms turned outwards, his body twisted like one of the branches in the fire and shuddering violently. Another roll of the drum and suddenly he sprang into the fire.

Three men ran and pulled him out and stood him upright. He stayed put, his eyes and teeth showing white. Then, his legs astride and stiff as a trestle, he swung forward, swung right, swung left, sometimes threw his arms up, sometimes with both hands touched the back of his head where a little wisp of hair whisked about.

Soon another, leaning forward, his jaws chattering, his shoulders and elbows shaking, dived into the gulf of fire. They put their arms round one another's necks and leapt together while the seats of their trousers, hanging and torn, shot up in recoil.

Meanwhile, others kneeling before the fire were taking handfuls of embers with which they rubbed their faces and breasts. Those who had kept their senses hurried to the help of the senseless who were now rushing into the flames or in the other direction, towards the precipice, but sometimes the rescuer lost his head too and saver and saved would rush back into the fire arm-in-arm. The drum kept raising others, driving them into the infernal dance and into the very furnace.

The man with the turban came and went freely in the tumult. Among the convulsions of these people in the throes of madness, he alone was dancing. Master of himself, Master of the game, handsome as Shiv, he danced a kind of Tándava[1] upon the disastered crowd and the raging, end-of-the-world fire.

Making his drumsticks gallop on the plate of skin, he advanced on tiptoe, bent his right knee, pivoted on his left heel, swung the drum in a circle on the grass, then rose to the assault again head high, mouth open, and pounced with a renewed growl of the drum on whomever dared resist him.

He was a great seducer. He had a precise knowledge of the working of the convulsions he was inducing. When he paused, pawing and stamping, in front of a man who seemed to be asleep with his arms round his legs and his head on his knees, it was because he alone knew what lay beneath such sleep. Indeed, the man soon raised a face ravaged with sacred horror. Then, prodding and whipping him with sound the seducer would cast him headlong into the divine storm.

One after the other, the frantic fell down stark as if dead. With the utmost indifference, their companions dragged them out of the way by the feet and poured a bucketful of water over their heads.

When they had all fallen, the seducer changed his game. He made for a group of pariahs who, further away from the fire, had, up to then, been affecting detachment and were talking and laughing together.

He placed them one behind the other. Each of them put his arms round the body of the man in front of him. In this way he turned them into a long, floppy chain with rags hanging down which, as soon as the drum had started up again, became a serpent and undulated. They sang a lament, low and dragging at first but growing quicker and quicker, and the words were:

'Lord, every fruit belongs to you
Since the world is your garden . . .'

and at the end of every line they jumped sideways from one foot
to the other. But they were not allowed to lull themselves long in
this manner. Their procession had scarcely worked its way round
the fire when a last roll of the drum, followed by a sharp command
to separate, plunged them all into frenzy. They raved, howled,
gesticulated, collided violently with one another, rolled in the fire
hugging the blazing logs and finally lay wherever they fell like
butterflies round lamps.

Happy Christmas. Thus did the great day end.

                    *   *

The mountain people come from long distances to take part in this
sort of revelry. They are sober feasts. Nothing is drunk. The
drunkenness has a higher source and goes further. Some loaves of
brown sugar are broken up and the lumps are distributed. That is
all.

Those who have entered the dance learn of it next day from
their friends. They have no recollection of it whatever. Those who
have thrown themselves into the fire have not a trace of burning.

At a certain moment, the man with the turban turned in our
direction. Indeed, not far from me, a young Brahmin was showing
signs of agitation, but his friends held him back by the shoulders
and while the poor boy was quivering like a fish out of water, the
Brahmins shouted threats at the master of the game. The latter
chose to turn away, not without carelessness and dignity, leaving
his victim struggling in the grip of decorum.

I learned to my astonishment that the turbaned seducer, the
king of the feast, clad in the glory of Shiv, was a Chandal, the
lowest of mortals, untouchable even for the Untouchables.

7

A little above Kotwalgaon rises one of the most sacred temples in
India. It is dedicated to Gananath, or Ganesh. My friend was
afraid that, being a foreigner, I should not be allowed into the
inner enclosure. But, on the contrary, I was welcomed with the

most unexpected honours. The High Priest pressed his forehead
on my feet and, when he stood up again, put flowers on my head,
for it isn't every day that one receives the visit of a mahatma from
Europe.

He therefore invited me himself to 'take the view' of the Holy of
Holies and led me into the heart of the temple where I saw the
Lingam of Shiv for the first time. It is an upright stone tapering
to a rounded top and blackened with grease. Garlands of white
flowers are piled up on the stone tables and wicks burn in oil. The
temple is half cave, half wall, half whitewashed, half reddened
with 'geru'.

A chunk of jungle forms the roof of the cave. Stone tanks full of
green water gleam down below and from above, a spring flows
through the hanging liana. On one side the pilgrims cook a meal in
copper pans for themselves and the god. On the other, the musicians blow horns and clash cymbals. The horns reach to the ground
where they twist up again and come to an end in a beak which
utters a stupefying, prehistoric, cavernous sound.

A grey monkey flashes across the green curtain that hides the
sky and the mountain slope.

8

We push on by short stages towards Gangoli, all day picking our
way dizzily along the edge of sheer valleys under gigantic, long-
needled pines or through forests of mighty oak-trees bearded with
lichen.

Pines and oaks, some radiant in straightness and benediction,
others flinging themselves apart in gestures of fury and perhaps of
pain, do their utmost to fill space and time with their multiplied
growth, for space and time here are boundless and unmeasured.

In the evenings, we reach snow-covered summits and shelters
open to the four winds, where we lie down on dry leaves.

*　　*

'You will remain silent all day,' my venerable friend said to me as
we were arriving. I obeyed without asking why, since there are
always good reasons for doing penance.

At Gangoli there are caverns dedicated to Shiv where no one

but a Brahmin may go, where no foreigner has ever set foot since the Himalayas rose. I was taken there with a group of about ten Brahmins. The guardians of the place could not tell me from the others behind my mask of tan, beard and silence.

My venerable friend explained himself later:

'I didn't want to deprive you of the benefit of entering such a holy place,' he said. 'On the other hand, I did not want to tell a lie or make you lie outspokenly. I don't think that the deception can be imputed to me as sin for I am assured that in the eyes of Brahma you are a Brahmin like us. But it is not always easy to convince people who don't know you. So I thought it preferable to avoid any discussion.'

We slid into the cavern one after the other, through a narrow neck, our feet feeling their way in the darkness and our bellies on the rock, till we reached the heart of the mountain. Then, each carrying a torch, we went down into a black forest of rock and its banyan- and banana-trees and liana of stone. In the course of the centuries, soot from torches has coated everything, and water oozing from the rock makes the dark hulks gleam like bronze. In the most secret recess lives the lingam.

Emerging from this darkness, one comes out on to the plateau again. It is carpeted with short grass and over its edge the view drops into a valley six thousand feet deep, and beyond this green abyss there rises a wall eighteen thousand feet high that shuts off the horizon and half the sky. It carries that crushing mass of pearls and precious stones: the everlasting snow.

And there, mortals of a purer kind than we live naked, finding in prayer and breathing the eternal benefits of sacrifice.

9

In Almora we rejoined the brother and lord of my friend and his family and with them travelled towards the plain.

The existence of buses and railways and their use have scarcely affected the Indian habit of migrating in caravans. The women (for whom a separate camp is set up each time in the compartment), the children, the relatives and their children, the wife's relatives and their relatives' relatives, the servants, the coolies, the dependants, the mountains of rolled blankets and bags, the bedding, the baskets filled with sweetmeats, the copper pots and pans, the water jugs, the bunches of bundles, make progress impossible and the sight of them discourages any desire to go anywhere. At night, we stop over at houses which seem to have been emptied to receive us; braziers are lit in the middle of every room and the cook—who is each of us in turn—having stripped himself as the job requires, squatting in front of the fires, smacks the dough between his hands. We camp in the same style in any station that is handy when it is felt that we have travelled enough. But whether travelling or at a halt, we spread our beds out everywhere and take up residence in stability. 'When shall we get there?' I would sometimes ask.

'Tomorrow certainly, or else the day after, or perhaps some other day . . .'

10

Back at Dehra Doon, I found a letter from the Mahant of the temple at Rishikesh, inviting me to his son's wedding. My friend was also invited. Next day, another letter came from the Mahant, insisting that we should come. Shortly afterwards a messenger came and insisted vocally, and soon another messenger arrived. 'I think the wedding is unavoidable,' said my friend. 'Besides, I am greatly indebted to the Mahant.'

Indeed, my venerable friend, having learnt from his master in the Punjab how to cure illness by amulets or by placing his hands on the sick person, cured the Mahant's wife of a heart disease—or so I have been told. There ends his 'indebtedness' to the Mahant.

We shall go. I am rather looking forward to seeing the Ganges again and taking farewell of her, green and shivery now in this light season. Also my hut with the pumpkin on the roof.

RISHIKESH

The three of them are seated cross-legged, one behind the other, on the platform of the temple. They are musicians, and they are playing, or, rather, working. Indeed, they have been working on my ears and entrails since daybreak.

The first, seated on the edge of the block of masonry that over-looks the alley and the esplanade, has a pot-like drum in front of him which he kneads with both hands, giving the sound an im-petuous pace, but the impetuousness is perfectly even and un-varying and induces an uneasy drowsiness.

The second, facing his back, aims at his neck with a straight cornet by means of which, his cheeks blown up and his eyes fixed, he produces one note, a furious, flawed note which, without trembling or weakening, has lasted for six hours.

The third, behind the second one's back (as if to underline by their position that the sound of the three of them is a single goad of which one holds the pommel, the second the stick and the third the prick), armed with a penny whistle, keeps forcing three little squeaks out of it, three little sprightly, shrill and venomous squeaks; three little stabbing, bloodthirsty, rending squeaks, three notes like a demon sneering and a dying shriek.

Towards noon, something took place in the sky that we did not at first understand. We looked up and suddenly breathed with a gasp of joy. Oh, it was true! The music had stopped! Silence descended upon the soul from above and flowed over the body like a soothing stream.

*   *

After a meal which lasted from midday to midnight, at last fed, we took the train for Bareilli where the wedding was to last ten days to the beating of drums and the eating of greasy cakes. For Bareilli was the town where the bride's relatives lived. I followed the procession through the provincial streets, con-stantly urged into the front row among personages wearing ties, although I myself was barefoot and clad in a small loin-cloth. However, nobody minded the contrast: there were plenty more to be seen.

The bridegroom was enthroned on an elephant hung with gold-embroidered purple trappings. A man with a green turban was seated on the elephant's head and guided it with a bronze crook; another, with a white turban, seated in the silver howdah behind the bridegroom, held a gold-fringed parasol, another was driving the flies off with a distaff-shaped, white, woollen fan. The bride-groom, draped in snowy silk, was wearing a gold crown from which a curtain of pearls fell over his face and above the pearls was a chain of tuberoses strung like beads.

Advancing behind the elephant was a black omnibus, high on its wheels, decorated with the paper flowers you can see at wedding celebrations in French wineshops on the outskirts of the city, and behind that, a file of overloaded vehicles of all sizes and all kinds, from landaus to the high carts in which, there being no seats, the people sit squeezed together with their legs drawn up.

In front of the elephant's trunk were the next of kin, on foot. (For a reason known only to God, I was among them.) The Mahant walked in a black frock-coat and a red turban with his cotton robe pulled up between his legs revealing sock-suspenders and black-buttoned shoes; the bride's two brothers were firing shotguns into the air and when the cartridges exploded above the house-tops they released a shower of fireworks; the cousins, in tight-waisted checked jackets and scarlet ties, dark of skin, with short, well-oiled, parted hair, looked like dashing South American brothel-keepers. One of them was wearing khaki riding-breeches without boots, purple silk socks and slippers of two colours.

We were preceded by a ragged orchestra, also on foot, their legs bare up to the top, who beat their drums with increasing fury as the cool of evening fell. In front of these, another wretched procession was carrying long poles at the ends of which hung oleographs framed in black and gold and depicting Krishna, Mahatma Gandhi, Jawaharlal Nehru, the god Ganesh, a romantic moonlit scene, Shiv and others. And in front of them, another ragged crowd leapt about keeping time to the music, armed with sticks with which they also beat time on the next man's stick, now right, now left, now in front, now behind, whirling round as they advanced. Leading the procession, one more ragged orchestra was playing 'God Save the King' on trumpets and bagpipes.

The balconies and roofs were crowded to breaking point. Little, poor girls in faded saris stared wide-eyed in an attempt to guess what the flower and bead-masked bridegroom looked like.

I asked my neighbour where the bride could be. He stared at me, unable to understand the incongruous question. Indeed, the bride could only be in her room, watching through the lowered blinds of her window her own wedding procession go by and wondering what face was hidden behind the flowers and beads.

Not till, back at Rishikesh, the procession of the seven rounds of the altar has taken place, will bride and bridegroom be allowed to discover and surprise each other.

The bridegroom forces a smile to his friends. He looks ill. He is in love with another girl. That's why his father is marrying him.

*   *

Blood-curdling screams disturbed the feast. An army in uproar surged into the room. It was the monkeys returning from a raid on the kitchens. Pulling, pushing and tumbling, they were dragging a pot in their wake and the boiling sauce was splashing out at each jerk and scalding them, and half-naked cooks were rushing after them brandishing ladles and shouting threats. Whereupon the aggressors, seeing that all was lost, capsized the pot and fled, leaving behind them nothing but black, steaming mess.

*

When we believed we had sufficiently enjoyed these festivities to fulfil my friend's obligation to the Mahant, we took the train back to Dehra Doon.

Feasts such as this are not at all rare here. Neither the Mahant nor the young bride's father are wealthy. Custom in India requires that a wedding should be as brilliant as possible. It even happens that the families overstep their means and lose their whole fortune in these celebrations. Vanity has no part in it. The show is a form of sacrifice. Pomp, like worship, like austerity, is ruled by the sign of fire. To fulfil himself, for a Hindu, is to burn.

11

DEHRA DOON

The moon. She appears like a mountain of gold between two mountains, rises clear of them, rounds herself and leaps from cloud to cloud like a sailing-ship smacking against the waves as it goes out to sea. At midnight she hangs like a lantern from the cupola of the sky. Then I lie down flat on my back on the earth and receive her in my eyes as in a well.

In remote courtyards. The drums of Kirtan are beating in her honour as soon as he sees her, my venerable friend bursts into loud prayer. The greenery is uplifted in the windless air. All the women implore Rama and the dogs all rave and howl.

*   *

The holy light of day fills my heart. It rests on the banana-trees yellow with sun, green with shade, blue with reflections; it sparkles and blazes in the flowers in the yard. In the countryside, grasses twice as tall as a man have pale plumes the colour of the mist at dawn and, higher still, tufts of cloud spring up in the tender blue.

And in a week's time I shall have been bundled from a street to a station, from a train to a boat . . . Why, Oh God? Where am I going? And what for? Bapu-Jee is no doubt right: I am called by nothing and by nobody. Why then have I got it into my head that I have something to teach to others? Oh, what an importunate illusion! What vulgar petulance and hateful pretension! It is clear that they all know what I have to say but don't want to hear about it. And what shall I do myself with the little I know? It is too much for me and my happiness.

For me and my happiness it is enough to sit on my heels on the edge of a great plain under a sky touched like this one with tufts of cloud, and to fill my eyes with the holy light of day.

12

Just as I was leaving, my friend gave me a sum of money sufficient to pay for about half my journey. 'I feel no anxiety about letting you go off unprovided,' he said, 'because I trust in God. He will not fail to provide for you during the second half of your journey.' I laughed and said to him, 'My venerable friend, trust in God entirely then, and let me go without any money at all. Since you know that He is going to provide for the second half of my journey, why are you worrying about the first?' He answered, 'He has already provided for it. I render thanks to Him for having used me as the means. I shall be grateful to you for accepting this little help as coming from Him.'

To bid me farewell, the whole family stood in a group on the steps, their hands and faces appearing here and there against the colourful background of saris and turbans. Each of them smiled with his own note of sadness. Oh, the beautiful picture that I shall never paint!

Rolled up in my blanket were the gifts they had pressed on me; from my friend, a big handspun Kashi silk scarf; from his wife, a golden brown sari 'for my venerable mother'; from the bearded brother, a Tibetan dagger with a jewel-encrusted handle which was to serve me if I had to 'cross great jungles full of wild beasts' and which did, indeed, serve to sharpen my pencil.

I have not a home, I have not a family; I have many homes and many families throughout the world.

13

BENARES, *February 1938*

I chose to go through Benares where I was the guest of the famous Hindu University. They received me very cordially and left me with a very unpleasant memory.

Since I had left Europe, I had become unaccustomed to hearing speeches on the Fatherland, Progress, Revolution, Science and the Glorious Future and discussions concerning the pedantic rubbish of Marx and Hegel. They bored me just as much as they used to do.

Like most nationalists these seem to be in a great hurry to deprive their nation of everything proper to it. I said to them, 'What no foreign conqueror has succeeded in inflicting on your country, such as breaking its traditions, flouting its faith, destroying its purpose in life, striking at its very soul, is what you seem to be doing your utmost to achieve, my young friends. You want independence for India, and greatness and glory. If you have your own way, in ten years' time there will be no India at all.'

Not far off stands the temple of Our Mother India. This magnificent building of reinforced concrete looks, as it should, like a cinema or garage. I have seen this kind of artificial idolatry at work elsewhere and know that it has perpetuated the custom of human sacrifice.

*

But a true sanctuary of India, and worthy of her, is the town itself, already very sacred, very illustrious and very ancient twenty-five centuries ago. The whole of India comes here to wash the living in the Ganges and the dead in fire.

Cupolas people the roofs. Time has kneaded the mass of stonework so thoroughly that one goes through houses to enter temples. The narrow streets twist between walls as black as roots. The city plunges great staircases into the river and the crowd there is so dense that the human heads look like the seething shreds in a boiling soup. A multitude in quest of purity. This people knows that life is a piece of linen one must wash, beat and wash again. Further on, the never-extinguished funeral pyres are crackling in the sun. Thus, no filthy, evil-smelling remains sully the earth and no tombstone is engraved with some name more vain than the ashes the river sweeps away.

*   *

Said Bhartriheri, 'The Ganges falls from the sky on to the head of Shiv, from the head of Shiv on to the Himalayas, from the Himalayas into the wide plain, from the wide plain to the wider sea. Thus the great soul, coming down and down, falls into immensity.'

14

Out in the country I went searching for the places where Buddha first preached. I stumbled over some stones in the grass; the cities to which he taught Deliverance. But a thoroughly new, thoroughly ugly temple had been put up to his memory and some Buddhist community had settled there not very long before.

A young monk in a yellow robe[2] came up to me and, seeing my cross, asked if I were a Christian, then added in a jeering tone, 'So you believe in creation, then?' and without waiting for an answer, took it upon himself to show me the absurdity of such a belief.

'How can something come out of nothing? And, to begin with, there is nothing that is a thing.'

I answered, 'You find it more reasonable to say that nothing has come out of nothing since, for you, this world is only an illusion, and these objects merely holes in nothing and disguised as shadows of smoke.'

'Exactly,' said he.

'But what are you talking about then? And who are you who are talking? Indeed, who can affirm nothing, but nobody? Denying the reality of the world in order to set against it Absolute truth is following wisdom, but setting it against nothing is absurd. For the illusion that you have nothing to set against, itself becomes reality, for that very reason. In absolute nothingness there is no more room for illusion than for reality. And if the existence of the world requires an explanation, that of illusion without existence requires two. But your Lord Buddha said, "I have not spoken to you of existence or of inexistence, nor of whether there is a state that is neither. Why have I not revealed these things to you? Because it is not edifying, because it has little bearing on the essence of the law, does not lead to the conversion of the will or the cessation of desire or to repose, or the acquisition of superior powers or supreme wisdom or Nirvana." I am quoting from memory, but you must know the passage. On the other hand, unless I am mistaken, your Lord Buddha numbers metaphysics among the sins. Consequently, instead of molesting passers-by with quibbles, you would do better to go and meditate in silence. Seek in silence the reasons for your Lord's teaching. Like him, be "your own lamp". And find out, through experiencing it, that Nirvana is not Nothingness, but Bliss.'

*

To the Brahmin ascetic who said 'Thou art That', 'I am He', 'God is myself', there was only one answer after some centuries of assiduous meditation on the self and a thorough study of it by the methods of Brahmanic yoga: the answer of Buddha discovering that 'I am not this self; the self is nothing.'

*   *

Every time that I have tried to define the difference between the Hindu and Buddhist doctrines, I have found some text that contradicts my definition.

The difference is primarily in their conception of the Atma, the Self, for the Hindus affirm and exalt it and the Buddhists deny it.

But when one goes into the meaning that lies under definitions, and when one considers the sameness of the methods prescribed for realising that content, which, for some, is an absolute that cannot be positively defined, and can be reached only through emptying oneself completely; and for the others an emptiness absolutely distinct from nothingness, then one perceives that yes and no coincide in this point beyond the reach of words.

It should be added that at some indeterminate time, probably that of Shangkar, the Brahmins may have reintegrated some of the teaching and practices of the new school and passed them off as their own. This is probably how the Buddhist community was edged out, not because of persecution, of which the Hindus seem to be incapable, and not because Buddhism contradicted Hindu tradition, but because it was a needless repetition of it.

15

THE PLAIN OF BENGAL, *February*

I have crossed Bengal, an endless wet plain of black earth, lotus ponds, rice-fields, cotton-fields, age-old banyans multiplied by the water.

Rolling through the pot-holes, ox-carts with solid wheels.

The Bengalese differ from other Indians in that they are more active and more aggressive by nature and intellectually quicker and more inquisitive. They have a certain taste for music, poetry and art which has almost entirely disappeared from the rest of India.

From Kashmir to Malabar, India still possesses wonderful craftsmen, who for centuries have never departed from the traditional canons of their art. But the young people who call themselves artists simply copy the coloured calendars printed in Europe. I have been in middle-class houses where the style is quite oppressive and quite as ugly as that affected by the Western newly wealthy. In the palaces of the Maharajahs, bad taste reaches unimaginable refinements of cruelty. Why? How can it be, in a country as rich as this in beautiful buildings, a country where every sphere of art once reached such a high degree of splendour and perfection? We might ask ourselves the same question. Are insignificance, the idiotic mixture of forms, disregard for the great elementary laws, unbridled invention and the collapse of the constructive spirit contagious evils to which all the peoples on earth will little by little succumb? Is the human race sick at the root? Or is this world-wide disease of ugliness due to some sinister planetary influence?

Not that one comes across any very great artists in Bengal, but at least one feels a longing, a striving, a hope.

Tagore and his followers respond to the best of their ability, and the old Master assumes, almost single-handed, the teaching of poetry, singing, music, dancing, drama, philosophy and painting and has left his imprint on each: it has a certain candour and a certain grandeur.

I went to visit him at Shantiniketan and stayed there for three days.

It is a beautiful school in severe, silent countryside. Languages and the grey sciences are taught there, but also music, dancing and the various arts. The classrooms are bamboo huts, full of light, scattered at some distance from each other in a fine park. With a sinking of my heart I remembered our dusty colleges, when June brought the buzzing of flies to the window-panes and we, the back-bench lyrical dunces, dreamt of fragrant meadows 'Where the grass it is so green, Oh!'

*   *

The poet lives in the adjoining garden in a house cumbrously and richly ugly.

He received me on a terrace where he was writing. White with age and illness, he is serene and royal in his whole appearance. The light flowing over his hair and his beard, the slowness of his gestures, the measure and simplicity of his language, clad him in glory and majesty. I could not help but feel his courtesy was worthy of a king.

16

When a musician here has got hold of four notes he does not
let them go from morning till night and perhaps from night till
morning. One of the four will be wrong, vicious and pernicious
but insistent, and in every repetition, fatally and inexorably
faithful to its initial wrongness, so that it will probably end up
by justifying itself even to other people's ears. But other people's
ears are of little interest to the Hindu musician. He sings for himself, and if he happens to be among other people, his song will
forge solitude for him. In any case, the others have pulled their
blankets over their heads and are sleeping or else talking to each
other or reading the newspaper aloud like a chant, or praying
aloud or singing something else. Only the singer listens to his
song and he hears nothing else. Singing is turning in upon
oneself; that is why the song also keeps turning back upon the
same four notes.

Their music is adventurous to the smallest possible degree.

The theme is not developed in the repetitions. No variations
encumber it. But a practised voice can swim under the note and
modulate freely in the interval of a tone; it can explore the inner
space of each tone.

The song can go on indefinitely or come to a sudden stop. Its
end is not foreseen from within. It goes on as an example of the
senseless infinity of the perceptible world which, being nothing
in itself, could just as well stop for no reason.

The silence that follows it astonishes the intelligence and relieves
the heart.

The finest and most complete instrument they have is the drum.
It is the voice of all speech, the *Aum* of all hymns, the foundation
of all music.

The drum is the bond between the musician's voice and his
body, between his body and the music to which it gives the earthly
consistency of the steps it raises.

The notes of the flute hang on it, looped like a snake winding in
and out and in and out of the holes in a stone. The drum gives
birth to the cry of the human voice, now rending, now raving,
now dying away.

All laments come home to it, laughter chuckles in it, desire comes to rest. The drum has them in its keeping. It suffices to replace them all.

Beaten with sticks or hands, with fingertips or the palms, it flees like a herd of gazelles, stops, takes fright, dies out in a whisper, shoots off again with the spring of a wild beast, rattles like a snake, shivers like a tree in the plain, becomes earth again. Then it swivels round and strikes the earth with its heel, flies up with a cackle like a bird, bursts into sun, thunders and strikes the mountain down with lightning, beats like a waiting heart then becomes earth again, yes, becomes earth again.

By the rolling of the drum, Shiv gave life to the elements and summoned shapes and names out of chaos when the Egg of Gold floated on the primeval water where Brahma non-manifest had placed it so as to come out of it his manifest self.

17

DELHI, *February*

At New Delhi, I went and rang a Norwegian banker's doorbell. Some friends had recommended me to him.

When the door opened, I was seized with astonishment. The fact was that this house bore an astonishing resemblance to all the other houses in which one visits friends, and to those I used to live in myself.

As soon as I entered the drawing-room, with its pale green hangings, the chairs, piano and other pieces of furniture standing on legs surrounded me familiarly.

The lady of the house entered looking exactly like herself, I mean similar in everything to any other lady. She said to me what one says in these circumstances; I answered what one answers, as if by heart.

It was decided that I should stay till the following day.

I went and took a hot bath in a bath, which completed the estrangement of my body. I abandoned my novice's robe which was not proper here, for grey flannel trousers lent to me. The lady's husband being of Norwegian stature, his trousers fitted me, so did the silk shirt, and the jacket seemed to have been made for me.

Thereupon I sauntered around the house just like any other of its occupants. Among all these useless but pretty objects, my gestures had an ease which caused me some disquiet. Was my life going to fall back into its old folds again? Am I, as soon as I get back to Europe, going to take up my personage again at the point where I left it or, rather, am I going to be taken over by it?

And we lunched and we dined, for they lunched and dined all the time in that house, and there was silver and crystal galore and, more precious than all that, a crusty golden bread roll.

It was there that money fell out of heaven for me. My venerable friend, who is a good astrologer, must have calculated at what point it would fall, for I had precisely nothing left of the sum he had given me. A friend of the lady's gave me an order for a gold locket and paid for it beforehand. I was to engrave it on the way and send it by post as soon as I had finished it.

18

Next day, I was walking along the roads of Rajputana. Sultry light lay heavily on the landscape of rubble, sand and thorn-bushes; there were neither grass, nor leaves, nor flowers in this countryside.

I had got off the train. The next one was due ten hours later, so I took the opportunity to see and touch the country. Its name means Land of the Princes. It is the cradle of the warrior races of India.

The roaring of a distant lion rent the air.

The hills pointed their even cones towards the flat sky. Crowning a mountain, barring a gorge or some dry river-bed, a rose-coloured wall broke into the blossom of its battlements.

The ruins of a fortified town stood agape on the grey shingle of this great lonely waste. A black elephant draped in green came out of a gate, sailed forward, passed me and disappeared into the distance like a man.

At a turn in the road, a little temple that looked like a cactus.

Sometimes from the dusty road a dust-coloured dromedary would loom up; a most improbable animal in spite of its apparently very real burden and its always very real anger.

Women there do not wear saris but long wide dresses hooked

at the waist, half yellow, half vermilion. They are harnessed in jewellery which also serves as brakes.

Families wedged into buggies formed vivid patchwork squares from which heads stuck out; the heads of men, women, old people and apparently legless and armless children all squeezed into a single block which receded with the thin galloping horse.

A fringed hood swayed above the turbans; the vehicle was a bamboo carriage, on two solid wooden wheels.

Back at the station, I discovered that my ticket had disappeared. Likewise, the money that had fallen to me from heaven had completed its predestined course by falling on the ground. What could I do about it? I had got out of the habit of carrying any. I refused the temptation to entertain any despondent thoughts on the subject. Indeed, all I had to do was to remember that one loses nothing by losing money, since it is of no use so long as one keeps it. It only has any value when it is exchanged for something else, and the only time it serves us is when it goes. It is of the order of abstractions, a mere conventional sign, like figures and words. It is not as if I had lost my well-beloved stick, or my calabash adorned with my emblems, or my graver—the very thought makes me tremble—or the gold locket I have begun to engrave, or my faithful pencil, or my dear little rubber.

19

To bid Gandhi-Jee farewell, I was to join him at Haripura. All the members of Congress were meeting there for a great national festival and an exhibition of the products of village industry.

I got on a train jammed with people and found a place on the luggage shelf above the other passengers' heads—a narrow place between two iron trunks. I took up the lotus position in this niche. My ten hours of walking having tired me somewhat, I rested my shoulders on my knees and my forehead on the shelf and very quickly fell asleep.

When I raised my head again, my eyes fell on the people packed together on the benches beneath me, and I saw that a good many of them were wearing the Khaddar robes and smocks by which one can tell Gandhians. I concluded that like myself they were travelling to Haripura. I even seemed to recognise one of the six ministers I had seen at Gandhi-Jee's feet the previous September. He was now standing in the corridor. As a matter of fact, the whole government was in the train. Now, we were in a third-class carriage with wooden seats. Ministers and members of parliament had recently passed a bill reducing their own salaries by half and had made an official recommendation that they should set an example of simplicity in their manner of dress, their habitations and means of transport. They had concluded by declaring that the National Government was there to serve the people and not to weigh on it—a thrust at the Viceroy.

They recognised me too as being one of them and we were soon in conversation. My position in the niche was glorious but very exposed. Anybody could ask me questions on any subject, from Shamkhia philosophy to international politics.

I was obliged to know everything and find an answer to everything, or else be considered disdainful. People were coming from neighbouring compartments to listen and consult me in their turn.

When the ticket-collector came along there was fierce competition, verging on violence, as to who should pay my fare.

One evening, in sandy countryside, under a new moon, the train stopped and let us out. A car whipped me off with the others.

20

HARIPURA, *February*

In a wilderness on the edge of a river, this town of tressed straw and palm-leaves took only two months to build and can give free food and shelter to three hundred thousand people. An immense crowd comes and visits the exhibition of specimens of the country's revived craftsmanship. There are no flies, no rubbish, no disorder of any kind. Schoolchildren armed with bamboo sticks replace the police.

All the approaches to the house where Gandhi-Jee was staying, were strictly guarded. I had to spend the night in one of the straw huts. In the morning I was able to send him a message. A man came to fetch me.

When I had made my way through the crowd I had a delightful

K

surprise, for not only did I find Gandhi-Jee again, but Segaon as well, and even the perfect silence of Segaon.

The organisers of the festival had managed to seclude Gandhi-Jee in his own home right in the midst of things. They had done so by reconstituting the familiar hut on an island in the middle of the river. And while the crowd vainly besieged the bridges, there reigned in the island the humming of the spinning-wheels and the sweet peace of the rule. Only, instead of the dreary steppe at Wardha, a stretch of water lay before him.

Bapu-Jee smiled to me and nodded, but without saying a word. For a moment I was bewildered, then I remembered and was reassured: Monday was his day of silence.

I made up for lost time the following day. He gave me a long and very comforting interview.

During the last hour, he was lying on the threshold of the hut on a small mattress, surrounded, as usual, by the pure whiteness of linen.

Kneeling beside him, I said, 'Bapu-Jee, the time is drawing near when I must go and lo and behold! my great eagerness to go home to my own country has quite abandoned me: I feel that it is now that I am leaving my country and my father for ever.'

Then in an almost exhausted voice he said to me, 'I shall miss you. So long as I knew that you were somewhere in India I thought of you as one thinks of someone who is absent, but now I shall miss you. And yet, it is right that you should go, that you should be put to the trial you are looking for, away from me. You will see if non-violence is strong enough in you to impose itself on those you live with. A lukewarm thing loses its heat when it touches something else, a burning thing sets fire to everything it touches. You will write to me. You will write to me from Palestine if you succeed in making your pilgrimage. You will be able to see the struggle between the Jews and the Moslems at first hand. It breaks my heart; you will tell me what you feel about it. But you will write to me before that and afterwards too. Now the time has come. Go.'

I touched his feet without saying a word, and fled without looking back. Grief was nearly choking me. I shall never again see his face, not a handsome face, but so much dearer than a woman's, or his eyes, like a playful doe's, and his nose that wrinkles when he laughs, never again see the whiteness that surrounds him and comes from him.

21

I went through Bombay without stopping, without opening my eyes more than was strictly necessary, so ugly was everything I saw there in spite of myself. Under the tropical sun, sad in itself, lay the mean desert of asphalt and concrete. Noise and disorder of trams and motor-cars, and all these men let loose in the street in underpants and flying shirt-tails.

*

I have all I need. The man who paid for my ticket in the train sought me out in Haripura, having taken it into his head that it was up to him to provide for the rest of my journey. I made a sincere attempt to persuade him that this was not at all the case, but he would not listen to me.

*   *

At Bombay I boarded the ship for Goa. The third-class deck was paved with human bodies of all colours, of every age and clad in every style: each on its rug. Having found one square foot unoccupied, I folded my blanket in four and squatted on it. To move from that place and that position, stride over the other bodies, lean on the rail and look at the sea, I should have had to defy all the laws of nature. A patch of sunlight kept swinging from my head to the feet of a man lying asleep, and back again. The boat rolled, the awnings smacked in the wind. Sickness slid from belly to belly like a wave. The smells of vomit, food, tuberoses, sweat and spindrift mingled. I remained there, swung and heaved in the same position, for a day and a night. I finished engraving the pendant.

22

Here is Goa the Red, red earth and red rocks, and the yellowing green of rice-fields. Peaceful splendour of palm-groves.

The purple that the women wear saddens into violet when they pass through shade.

The men one can see dragging their boats on to the beach or breaking stones by the roadside have naked, glossy bodies at the top of long legs, and look like idols of ebony. A red handkerchief passes between their thighs, a silver chain round their loins and a tiny cross shines gold against the black of their chests.

The Portuguese converted their fathers forcibly and separated them from the rest of India.

At cross-roads there are stone crosses such as still stand by the side of our old country roads, but here, lower down, in a niche in the wall, there is also the worn head of some heathen god who has been consoled with a garland of fresh flowers.

A whitewashed church stands beside the village of tressed palm-leaves.

The ancient temple on the top of the hill has been masked with a baroque façade, and at the top of the façade is enthroned the Holy Virgin, who has robbed the goddess of her jewellery.

On the ancient feast-days, the Brahmin Hindus assemble as before and pay the vicar to celebrate mass instead of the old rites.

When a man is dying, the priest is called to give him the last sacrament, then the Brahmin is sent for to recite the mantras, and water from the Ganges is poured into the dying man's mouth as it was for his fathers.

The same drums and the same flutes as in ancient times escort the wedding procession and the five-year-old bride.

There are Brahmin Christians and Kshatriya Christians who will not eat with each other. But both eat meat, drink alcohol and on Sunday mornings wear khaki trousers and sun-helmets to show that they are Christians. The reawakening of India has not woken them yet.

*

After they had landed, the Portuguese conquerors were ordered to settle in the new country and marry native girls.

They did not merely superimpose their faith, their law, their customs and their style on those of the people they had defeated, but established them within the bonds of marriage.

They were no doubt guilty of much massacre, extortion and destruction, but they have given as well as taken. They came here with their faith and their blood. They assumed risks and obligations by taking root here. Something has sprung from their embrace which is not a mixture but an alloy.

Their contribution has therefore been accepted by the land. Elsewhere in India, everything that has come from Europe, whether it be the tin roof of a hut or the palace of a governor, jars on the landscape and looks as if it had been dropped there like an empty tin or so much rubbish fallen out of the dustbin.

But the old Portuguese residence, with its thick walls washed with ochre or powdery blue, its patio overgrown with green, where water trickles from a fountain, and its paved and vaulted rooms where slatted blinds jealously shut in the shade, has its place here in the midst of the banana-trees and rice-fields just as much as among the olive-trees and vineyards of Coimbra. It suits this climate better than the Hindu house open to wind, dust, flies and snakes and the furious heat of the day.

*   *

In Goa, where great church and convent walls still stand, and St Francis Xavier sleeps in his tomb of solid silver, there, in the city laid low by fever, the meaning and the beauty of the baroque style were first revealed to me.

These façades agitated by scrolls, balusters, plumply naked statues, stone drapery swollen by make-believe wind, white-washed, rough-cast, stucco cornices, convulsed protruding marble, twisted columns, fleshy allegories whose meaning is suffocated by their carnal luxuriance, emphatic, insolent, gilded lies, bloated domes, everything that irritates us by its intrusion on our cities stamped with proud medieval grace and classic sobriety, has found its place and taken root in Goa the Red, where it flaunts its faintly funereal triumph.

Under the cupola of the tropical sky borne on cumulus cloud from which the sun darts occasional rays of bronze, among glossy banyans smothered in liana, the banana-trees with their heraldic purple flowers, the elephants arched over their five moving columns, the perpetual blaze of the funeral pyres, the ever-flowing rivers and the ever-streaming crowds, the baroque façade rises, no longer a presumptuous and ridiculous artifice, but the exact definition of the monstrous and hollow grandeur of all created things.

23

CEYLON, *March 1938*

I arrived in Colombo ten days before my ship was due to leave and hastened to put my affairs in order. I had not a halfpenny left. My passage was booked on a good ship of the Bremen sailing company. The customary tips to the crew were causing me worry that no philosophy could dispel. I can go barefoot as much as I like, that's my business: it should not concern servants or harm those who earn their living.

*   *

It formed a heap of lard and hide and was the colour of ripe tomato in parts, and in others looked like overripe, running cheese, and it was a man sitting at a table on the café terrace, a white man, that is to say, red and bluish, visibly gorged with beer and pork. And I thought, 'There!—it's them—it's us! . . .'

I had not seen a European for almost a year and a half, not even myself, for I did not possess such a thing as a looking-glass.

On a loose leaf, in pencil-strokes, I drew a hideous caricature of this one.

He noticed what I was doing and got up. He wanted to see the caricature. Having seen it he broke into gesticulations and exclamations. '*Kolossal*,' he said in German. 'It's colossally fine; you are a great artist and a true friend.' And he ended up by inviting me to drink with him.

We talked. The man told me that, feeling his age, he had just retired from business. He had spent thirty years in the island, hunting elephants and wild beasts in the thick of the jungle, not to kill them—which was too easy—but to deliver them up alive to menageries and zoos.

He took me home with him. And there I drew his portrait. A large, clear drawing, a touch of silver in the pearly shadows where I concentrated on bringing the man's original structure

out of the flabby mass of flesh in which it was buried so as to
reveal what had enabled him to become a wild beast among
the wild beasts, an elephant more cunning and savage than those
of the forest.

He gave me the price I asked for, which relieved me of worry
about money.

I sewed the sum I should need for tips into a little canvas bag,
determined not to lose it this time. There were a few nickel
coins left over which I took to an Afghan money-changer in order
to get some small change for my landing in Egypt. He gave me
three piastres for them.

And then, as there was over a week left before the liner was
due to sail, I went walking along the shore and in the woods,
feeling free and light of heart.

24

A sweet, venomous country. The sweetness strikes you first.
Flowers mask the paths into the jungle. The sickly sweet air,
warm like flesh, cloys the throat; it feels like the contact of
another body, neither loved not hated, and very soft to touch.

The human form here attains peaceful, plant-like beauty.
Poised on the long stem of the legs, the figure widens and flowers
in the shoulders and the bronze mirror of the face is offered to
the sky.

You come to know the poison as you go deeper in. The sea itself
churns up ferments and miasmas; the scent you breathe from
the cups of the flowers carries with it animal dust that attacks the
nostrils and makes your head spin. Insects you can neither see
nor feel leave whitish red-ringed pimples on your skin, and watery
blisters.

My clothes are going mouldy in the blanket; the dagger has
rusted at my belt. The two contrary monsoons have brought an
equal downpour of rain. The clammy air cannot carry the great
masses of lightning-lit cloud piled high on the horizon.

The vapour rises with the sun and the mornings are clear,
but when the sun sinks, it lets the waters of heaven fall on the
thick, slippery, fleshy leaves and the thrice-rotten earth, and they
flow back into the steaming sea through myriads of channels

between the rocks. No breezes stir the listless plumes of the coconut palms on the shore as one after the other breakers rise on the
horizon of the globe and run in to dash themselves against the
breast of the wide beaches. In the still immensity of blue their
thunder rolls ceaselessly.

Useless to hang linen up to dry after washing it, useless to
take your robe off before bathing. In any case, without its layers
of cloud, the earth would crack when the sun falls on it like
quicklime or molten lead, just as the skull and shoulders would
crack without their compress of moist clothing.

The effort of walking seizes the calves of the legs with cramp
just as swimming does. Too great or too prolonged an effort
makes the heart stop in helpless anguish. Every elevated impulse,
pity for your neighbour, admiration for things, is suffocated by
the sweltering heat. The only emotion that shakes life to its
foundations is fear: fear of cracking noises, of things that brush
you, of sounds of flight, of the sudden touch of slimy things.
Then you shudder like the flappering head of the coconut-palm in
a squall.

You can understand why this people vegetates without art or
philosophy or religion, and why only witchcraft and diabolical
dances can stir its blood.

I followed the road along the coast, monotonous with its
palm-trees leaning over the shore, and the mirrors of rice-fields,
uneven but always the same.

Yet the torrential rains, the overpowering sun, the earth so hot
that you shrink from putting a foot on it, the clouds of mosquitoes
that assail your ankles even in daylight as soon as you pause,
the sultriness of the air that the lungs can scarcely move in, are
all more bearable than the mob.

The road leads out of one village only to fall into another, and
round the pilgrim another swarm of people cluster, pushing and
jostling, grinning idiotically, asking the same questions again in
every language, calling and jeering.

I go through this crowd dumb and frowning, sometimes waving
them off, sometimes turning suddenly, which makes them flee
in panic. But the runaways rally on the bank and begin to
howl like a kennelful of dogs. In the evening, in pouring rain—
for evening and rain are the same thing—I take shelter in the

temple of Buddha. The bonzes, clad in yellow and with shaven heads, remain dumb and blank when I ask—by means of signs— for permission to sleep on the verandah of this open shelter. They make a pious point of ignoring every language except Cingalese and perhaps Pali, and I have never been able to exchange an idea with them or find out what they think, or whether they think. But never has their hospitality failed me. Presently a servant comes out with a mat and asks—by means of signs—whether I have dined.

And once, in the middle of the day, a storm having beaten me on every side, I was sheltering near a dagoba. Sitting under the roof, I was admiring the various leaves and watching them play in the downpour, tasting it with their feathers, their blades, their tongues, and glistening blue. Then I noticed that on the other side of the yard, on the threshhold of a bamboo hut, a priest was signing to me. When I had gone through the rain towards him, he was no longer in the hut, but soon I saw him again signing to me once more from inside a house further off. In this room I found a mat spread on the ground and a dish beside it. Other bonzes sat down round the room, their bowls on their knees; a black child dressed in yellow kept smiling at me. I picked at my plate of curry, in silence like the others, having put aside the pieces of fish, for I noticed that these people eat it in spite of their Master's commandment, 'Thou shalt not kill.'

25

I reach the village during market time.

With annoyance, I see the crowd moving round me. I turn my head right and left to avoid catching their eyes.

I can't help being aware of one of them gesticulating and bawling. Apparently they are looking for someone who knows English so that they can ask me the list of questions.

Finally, they find their man and push him forward. 'Master,' he says, 'these people want to treat you and are very anxious to know what you would like.'

I stop frowning and beg him to tell them that their kind intention is enough and that I thank them with all my heart. I look at them with a smile and give a friendly wave. The crowd hollows into an apse before me, a gleaming wall decorated with eyes.

There is a long moment between us. I touch my forehead in greeting, break the circle and go off.

*   *

Now that the bush and the great jungles are nearer, men are fewer and not so spineless, and they greet the lonely man from the wilderness with respect. I have been offered more tea, coffee, coconut milk, semolina buns, rice cakes and bananas than I could eat.

They no longer ask me anything: the bus passengers who came home last night have spread the news. The commentary follows its course and the words keep turning up: Europe, Himalaya, Christian, Roman Catholic. A little further on I seem to understand that I have become an Abyssinian.[3]

Then come the great stretches without a roof or a face to be seen: fifteen miles of bush streaked here and there with candelabra-shaped cacti the colour of bird-droppings, and salt lakes where buffalo lie. The low landscape gleams.

Over the sleeping waters here comes the thunder of the sea beyond the dunes; and over the other horizon the thunder of a great herd of storms.

26

At Hambantota on the edge of the salt lake, the fatherly welcome of an Indian Catholic priest who seats me at his table, gives me a room, lavishes touching attention on me, blesses me before I leave and puts the heart back into me.

27

TISSAMAHRAMA

An ancient capital. A few houses scattered in the waterlogged fields. Rain has flattened the rice stalks. The crop is spoiled.

Against the stormy sky, the roundness of a dagoba the colour of a stormy sky. It is much smaller than the one at Anuradhapura, but intact and complete, the most beautiful one in the Island, I think. A huge dome rising out of the earth, decorated at the four cardinal points by a Bodh-leaf the size of the roof of a house, with the tip pointing downwards; above this, a four-sided coffer, on top of which is a round wall, on top of which is a cone, on top of which is a ball with a spike.

The dome is smooth, black with whitish chips; the coffer and the wall are decorated with classic discretion. A temple without an opening, turning its back on everything; holiness concerns only the man who possesses it. Worship remains lateral and secondary; it takes place in the small kiosks stuck on to the foot of the wall.

The Buddhist religion presupposes such a high degree of perfection, requires such rare purity, that it gives nothing to ordinary humanity and asks for nothing from it.

It is not concerned with those who are suffering because they believe they are; it can do nothing for them. It pities them without consoling them.

It has much more pity for those who do not suffer from their own wretchedness, and in their incurable ignorance believe themselves happy; those who hope only for the gratification and not the cessation of their desires.

As a popular religion, it confines itself to an offering of flowers at sunset.

28

A yellow river under huge boughs marks the solemn entry into the jungle. Cries of relief everywhere after the terrors of the night.

Lapis-lazuli birds with red heads, birds that look black, but closer up are blue above and red beneath, with long pointed beaks which they poke into the heart of the flowers in order to drink while they hover.

Cracking of branches, whispering of rain; a monkey's tail like a flash of lightning through a cloud.

Another storm that makes the earth tremble: a herd of elephants. Contradictory vehemence of their trunks, pounding of round feet. They disappear in whirlwinds of leaves.

I have come through forty miles of the most dangerous of forests armed only with my faith in non-violence.

You must have good jungle manners and adopt the suitable attitude towards each animal.

In dealing with the snake: wariness. You must be careful where you put your feet, and prod the thickets with your stick.

In dealing with tigers, boldness is advisable. I have a copper pan which safeguards me from attack. Man fills wild beasts with a certain horror, just as reptiles and toads are repulsive to us. Animals are loath to touch us. But a cat has only to see a ball of paper rolling, to put its paw on it: in the same way, the tiger strikes with a lightning leap the fool who tries to run away.

So you can only face up to him, assume an alarming attitude, make some unusual noise; the saucepan did wonders.

I recommend the *Gloria*: it is the most powerful spell. I put a black panther to flight by chanting the *Gloria* like a village precentor.

Towards an elephant you must behave with discretion. If you defy him, he tramples you and leaves only a little spot of you on the ground.

In dealing with water: caution. The crocodile lies in the river, the shark in the sea and fever in pools. Prolonged bathing does not refresh the skin. The same moistness reigns everywhere.

Without false philosophical shame, I declare that no man ever loved life more ingenuously than I do—so I like to risk mine, even for nothing. Is not freedom the essence of life? But what is freedom without risk? Life without danger loses its savour. I therefore maintain that it is wise to dare.

*

The butterflies seem no bigger to me or more beautiful than those that flit among the buttercups in the spring meadows at home, but they rise from the ground in columns that flutter round my head and bewilder my sight.

And then, above a pool, there are two of them, as big as hands; two limp hands greeting each other, a couple, dark with light yellow tails: they tumble each other in the clammy air, let go,

draw close again, shuddering before each other from tip to tail
and tiring themselves untiringly.

*　　*

Here the jungle stays short and rough with glossy tufts and stubborn scrub. It is ground recently won from men by the trees.
The fields and the villages have gone back into the earth and the
tanks of the kings have turned into these vague marshes of pink
lotus where white grebes fish and circular trees with crests of
drooping stamens look at their own reflections.

A little crocodile drags himself up on to the bank and clumsily
pushes the reeds aside, hampered by the attributes of his ferocity,
which he cannot help. I find him touching; I should like to stroke
him.

29

After Vellavaya the mountain begins and immediately the forest
becomes high and hanging.

Trees spring up carrying their skeins of liana over the road.

Sometimes the liana is as thick as the trunks it depends on: it
reigns over a far-spread people of trees. Its wood curls like the
crest of a breaking wave.

Sometimes the tree the liana clings to is all liana itself, or root
up to the top. Then the whole thing becomes a cave, shut off with
curtains of greenery, curtains of sunlight, and here and there
a heavy curtain of rain.

Sometimes liana—or ivy—covers everything. The bushes
become nipples, the trees are the domes of temples, the huge trees
hollow mountains made of shadow.

White orchids with gold hearts cling to the bark and insects
cluster round them, for they give off a strong sweet scent.

The richness of the foliage is a joy to see. The green attains such
strength of colour that it spreads in haloes. The centre of the
bunches of leaves browns, reddens, and changes into light
bronze. Everywhere blossom flourishes on the high branches.

When you come out of all this shade, you find yourself at the
foot of a mountain under a wall of black rock that touches the
sky, and from the dizzy summit of the mountain under the belly

of the clouds flashes the white blade of a six-hundred-foot-long waterfall. It rushes under the trembling bridge I am standing on and plunges into the dark sheath of the forest below.

1. The dance of Shiv the Destroyer.
2. The yellow robe is worn by a Buddhic monk.
3. The recent Italo-Ethiopian War had made Abyssinians popular all over the world.

VIII

EGYPT

OR THE THREE PIASTRES

PORT SAID, *March–April 1938*

The engines of the liner have stopped droning: we have fallen into the bottom of a great silence which awoke me this morning. I stick my head out of the port-hole. The cold flame of the tranquil water fills my eyes; we are in port. A man in khaki trousers, a black coat and a blue turban is rowing with short strokes in a green boat between the sky and the sea. Dhows and barges are beginning to cluster at the foot of the white wall of our newly arrived ship. A stevedore, wearing a grey jacket over the azure-coloured robe that hides his bare feet, is staggering under the weight of the sacks. On the bridge of the stationary tug two others are having an argument; they shake each other by the shoulders, wave their flat hands about and their smacking tongues are going hard at it. A ferry-boat is carrying off backwards a mass of men standing shoulder to shoulder, draped and hatted with bags of coal. A yellow tongue lies between us and the high-sea, the Great Green One as the Egyptians called it. A row of fragile-looking white buildings holds back the desert from us.

*   *

I go up on deck. It has already been invaded by troops of hawkers selling postcards, trinkets and oriental fakes manufactured in the East; as well as by the fez of the Customs officers and the police. The superintendents have taken possession of the saloon and are sitting at a table with their rubber stamps, ready to examine passports. When my turn comes, my papers are in order.

'You have come from India, sir?'

'Yes.'

'Why do you want to disembark in Egypt?'

'I am only passing through: I am going to Palestine.'

'And what are you going to do in Palestine?'

'My pilgrimage to Jerusalem, sir.'

'Pilgrimages have been suspended; the frontier is closed, there is civil war in Palestine, didn't you know?'

'Yes, yes, I know.'

'So . . . ?'

'So what?'

'You are going to disembark all the same?'

'Of course!'

'What means of support have you?'

'Sufficient', I said with self-sufficiency. But he insisted.

'Our law requires me to ask you for proof,' he said. 'Show me your cheque-book, your money . . .'

'Does your law require me to have a bank account?'

'At least show me the sum of money you are carrying.'

Taking my time, I searched in my pocket, which was deep, and dug out three coins which I placed on the table.

'Three piastres!' he exclaimed. 'Is that all?'

'Yes, that's all.'

'And how will you pay your hotel bill?'

'Does your law require me to put up at a hotel?'

'And how will you pay for your food?'

'Is that my business or yours?'

'I'm sorry, I can't let you land. But wait, we'll see to you presently.'

2

As a matter of fact, with nothing to do and a pleasant smile, I waited for nearly ten hours. During that time, there was a great fuss going on. They asked the Consulate if it would stand surety for me. For reasons it would take too long to relate here, the Consulate refused.

The captain suggested taking me on to Oran, which was the next port of call, but I hadn't even a passport for Oran. Well, Dover then. We moor for a whole day there. But between here and there I shall have acquired neither passport nor money. All right, Bremen then, where we berth. But you can't land at

Bremen without a visa either. So then the captain let out an oath
which it would take too long to recite.

I lean over the rail. Below, the diver is kneeling in his boat,
his hands on his forehead, his elbows raised. He raises his
hands towards the first-class bridge, implores, protests, promises,
beats his breast, points to the water, forms a figure with his
fingers. A coin drops into the sea, he kneels in the water and
immediately reappears with the coin, climbs up again and repeats
his performance till he is out of breath. A charlatan's patter, a
slave's alacrity, a beggar's look, and an athlete's body, but bent
at the knees. Poor poor-man.

The captain comes up to me.

'Well, are you getting off or not?'

I answer placidly, 'I should be only too pleased to oblige you
but for the moment I can only see one solution.'

'What's that?'

'Since I can neither be on board nor land, you will just have to
put me into the sea.'

The captain's face swells like a cheek blowing out; it reddens,
becomes purple and spits its two eyeballs at me. Then he goes
off, repeating his oath.

Somebody tries to talk me into reason. 'Come now,' says this
somebody, 'you are bound to have some resources—you had a
berth on this ship and the tickets are very expensive.'

Indeed, I had had one. But everything comes to an end. I had
kept the return ticket for two years. That was how, after living in
jungles and caves, I came to take up residence in this ridiculous
little floating Grand Hotel full of music, sausages and love.
No, truly, I have nothing. I am sorry it worries them more than me.

If it pleases God that I should go on this pilgrimage, things
will have to arrange themselves so that I can. If not, I shall have a
sure sign that I shall have to steer myself some other way.

3

But the time for decision has come, for the signal for departure
has been given and the flags have been hauled down, the water is
churning at the stern and chains are creaking. The argument
concerning me has risen in pitch.

At this point there comes on the scene one of those tall English-men on whom a large, loose jacket is hung, and who see without looking and speak without opening their mouths. He asks off-handedly what all the noise is about. Having been informed, he states, 'I'll stand surety for this man,' and immediately begins signing all the papers presented to him.

'And now, my lord,' a policeman points out to him, 'if this gentleman takes it into his head to move into the best hotel in Cairo for six months, you will receive the bill.'

'That's exactly what I mean,' answers the Englishman, getting up. Then, with surprising energy, he shakes hands with me and goes off as if in a hurry.

At last the ship has deposited us on the quay. We pull ourselves together for a moment in order to deliberate—we, my calabash, my stick, my sandals, my beard and I.

When a tourist disembarks, he is hailed, tugged at and harassed by pedlars and would-be guides of all kinds. As for us, they leave us to our fate, which is none the better, since we fall prey to the starers.

I cannot stop at a street corner or look at a building without a crowd gathering immediately. I have to quicken my step to shake off my persecutors. And so I go through the city as if I had nothing more urgent to do than visit every side street. A city of dust, of mud, of flies and mixture, plastered with posters, advertisements and street signs. Between them, glimpses of an Italian flag, a French one, a Union Jack, 'Pharmacie de Lesseps', 'Prix in-concurrables', 'Patisserie Syrienne', 'Alla Bella Sicilia'. Big yellow buildings in the Milanese style; in false modern style. Italianate arcades in the main street, wooden hovels squeezed in between concrete walls in the narrow ones.

The façades in the Arab quarter overhang the street on rickety beams. The windows have wooden lattices. Women wrapped in black, black nets over their mouths, wooden trinkets on their noses, A Negro, two. A messenger on a bicycle in a big cover striped like a mattress and ballooning in the wind. He is whistling. Here and there, a blue turban like a patch of sky in a puddle. A rich, pot-bellied man lets his silk coat flow out in the wind. Hairless cats are sharing a heap of filth with a nanny-goat.

4

The greengrocer is a big man with powerful shoulders, made bigger by his green robe. His European coat has been so well darned with string and decorated with patches that it looks like an antique carpet. His week-old beard is going grey, his voice is hoarse with shouting as he shoves his cart along. His little invalid daughter is lying among the fresh vegetables.

5

I am still on the run, hounded by my escort. Sometimes they arrest me and take me to the police station. They release me and at the next street corner arrest me again. They have already taken my papers away from me and ordered me not to leave the precincts of the town. The police, professional starers, have the right to look at me and question me at leisure.

And seated in the centre of the ring they form, I look at them. Their heads, topped by the fez and its pom-pom, look like a row of pine-apples on a stall. I think it is above all my beard—a survival from my forest days—that they have a grudge against, for they all have the same way here of cultivating their swarthy, ferrety faces, and wear under their noses a sort of squashed fly made of nibbled hair, which puts the finishing touch to their pruned, pleasure-garden heads.

Going through certain popular quarters is becoming dangerous, for there curiosity verges on rioting, and in the neighbourhood of schools, gangs of children stone me.

6

In the evening I slip along the side of the canal, and the desert has soon rid me of followers.

Something gets off the ground and takes shape: a camel stretching his legs, and his shadow stretches to the furthest horizon, for the ball of the sun is sinking and has touched the sand. The ground changes from ash-coloured to straw, from lava-coloured to heather-in-bloom. A blue lagune opens behind each mound.

Now the earth is cloud-coloured, flares for a moment on its crests,
smokes violet and goes out. Now the earth is moon-coloured.
It is night. The earth makes one with the moon, but a warmer
tone, for the earth is body and not corpse. Like Mars and like
Venus, she is a planet and shines in space.

I lie down on the sand, and whether I keep my eyes open or
shut, the stars penetrate my face.

7

I was beginning to get tired of doing the rounds of the same
streets and tramping the ring like a circus horse to the accompaniment of booing and jeering.

I hoped the people were going to get tired too, get tired of the
pleasure of seeing me, so tall and bearded, so funny and so ugly.
But their pleasure seemed to redouble at every turn and my
popularity was increasing hopelessly. The fact was that the company was constantly being renewed for I was carrying it along
in my wake at the speed of my legs, which are long, and the
teams of whistlers and stone-throwers were relaying each other.
Only two personages remained faithful to their post although
they were out of breath and dripping with sweat. They were
dressed in grey and had the conspicuously ordinary look that
distinguishes plain-clothes policemen the world over.

8

The hot hours of the morning came; and with them the stinging
flies. The crowd dwindled and I even found myself almost
alone with my two spies twenty yards off. I led them into the out-
landish quarters where one can see the sands between the thin
planks of new houses.

A train whistled, two rails disappearing into the desert caught
my eye like a flash of lightning. 'The Cairo train,' I thought, and at
the same moment made up my mind. Turning my back on the
rails, I set off with long strides, suddenly turned the corner of a
half-built house and, as soon as I was out of sight, raced towards
the ballast, leapt over the rails and jumped into the train which
had slowed down at the switching.

The little train set off at a gallop for all it was worth and rushed
into the desert in a cloud of fine dust.

The robed man sitting in front of me entered into conversation.
I asked him what the fare was from Port Said to Cairo; he named
a sum which I have forgotten but which was beyond understanding. He treated me to one of those flat Arab loaves that are
tressed like the bottom of a basket. I ate it hungrily for I had eaten
nothing since the day I had disembarked. The man pointed out
the best place for dropping from the train before it entered the
station.

9

In the centre of the town, I wandered for some time in streets and
squares full of tram-lines. At a corner I met a Spaniard who asked
me if I was Spanish. I said I wasn't, but said so in Spanish, and
we became acquainted.

He took me off to lunch in a cheap café and ordered 'fool', a
kind of soup made of beans and seasoned with onions and herbs.
I think I have never eaten and never shall eat anything so good.
When the meal was over, it almost seemed for a moment that I
was no longer hungry.

As it cost one piastre the plateful, I made plans for the future. I
thanked my host, who was going back to work (he was a cobbler),
and went off. I was looking for colourful, shady streets. It was a
mistake, for the crowd gathered as at Port Said and I received
the first battery of stones. I went up to the Citadel that stands
alone and apart and looks out on the town, the Nile and the wide
horizon.

I went through the Arab quarter to the old gates, along the
necklace of beautiful mosques. The geometrised cave of their doors
is a crystal seen from the inside. Shade cuts the wide, flat courtyards in two, and makes the green of the pools blaze. In the shady
rooms, under the arcades, the worshippers kneel and squat times
without number in front of the decorated wall that halts the eye
and fixes faith.

10

At last I took the road to the Pyramids. It is less than ten miles to Ghiza. It would have been easier to walk thirty over stones and sand and I should have done so more willingly. As soon as I set foot on it, I thought, 'This is bad, very bad.'

It was a wide, asphalt road along which trams ran, and sometimes big, roaring cars shot up it. Right and left rose rich, white villas standing in gardens. Then stretches of market garden. From time to time, a huge hoarding exalted braces or a tin of corned beef. It was getting worse and worse. At the end of the promenade there was a round place where the tram-lines turned and there, as in nightmares, loomed a stupefying yellow building. On its roof-top was the inscription: 'Grand Hotel of the Pyramids'. My calabash, my stick, my beard and I were struck dumb.

In front of the steps and the glass of the Grand Hotel of the Pyramids a Bedouin in a burnouse was leading a dromedary by the bridle: it was caparisoned with red in the grandest style and on its summit the tourist had been placed, crowned with his sun-helmet, adorned with admirable plus-fours and field-glasses that bounced here and there as the advancing animal swung him backwards and forwards or from side to side, while his hands, melting in suède gloves, vainly sought support in the void.

And not far off, a dromedary just like it, crowned just like it, was pitching and rolling the blushing spouse of the said tourist.

11

I followed them by a road that climbs and turns. At the last bend, which leads on to the esplanade at the top, the tourists thinned into the splendour of the day and vanished, and below trams, cars, hotels and all the other muck also disappeared.

The blocks of the Pyramid of Cheops, growing higher and higher, advanced on me.

The brown stones are put together with no other lime than heaviness and precision and jut out slightly by a corner, which makes a prism of shadow the colour of the sky. Thus the celestial substance, playing like the infinite in the series of numbers, runs across the great geometrical harp and makes it sound.

A notice-board bars entry into the subterranean passage, a notice-board bearing these words: 'Entry: 5 piastres'.

Three Arabs, grunting and jabbering excitedly between the grunts, are doing their utmost to heave a German in an alpaca coat up the face of the pyramid by pushing up his behind and pulling the skin of his neck.

From up there, you can see the golden wilderness everywhere you look. The three pyramids are the boundary marks of the desert; they brave it, pit themselves against it, and stand up to it just as the spirit in these tombs dictates limits to death and rises stronger, harder and more lasting than death.

Unlike most ordinary monuments, they grow bigger as one goes farther from them.

12

I was hunting for the Sphinx. The pictures I had seen of it had led me to imagine that whole caravans could have camped between its paws, so I was surprised to see, on the rocky platform where I was looking for it, only vague excavations and rubble.

I came to a railing from which, on looking down, I discovered its rump and a flank scoured and grooved by the sand of desert winds. Its forehead is no higher than the roof of a modest bungalow.

But one has only to contemplate it for a moment to see it outgrow all human dimensions.

There it lies, the divine Beast before whom generations have meditated, placed at the beginning of time at the opening of a secret road.

Whoever first saw 'the smile of the Sphinx' must have been a witty man and I should hate to slight him, but for at least three hours I contemplated that closed face without seeing a quiver of indulgence light its accomplished silence.

The Sphinx does not smile. Its mouth is straight like the horizon, straight like the separation of the waters above from those beneath, straight like righteousness and virtue, straight like the glance of those who know.

To the riddle of the Sphinx, Oedipus answered 'Man'. To the riddle, 'What is the Sphinx?' I think one must answer 'Man'.

If there is one thing the Egyptians have taught us better than any other, one thing that we Christians should know—it is that man in his fullness goes infinitely beyond the limits of man.

The testament of the Word Incarnate comes to us carried by four animals. The Ox, the Lion, the Eagle and the Angel together form the Sphinx. And the Sphinx says, 'I, the Son of Man.'

13

As day was going down, I turned away from the Sphinx and climbed down to where Moslem tombs with their loosened stones lie in a valley of sand. While the sightseers abandoned the pleasure of the ruins for that of supper and a cigar, I went my way into the desert.

Like the sea-bottom, the desert is carpeted with weed, and there are fleshy-leaved plants with livid or red blisters that wet your feet when you tread on them. I climbed on to a small, rocky escarpment of which the highest platform dominated the distance and looked on to the pyramids. I made this my dwelling-place, unrolled my goat-hair blanket and collected some stones to keep animals at a distance should they attack me at night.

The sun drowned in the heat-haze and went out. A rose-coloured turban dawned on the eastern horizon, glided to the top of the sky's head, which became violet, and turned the evening star green. Night came with a sigh.

The sounds of the last village came to me from the left with the barking of dogs, while on my right the great silence was crystallising. In the sapphire of the night, the pyramids were darkening, their prism rose like the outermost landmark between the world of the living and the mineral kingdom. Sirius, the star that is said to have served for the determination of their tip and their angle, suddenly shone bright. Waterfalls of stars sprang from the zenith. Stardust was resounding between two stars. I felt the wheel of the earth turning dangerously in immensity. I lay down. More than fatigue, the beauty of the world crushed me against the earth. Sometimes my teeth chattered when I looked at the sky and I would pull my blanket over my head for respite from marvelling. I was dry and sealed like the mummies whose entrails have been replaced by balm. A little, chilly wind that seemed to come from between the stars rose and stood on my rampart of rock, threw a handful of dust in my face and fell again with a moan. My eyes and ears were more than awake, just as the transparent night was more than awake, and a line from Rilke rang in my memory: it says that beauty is the beginning of the terrible, for it is the touch of the Angel who disdains to destroy us. Those who seek Beauty at their ease and take it for another pleasure will never know what Beauty is. But this hunger, this thirst, this utter abandonment, this ardent vigil at the feet of naked night have made her shine in my blood, more present to me than myself, Beauty, the 'truth of forms', the 'splendour of the true'.

Beneath the bright triangles of the stars, I contemplate the dark triangles of the three tombs.

How wise you were, Oh Pharaohs, to see death awaiting you as the health of the sick, the perfume of the olibanum, rest under the sail on a windy day, return to the harbour we were thirsting for.

Oh master craftsmen in the workshop of the gods, oh indestructible in the orb of the solar disc, how wise you were not to see your great-great-nephews fallen into confusion and ugliness, how wise you are not to hear me, the troubled, wandering, ignorant dreamer that I am.

You have gone over the horizons of glass, gone through the convexity of the worlds, the holy constellation Sahu.

You have stood before the Blue God, the Steadfast of Heart, the Stable Son of the Stable Self conceived and born of Himself in the Territory of Stability, and in the Hall of Truth before the Forty-Two, you held your heart and said, 'Here on my palm is my heart, my mother's heart. Ah! let it be weighed, this heart, in the scales of truth, balanced by the hieroglyph of truth: it is pure.'

Luminous ones of today sprung from yesterday's womb, led by the Guide of the Roads, by the Lady with crimson hair who reigns in the Southern sky, by the Divine Hatcher, you have climbed the steps and passed the Twelve Doors, armed with

powerful talismans, the insurmountable Khopesh, the Cross with
a handle, true voice and truth of word. The sky has opened, the
four angles of the horizons have opened and you have entered the
Dwelling-place of Hearts.

You have entered like the hawk seated on its angle, like the
swallow that flies where she wills. You have found the Divine
other side of things, you have found it.

You have reached the Country of Life where the beans are in
flower, where the wheat is seven royal cubits high, where there
is a painted house and a lake where water-lilies blossom and
gardens full of flowers, and in the shade of the acacias, your
beloved one is beside you and her breasts, to make a day of joy,
to make a day of joy.

O beloved of the gentle-eyed Lady of the Sycamore, she has
laid the coolness of her hands on your forehead, and the northern
breeze in your mummified nostrils and you have said, 'Here is my
heart returned to my breast, here is my tongue restored to my
true mouth, and here are my eyes come back to me. And here,
in its accustomed place, is the solar sign of my virility, my member
from my father and my seven ancestors.

'Homage then to the Father of Fathers, to the one Hidden-in-
the-middle-of-the-pupil-of-the-eye, to the Radiant One who
hides himself away. I evoke and utter his great names except
His true name which only He knows.

'Come, oh Blue. Oh Blue, oh Blue! Come!'[1]

14

I left this place next day towards noon. There was not even a
mouthful of water left in my calabash and the flies that prey on
the thick-leaved, red-blistered plants as if they were meat,
were tormenting me. I passed the feet of the pyramids once
more and by the roundabout went down into the land of men
again.

*   *

And it was there, at the tram terminus, that I met the very human
policeman.

As soon as he caught sight of me in the distance, he spread

his arms out to bar the way to me and came upon me thus, his arms wide-spread. I thought, 'That's done it!' They had kept my papers at Port Said and had ordered me not to leave the place. I thought, 'This time, I am trapped like a rat.' 'You passed this way yesterday,' he said, 'and since then, you haven't been seen again. Where did you spend the night?' I answered, 'There,' waving vaguely. 'What?' he said, 'in the desert? And you're not afraid of wild beasts?' I laughed. He continued, 'I see, you prefer them to people. Come with me.'

We went into the corridor that smelled of urine and then into the whitewashed office. He offered me a straw-bottomed chair, sat down at the table and apologised, 'I must just finish looking at these papers. It will only take a minute.'

I waited, my palms on my knees.

In racks above my head hung rifles with iron-heeled butts. Through the half-open door I could see the row of bicycles. I thought of the different prisons I have stayed in. Whatever the régime and whatever the climate, they are all the same. I thought of the kind of immanent injustice which enables men who do not love freedom enough always to find some good reason for imprisoning those who love it too much.

At last the policeman raised his head and I prepared to face his questioning. 'How many days is it since you last had a meal?' asked the very human policeman. I did not answer.

'Come now!' he said. 'Come and have a meal on me. It's lunch-time.'

Now a tramp can accept anything from anybody, but not from a policeman, even a human one, so I replied, 'This is Friday if I'm not mistaken: it's a day of fasting.'

'It's me who's paying,' he insisted. I repeated my answer in an expressionless voice. He was a Moslem. With a laugh, he said, 'You Christians don't know how to fast; you eat fish instead of meat and you call that fasting!'

'That's true,' I said, humiliated. 'We don't know; anyhow, I am learning and practising a bit.'

There was a silence. The policeman raised his pen and squinted at the nib for a few moments. Finally, he asked, 'What can I do to be agreeable to you?'

'Let me go,' I answered without hesitation.

He cleared his throat and scratched his head awkwardly.

'All right, go then,' he said at last.

I went towards the door, but as I was crossing the threshold, I heard a loud crash which made me turn round.

The man was standing, he had knocked his chair over while getting up. He was red and his eyes were shining. 'I'm sorry,' he said in a choking voice, 'I'm sorry this uniform prevents me from following you: you are at least a free man, a free man.'

I said to him, 'You can get out of your prison too, if you like. You only have to want to,' and I went out.

15

Back in Cairo, I would gladly have spent one of my three piastres for a dish of 'fool' but I did not want to have told a lie in the presence of the very human policeman and I did not want him to have told the truth when he said that we Christians didn't know how to fast.

So, fasting and without a ticket, I took the little train to Port Said. We had been going full speed for some time when the cap of a ticket inspector appeared at one end of the corridor and made me go to the platform at the other end and leap feet foremost into space.

I found myself stuck into the middle of the desert like a pole, my mouth and eyes full of sand. My blanket had flown ten yards, my calabash thirty, and I had almost lost my dearly beloved stick.

16

By following the railway line for half a day, I reached town.

It was high time to see to my affairs: I had taken holiday enough. I had to find out now whether the pilgrimage was wanted and how I should leave.

So I went to see the bishop in order to receive fatherly advice. My Lord Bishop was a Frenchman with a very fine white beard, very silky.

He gave me fatherly advice to give up my plan. 'You know perfectly well,' he said, 'that there is a war on in Palestine and

that the frontier is closed. On the other side is the Great Desert—
you must not even dream of crossing it alone . . .'

The holy man little knew the thorn he was burying in the heart
of the ambitious, silly pilgrim that I was, when he said I must
not even dream of the Great Desert. Thereafter, I dreamt of
nothing else but the Great Desert, questioning nomads about
distances, wells, and the stars to follow.

Then I thought of the sea route which seemed much more
practical. Down on the docks, I got in touch with some Lebanese
sailors who were sailing for Haifa the following week. I offered to
man the sails in exchange for food. The captain accepted with a
shrug. Landing without papers was still a risky business. I was
to dive off the ship when we came in sight of the coast and swim
ashore.

17

The days had been going by and my three piastres with them,
two for the two plates of 'fool' and the last one for the flat loaves
I was gripping under my arm and from which I broke a mouthful
now and then as I fled. For the crowd was still chasing me
through the streets, sometimes throwing stones at me.

My ribs and a knee had been bruised with the stones, my forehead was bleeding. I felt sick, but in vain, since I was empty.
In the heat of the sun, I had shivering fits and broke into cold
sweats. My fingers trembled rather like those of drunkards. I
was afraid that as I weakened, impatience with my tormentors
might get the better of me, which would have given me a poor
opinion of my character. In short, everything indicated that I
was nearing a solution.

18

And indeed the solution was not long in coming. As I was passing
the post office, it came into my head to go in and see if there was
any mail for me. The employee put on a knowing look and
threw me a letter as if it were the most natural thing in the
world.

It was a letter from my mother, who had sent others like it to

several ports, not knowing where I would disembark. She re-
proached me gently with 'passing so near without making a
detour' to see here between two journeys and asked touchingly
whether I needed anything. She also sent me a copy of an invitation from friends of ours in Rhodes offering me a post as tutor
the following summer in order to prepare their children for
examinations.

This was the sign I was waiting for. Everything became clear
now. From Rhodes, nothing would be easier than to go over to
the Turkish coast in the autumn and from there all roads to the
Holy Places would be open, since I now had the assurance that I
would be acting by a will that was not mine.

It seemed clear to me, as well, that permission had been given
me to obey my mother and to go home to her until summer came.
Only then, because of the sudden furious joy that took possession
of me, did I perceive how much I longed to do so.

*

I went down to the port walking purposefully. There was a boat at
anchor carrying the Italian flag and sailing for Genoa that very
evening. I asked for the captain. I told him my name.

The captain knew my family. He could not refuse to take me
on board. Throughout the interview, his eyes remained fixed on
the rags of the blue jute trousers hanging round my ankles.
Apparently it was difficult for him to find a logical link between
the rags and the name. But he remained as discreet in his surprise as I in my explanations. He had me shown to a good cabin
and a meal was served me there, which was a diplomatic way of
begging me not to thrust my shocking appearance upon those
who honoured the big dining-rooms upstairs with their decorative
presence.

*

Farewell, Africa. I shall see the sweet land of my birth again.

On my eyelids, I shall feel the breeze rich with the freshness of
leaves and soft with rain.

The bells of morning and the bells of evening will ring in my
ears. Whoever has not lived long enough in a distant land cannot
know how the heart melts at remembrance of the bells.

I shall rest my eyes on the sweetest thing in the world and the loveliest to see: my mother's white hair.

And leaning out of the high window in the house of old stone, I shall travel, travel without sweat or danger, watching the gentle clouds go by.

1. From the Egyptian 'Book of the Dead'.